The Story of the Rhodesias and Nyasaland

uniform with this book

*

THE STORY OF SOUTH AFRICA
THE STORY OF NIGERIA
THE STORY OF MALAYSIA
THE STORY OF AUSTRALIA
THE STORY OF NEW ZEALAND
THE STORY OF CANADA
THE STORY OF ENGLAND
THE STORY OF SCOTLAND
THE STORY OF IRELAND

by the same author

*

THE BEGINNINGS OF NYASALAND
AND NORTH-EASTERN RHODESIA 1859–95
(published by the Oxford University Press)

Lobengula shortly before his Accession

The Story of the
RHODESIAS AND NYASALAND

A. J. HANNA

FABER AND FABER

24 Russell Square

London

First published in mcmlx
by Faber and Faber Limited
24 Russell Square London W.C.1
Second edition mcmlxv
Printed in Great Britain by
Latimer Trend & Co Ltd Plymouth

Contents

Illustrations

PLATES

MAPS

Maps 1, 2, 3, 5 and 6 were drawn by N. S. Hyslop

There is a cartoon on page 113

Preface to the Second Edition

The publication of a second edition has given me an opportunity to bring the narrative down to the dissolution of the Federation on 31st December 1963. I have rewritten Chapter 10 from p. 258 onwards, and have added a new concluding chapter. Elsewhere in the book statistical and other information has, as far as possible, been brought up to date. The second chapter has been extensively revised because, in its original form, it merely presented an accurate account of the salient facts and failed to reckon with the *zeitgeist* of the 1960s, which wishes to hide them from view under a cloak of anthropological technicalities. Only one real error in the first edition has been brought to my notice: I followed Marshall Hole, who has a very high standard of factual reliability, in stating that George Westbeech kept no journal, but recently, to my discomfiture, his journal has been published in the Robbins Series. I have, of course, altered the text accordingly.

By the time this edition is published both Nyasaland and Northern Rhodesia will have changed their names. But I do not think that there should be any consequent alteration in the title of the book. For this is a record of the era of British initiative and ascendancy, and it ends when that ascendancy ends; it is therefore appropriate that it should retain the British names of the territories. Of course this does not mean that it is intended as an apologia for either Governments or settlers.

Plates 6 and 7 are new in this edition, and I gratefully acknowledge the courteous helpfulness of Rhodesia House in making them available. I should also like to thank all those who answered my questions and gave me the benefit of their very

Preface to the Second Edition

diverse opinions when I visited the Rhodesias in the last weeks of the Federation's existence.

A. J. Hanna

University College, Nairobi,
4th April 1964

Preface to the First Edition

This is the first attempt to survey the history of the Rhodesias and Nyasaland in a single book, apart from the incidental treatment of it in Professor Walker's authoritative *History of Southern Africa*. The justification for making such an attempt at all must be found in the fact that since 1953 the three territories have been bound together, for better or worse, in a federation whose present problems can best be understood in the light of the history of its component parts. But their history is not so much a single story as a number of separate stories, more or less inter-linked, rather like the plot of *Pickwick Papers*. Southern Rhodesia and Nyasaland have not much history in common, and although Northern Rhodesia, which is intermediate in much more than a geographical sense, can to some extent be said to share its past with each of them, it is so far from providing the historian with a convenient bridge between them that for the most part it must be dealt with separately.

Where a common thread of narrative is lacking, the only available unifying element is the judgment of the historian himself, exercised through the device of comparison and contrast. Besides, in a comparatively short and comprehensive book such as this, a good deal of selection and interpretation are unavoidable if the work is to be more than a bare chronicle of events. But the historian's judgment and interpretation can only be his own: there is no such thing as 'the verdict of history'. My own preference in the writing of history is to try to minimise this subjective element, by marshalling the facts as fully as possible and letting them speak for themselves. I am, indeed, fully

Preface to the First Edition

aware that perfect objectivity is an unattainable ideal, but I nevertheless believe it is the worthiest ideal that the historian as such can pursue.

If, however, I have felt obliged by circumstances to be to some extent subjective, I have at least done my utmost to avoid being partisan. Objectivity is an ideal, but impartiality is an ethical imperative. I have done my best to be just to all concerned, and have tried to avoid over-simplification, especially where it would be politically tendentious. The present Federation has, unfortunately, occasioned such bitter controversy that in all probability some of its more zealous supporters and opponents will find it impossible to believe that I am not prejudiced against whichever side they are on—for, as Burke remarked, 'it is in the nature of things that they who are in the centre of a circle should appear directly opposed to those who view them from any part of the circumference.'

In the pronunciation of African names it should be remembered that the final 'e' in such a word as Kafue or Bandawe is sounded as a separate syllable: thus 'Kaf-u-ay', 'Ban-da-way'. In the case of the River Shiré (pronounced Shee-ray) I have departed from normal practice by using an accent to indicate this; the reason for the inconsistency is that without the accent the name looks like an ordinary English word. In the case of the Chewa tribe the 'ch' is pronounced as in 'cheese' and the word as a whole is 'Chay-wa'.

I am greatly indebted to Dr. J. D. Fage for allowing me to make full use of his thesis on *The Achievement of Self-Government in Southern Rhodesia, 1898–1923* (Ph.D., Cambridge, 1949), and for reading Chapter 6 in typescript and making a number of most helpful criticisms. I am likewise much indebted to Dr. R. McGregor for allowing me to use the abundant information in his thesis on *Native Segregation in Southern Rhodesia: A Study of Social Policy* (Ph.D., London, 1940); it is to this source that I owe the quotation on p. 186.

I wish to thank Miss Irene Fletcher for permission to quote extracts from correspondence in the archives of the London Missionary Society; the librarian of Rhodesia House, London,

Preface to the First Edition

for making available the photographs reproduced as Plates 5, 6 and 7, and for helping me to find useful information in the valuable collection of press cuttings which that library possesses; Messrs. Edward Arnold (Publishers) Ltd., for allowing me to quote at some length from Cullen Gouldsbury and Hubert Sheane, *The Great Plateau of Northern Rhodesia*, and the Delegates of the Clarendon Press for giving me a free hand to incorporate material from the book on *The Beginnings of Nyasaland and North-Eastern Rhodesia*, which they published for me in 1956. The quotation from the Orde-Browne Report (Colonial No. 150) has been made by permission of the Controller of Her Majesty's Stationery Office, and the substantial extract from the Clay Report (C.S.R. 3) is included with the consent of the High Commissioner for the Federation of Rhodesia and Nyasaland.

Messrs. Longmans, Green and Company have kindly made available the blocks of one of the coloured maps in Professor Eric Walker's *History of Southern Africa*, and Messrs. Robert MacLehose, printers of *The Northern Goldfields Diaries of Thomas Baines* (published by Chatto and Windus in the Oppenheimer Series), have made available the blocks for the frontispiece; this is reproduced by kind permission of the National Archives of the Federation of Rhodesia and Nyasaland. The original is in the Natural History Library of the British Museum, in South Kensington.

I wish to make grateful acknowledgement to John Murray (Publishers) Ltd., for permission to reproduce Plate 1 from *The Last Journals of David Livingstone*, edited by Horace Waller (1874); to Methuen and Co., Ltd., for Plates 2 and 3, from Sir Harry Johnston's *British Central Africa* (1899); and to Macmillan and Co., Ltd., for Plate 4, from *The Making of Rhodesia* by H. M. Hole (1926). The cartoon is published by permission of *Punch*.

A. J. HANNA

Southampton University,
20th January 1960

15

CHAPTER 1

The Country

The Rhodesias and Nyasaland occupy a wide expanse of the great African plateau, which, stretching from the Sahara far into the Republic of South Africa, is the largest plateau in the world. Their total area of about 475,150 square miles (not counting 8,680 square miles of Lake Nyasa, which lie within the boundaries of Nyasaland) is a little more than five times that of Great Britain.

Of the three territories Northern Rhodesia is by far the largest —it is almost twice as large as Southern Rhodesia, and eight times as large as Nyasaland—yet it has the smallest population; while Nyasaland, which on the map looks like an insignificant strip of land beside the lake, has actually the largest population of them all. As a matter of fact, if a map of Nyasaland is superimposed on a map of Great Britain drawn to the same scale, and if its northern tip coincides with Cape Wrath, its southern tip will reach to the Isle of Wight. But Nyasaland is much narrower than Great Britain, and for that reason has scarcely more than two-fifths its land surface. And although it is by far the most densely populated territory of the three, its estimated population of 2,340,000 in 1951 (they had increased to 2,710,000 by 1958) appears almost sparse when compared with the 48,841,000 recorded in Britain in the same year.

Much the greater part of the three territories, especially the two northern ones, has an altitude of between 3,000 and 5,000 feet. In the east there are various mountains which rise in places to 8,000 feet or more: the Muchinga range in Northern Rhodesia, forming the western edge of the valley of the River

B   17

MAP 1. *General*

Luangwa; the eastern border of Southern Rhodesia, especially north of Umtali; and the highlands which run almost continuously close to the western shore of Lake Nyasa, from the Nyika Plateau in the north to the Kirk Range in the south. On the south-eastern border of Nyasaland is the loftiest mountain of them all, the tremendous, towering mass of Mount Mlanje (9,843 feet).

The convulsion of the earth's crust which gave to Nyasaland some of the highest mountains in the Federation (and the finest scenery in all Africa) gave it also a deep trough between the mountains. This is partly filled by the waters of Lake Nyasa itself, and continues southwards by the valley of the River

The Country

Shiré, which flows out of the southern extremity of the lake and becomes a tributary of the Zambesi. The Great Rift Valley, as it is called, extends northwards by way of Lake Rudolph (in Kenya) and the Red Sea as far as the valley of the Jordan; Lake Nyasa and the Shiré valley are, therefore, merely its southern end. The floor of the lake is as much as 700 feet below sea level, though the lake's surface is about 1,500 feet above it. Because of its depth it contains a greater volume (though not surface area) of water than any other lake in Africa, with the exception of Lake Tanganyika, which, with its surface 2,500 feet above sea level and its bottom 1,600 feet below, is actually twice as deep.

In addition to the lowlands in the Rift Valley, south of Lake Nyasa and on a narrow strip along its western shore, there are the deep valleys made by the rivers. The greatest of these is the Zambesi, which is the boundary between the two Rhodesias. From Northern Rhodesia, on its left bank, it receives as tributaries the Kafue and the Luangwa, mighty rivers themselves; from Southern Rhodesia, on its right, the Gwaai, the Sanyati, and the Hunyani. In the southern part of Southern Rhodesia there are the Sabi, not far from the eastern frontier, and the Limpopo, which is the boundary with the Transvaal in the Union of South Africa.

Since all three territories lie wholly in the tropics, the more low-lying parts are hot, unpleasant, and unhealthy. The main plateau, however, is high enough to have temperatures ranging from the moderately hot to the distinctly chilly; indeed the Nyika Plateau in northern Nyasaland is so high that it is completely uninhabited, because the native Africans cannot endure its cold.

The rainfall is almost entirely seasonal, during the southern summer. It descends in downpours upon the parched land, and pours down slopes in torrents which quickly sweep away any soil left unprotected by trees or grass, or by contour ridges made by man to check the flow. The soil is all the more liable to erosion because much of it is sandy. When it is gone, all that is left of the hill is a mass of huge boulders piled on top of one another,

The Country

known in Southern Rhodesia—which has far too many of them —by the Afrikaans name of kopje.

The amount of rainfall varies greatly from one place to another, and also from year to year. Nyasaland is for the most part very adequately watered, and many of its streams are perennial. Most of Northern Rhodesia is adequately watered too, especially the more northern parts. In both territories, however, the rate of evaporation is high, and water conservation is essential to agricultural development. In Southern Rhodesia, the eastern highlands arrest more than their share of the moisture borne inland from the Indian Ocean by the trade winds, and the Sabi valley immediately behind them is very dry; elsewhere, the highest rainfall comes to the eastern part of the broad plateau which runs at a height of over 4,000 feet in a north-easterly to south-westerly direction between the Zambesi valley to the north and the Limpopo-Sabi lowlands to the south and east. The average annual rainfall at Salisbury is 32·8 inches, whereas at Bulawayo it is only 23·7.

This central tableland, known locally as the high veld, covers between a fifth and a quarter of the total area of Southern Rhodesia, and is regarded by both the native Africans and the immigrant Europeans as the most desirable land in the country. On either side of it is a broad tract of what is called the middle veld, between 3,000 and 4,000 feet. This area, which includes more than a third of the country, has much the same rainfall as the high veld, diminishing from east to west; it has, however, been badly eroded by the numerous streams which have gouged their way down it from the higher land above. The rest of the country, comprising the northern fringe and the broad southern plain, is referred to as the low veld; in the Limpopo valley the annual rainfall is as low as 15 inches.

The natural vegetation in both the Rhodesias and in Nyasaland is sparse, coarse grass in the drier parts and various types of forest according to altitude and moisture. There are over a thousand different species of indigenous tree in Nyasaland alone, the most famous and valuable being the Mlanje cedar. Northern Rhodesia, too, has valuable hardwoods, rather loosely described

The Country

as teak and mahogany; like the Mlanje cedar these are resistant to white ants. Near the rivers the baobab flourishes: a squat, enormously thick softwood which has a variety of uses. Wherever there are swamps there is a luxuriance of reeds and papyrus, and thousands of acres of river surface are covered with the fast-growing 'Shiré cabbages', which accumulate when the water-level is low, and are swept away as great islands of sudd when the floods come. The railway bridge across the Shiré at Chiromo was broken down in 1949 by the pressure of water rising behind a wall of sudd which had become stuck against the pillars.

The rivers and lakes are infested with crocodiles, which are a hideous danger to the African women when they go to fill their water-pots, and which have claimed a number of victims among the Europeans too. The wild animals of the country include the roan antelope, the zebra, the bushbuck and the buffalo; the elephant, the hippopotamus and the rhinoceros; the lion, the leopard, the hyena and the jackal. The days of uncontrolled big-game hunting are long since past, otherwise the elephant at least would have been exterminated on account of the high value of the ivory from its tusks. But the game are carriers of tsetse fly, whose bite invariably brings death to domestic animals and in some cases infects human beings with sleeping-sickness. Southern Rhodesia therefore resorted to a desperate, ill-advised policy of extermination in the tsetse-infested Zambesi valley, and in the four years from 1953 to 1957 about 130,000 wild animals were killed in these operations. Outside this area a distinction was drawn between 'game', which include both predators and prey, and 'vermin', such as monkeys and wild pigs, which have every man's hand against them.

A lion can usually break into an African's hut if it feels inclined to take the trouble; fortunately it does so comparatively seldom, since normally lions eat animals in preference to men. Nevertheless about a dozen Africans a year are still killed by lions in Nyasaland alone; the number was formerly much higher. Yet Africans consider the leopard even more dangerous than the lion. Was it really a happy inspiration to make him the emblem of Nyasaland, to illustrate the motto *Lux in tenebris*?

CHAPTER 2

A Hundred Years Ago

It has become conventional to deny, with emphasis and scorn, that there is any justification for referring to pre-colonial Africa as 'the dark continent'. Attention is directed away from the Congo and Zambesi basins (to which that phrase primarily referred) towards the east coast and the western Sudan, which had responded impressively to the stimulus of Islamic culture when it was at its zenith during the Middle Ages. It is pointed out that Egypt, so important in antiquity, is geographically and to some extent historically part of Africa. Even in the southern part of the African interior, which was almost wholly isolated from external influences, the knowledge of iron-smelting eventually penetrated all the way from the valley of the Nile, and the iron-workings in Northern Rhodesia have become a subject of considerable archaeological interest.

In the part of the continent with which this book is concerned, it is the ruins of the massive stone buildings in Southern Rhodesia which represent the most notable achievement of the pre-colonial era. The most famous of these ruins are the so-called 'Temple' and 'Acropolis' at Zimbabwe; the names represent early guesses at the purposes which those enigmatic structures served. They are evidence that in the past the inhabitants of the surrounding region had achieved a sufficient degree of political organisation to make possible a sustained collective effort, and that they had achieved it for a long enough period to permit them to develop a remarkable patience, and considerable skill, in construction.

The Portuguese, who penetrated into the area in the sixteenth century, found still in existence an extensive empire ruled by a dynasty named Monomotapa. This empire was notable for its gold-mining, which aroused the covetousness of the Portuguese, as of the British three hundred years later; it maintained at least a trickle of trade with Sofala on the east coast, and indirectly with India and China. But the Portuguese chronicler Bocarro, who gave a fairly detailed account of it in the mid-seventeenth century, recorded that in his time it was beginning to disintegrate. The practice of building in stone continued, however, and did not completely die out until the nineteenth century.[1] The important remains at Dhlo-Dhlo, west of Zimbabwe, can be dated fairly precisely, mainly on the evidence afforded by a Dutch gin bottle which was found there: the date was about 1700. Khami, near Bulawayo, is believed to have been built about the same time. Although these later buildings are less remarkable than Zimbabwe, they are in some respects of greater value to the archaeologist, because they escaped the attentions of the early British settlers, whose untutored curiosity and rough cupidity led them to commit serious destruction at Zimbabwe in their eager search for ancient treasure.

Equally interesting in its different way is the 'Inyanga complex', bordering on what is now the Portuguese province of Moçambique. Here there occurred a phenomenon which was exceedingly rare, if not unique, in southern Africa before the European occupation: the construction of an irrigation system and of terraces to prevent soil erosion. The Inyanga 'upland culture' is believed to have flourished from the early fifteenth century to the late seventeenth, and an offshoot (the 'lowland culture'), which emerged to the north and west, appears to belong to the eighteenth century.

Impressive as these works are, they are the achievement of a

---

[1] Archaeological investigations in 1958 showed that the earliest phase of stone-building at Zimbabwe began about A.D. 1100, and that the second phase, when the most careful and accomplished work was done, began about the fifteenth century and may have continued into the seventeenth or even the eighteenth. There was also a third phase, probably in the early nineteenth century, when the work was of a very crude and decadent character; most of these relatively recent walls have already collapsed.

people whose techniques were rudimentary, owing nothing to scientific inquiry or to the most elementary acquaintance with mathematics. In this respect the Zimbabwe culture compares most unfavourably with the brilliant Maya civilisation which arose in the jungles of Guatemala at an even earlier date, and in conditions of more complete isolation from the world's main centres of civilised life. The high, thick walls of Zimbabwe are made of small stones which required no mechanical equipment to raise them into position; they were constructed by men who possessed no measuring instrument whatever, and no knowledge of the arch or of corbelling. They show what could be achieved by a barbaric people when they set their minds to it under unusually favourable conditions, but they are not the remains of a lost civilisation.

The role of the Monomotapa was religious as well as political, and was so exalted that his subjects prostrated themselves whenever they appeared before him. Yet Zimbabwe, the centre of this rule and cult, has become a source of inspiration to a modern secular mass movement: the African nationalists of Southern Rhodesia proudly bear its name. Likewise, in Nyasaland, the nationalists have adopted the name Malawi, under which the Chewa tribe west of Lake Nyasa and the related Nyanja south of the lake were formerly united in an extensive kingdom. Just as two of the new republics of West Africa have appropriated the names of the medieval kingdoms of Ghana and Mali, the nationalists of south-central Africa are eager to root their emergent states in the pre-colonial past. A similar need has been felt by nationalists all over the world, and has been at once a stimulus to historical research and a source of patriotic myth-making. No people can master its difficulties without confidence in its own future, and its confidence in the future depends in large measure on pride in its past. There is therefore a compelling urge to represent tropical Africa's achievements during the centuries before the coming of the Europeans in the most favourable possible light, and to minimise the value of everything done by the white men during the brief period of their ascendancy.

A Hundred Years Ago

This does not mean that African nationalists really wish to return to the conditions of a century ago, or to shut out the modernising influences which the white intruders have brought with them. On the contrary, the nationalists wish to continue much of this modernising activity and to accelerate its tempo. They are capable of denouncing, in the same breath, 'reactionary tribalism' which tends to disrupt the unity of the new state, and 'colonialism' which has undermined traditional (i.e. tribal) culture. Although this is bad logic and bad history, it is good popular psychology, and is therefore politically serviceable.

It is this climate of opinion, far more than the findings of recent research, which demands that the old picture of 'darkest Africa' shall be discredited and destroyed. When the newly-independent Tanganyika decided to take down the statues of Livingstone on the ground that he was 'merely a tourist' who discovered nothing which was not already known to his African contemporaries, it illustrated to perfection a mood which, while it continues, will make the writing of balanced history an exceedingly difficult and thankless task.

Since African nationalism is acclaimed as a progressive movement throughout almost the whole world, this mood is not confined to Africans, but to a large extent influences students of Africa in Britain and the United States. For example, a well-known and normally discriminating British professor has referred to 'the racialist cliché that "the African never even invented the wheel" '. But a genuine fact cannot be a cliché; a fact which is elementary and obvious may still be highly significant, and it ought not to be subjected to a kind of academic censorship merely because it may be misapplied to support an unenlightened political attitude.

It is frequently asserted, especially by those who are not themselves anthropologists, that anthropology has disproved the 'myth' of African savagery. Living in an African village for many consecutive months in the easy-going 1930s, under the system of indirect rule which combined the *Pax Britannica* with the attempted preservation of traditional institutions and customs, the anthropologist gained a much more exact knowledge and a much closer understanding of the structure and functioning of African society than had been attained by earlier observers. A picture of great subtlety and complexity was thus built up, unrecognisably different from the crude violence reported by explorers and missionaries before the introduction of British rule. It was presumed that the new knowledge superseded the old, and that the nineteenth-century eye-witnesses had been blinded by their own Victorian prejudices. This, of course, is a reversal of the usual practice of historians, who normally attach more importance to contemporary evidence than to information gathered a generation or two later. It also implies a preference for what was intended to happen, when all went well, over what actually did happen, when things went wrong: as if the historian of the Middle Ages were to attach more practical importance to the doctrine of the divinely-ordained harmony and interdependence of the spiritual and temporal authorities than to the actual conflicts of Church and State, or as if Hooker's belief in the collaboration of Crown and Parliament were supposed to render mythical the strife and suffering of the English Civil War.

All the tribes of south-central Africa belong to the great family of African peoples known as the Bantu. Although negroid they are not pure negroes, but are of mixed racial origins, and members of the same tribe differ from one another in darkness of skin and in having or nor having negroid features. They form a linguistic rather than a racial grouping. Though there are many Bantu languages and innumerable dialects, anyone who can speak one Bantu language can easily learn another. Thus, for example, it has been possible to make a single language (Chi-Nyanja) an official *lingua franca* throughout the Nyasaland Protectorate. This obviously facilitates the fusion of tribes into larger communities, and the growth of a spirit of nationalism.

A hundred years ago these tribes were living in small round huts made of grass on a framework of poles, stuck together with mud or cow-dung. They cultivated the earth merely by chopping its surfaces with iron-headed hoes, and this was the work of women. They sometimes made a sort of cloth from the bark of trees. In degrees varying from tribe to tribe, they had skill in metal-working and in making baskets and mats from grass; they could hollow out canoes and catch fish. They had no idea of stock-breeding, or of using fertilisers or irrigation in agriculture, and those tribes who did not possess cattle could seldom kill enough of the abundant game to provide anything like enough meat for a balanced diet. Debilitating diseases were exceedingly common, partly because the ideas of sanitation and hygiene were usually crude or non-existent.

Many centuries previously the transition from the Stone to the Iron Age—without any intermediate Bronze Age—had marked a long step forward on the road from primitive to civilised conditions of life.[1] But the impetus had been wholly lost. Not only was no progress being made, but there had actually been a period of disastrous retrogression, which was due in part to internal decline and disintegration, but much more to invasion and conquest from without. The most destructive invasions followed upon a sequence of events which had begun fifty or sixty years previously, several hundred miles to the south, in what is now Natal.

For reasons which can only be conjectured, the relatively harmless pastoralists who had dwelt there in small tribes for three centuries or more had then become involved in a succession of desperate conflicts, leading to the absorption of the weaker by the stronger, until the whole country had been brought under the despotism of the Zulu king, Shaka, a great organiser and a cruel and relentless disciplinarian. It was he who invented the famous Zulu military tactics: the headlong rush of the enveloping crescent-shaped formation of warriors armed with the stabbing-spear and the long cow-hide shield,

[1] The Bantu had, in fact, undergone this economic and social revolution before they entered southern Africa. They had expanded slowly southwards from east Africa, arriving in Southern Rhodesia not later than A.D. 500, and probably reaching Nyasaland several centuries earlier. Their predecessors in the region were Stone Age Bushmen.

and worked up into a frenzy of blood-lust by a crescendo of ferocious war-dances.

Some of the defeated tribes, or sections of them, fled for their lives from Shaka's wrath. There was no escape to the south, where the tribes were piled up against the eastern frontier of Cape Colony. To the east was the sea, and to the west the barrier of the Drakensberg Mountains. So they went northwards, travelling slowly because they were driving their cattle with them, and devastating the country as they proceeded. They had adopted the customs, organisation, and tactics of their Zulu enemies, and they preyed upon less warlike peoples as ferociously as did the armies of Shaka himself. At least two of these hordes, known as Angoni, entered the former Empire of Monomotapa and proceeded right across it to the Zambesi. Nothing like this invasion had occurred before, for the invaders were not mere cattle-thieves but systematic exterminators wherever they went. Having butchered the men, they seized the women as wives and incorporated the children in their own tribal structure, training the males to be warriors as arrogant and murderous as themselves. The mountains and kopjes afforded places of refuge for the survivors, but what still remained of their tribal organisation had been broken in pieces, and their self-esteem and self-confidence had been destroyed.

The Angoni began their wanderings in or about the year 1821, and one of their hordes crossed the Zambesi in 1835. The exact date of the crossing is known—it was 20th November—because there was an eclipse of the sun when it took place. In the course of the following thirty or forty years they became divided into a number of independent chieftainships, and went their several ways; eventually at least five of these groups established themselves in the vicinity of the watershed which afterwards became the boundary between Nyasaland and Northern Rhodesia.

About the time when the Angoni made their flight from Zululand, or a few years later, there was another exodus of at least equal importance. This was led by Mziligazi, one of Shaka's own principal generals, who quarrelled with his king and fled for his life, taking his army with him. They crossed the Drakensberg and eventually settled in the western part of the country between the Vaal and the Limpopo, raiding prosperously in all directions. There the Matabele, as they came to be called, stayed for about ten years. Then, in 1836, some parties of Boers crossed the Vaal and began the settlement of what was to become the Transvaal Republic. The Matabele set upon them and wiped out one party, but they soon found that muskets in the hands of resolute men, protected by an encircling *laager* of ox-wagons, were superior to the stabbing-spears of a horde of yelling savages. Hearing that the Matabele had suffered defeat, the Zulus took the opportunity to chastise Mziligazi for his defection; they sent an army into the Transvaal, and compelled him to withdraw northwards, with his people and his cattle, across the Limpopo. He migrated to the high veld, and took possession of the western part of what is now Southern Rhodesia. To proceed farther was impossible, since the tsetse fly in the Zambesi valley would have destroyed the cattle.

In their new domain the Matabele resumed their practice of raiding in all directions. Each year, when the dry season began and conditions became suitable for travel, Mziligazi would launch his regiments against one or other of the neighbouring peoples. Like the Angoni, they seized not only cattle and other loot but also women and children to reinforce the tribe. But unlike the Angoni they did not become divided, but continued to form a single powerful kingdom covering an extensive territory and overshadowing a very much wider area than they themselves occupied. Their principal victims were the tribes to the east; these were the nearest at hand, and the most defenceless and unorganised, having already been shattered by the Angoni on their slow northward migration. The Matabele lumped these tribes together under the single contemptuous name of Mashona. And so it is that Southern Rhodesia to this day consists of two parts, known respectively as Matabeleland and Mashonaland.

The tribal distribution in Northern Rhodesia and Nyasaland has no such convenient if artificial simplicity. In a memorandum issued in 1934, Mr. Moffat Thompson listed as many as fifty-one tribes living in Northern Rhodesia alone; they spoke six different languages, and ranged in numbers from the Bemba with an estimated population of over 114,000 to the almost unknown Mbowe and Luchaze, with only about 5,300 each. Most if not all of these tribes and tribelets were already present, though in even smaller numbers, a century ago. In southern Nyasaland the original inhabitants were a loosely organised and easily dominated tribe whom we may call the Lake people, since their name, Nyanja or Manganja, is the word they use for a large expanse of water—it is the equivalent of Nyasa in the Yao tongue. The related Chewa, who lived in what is now the Central Province of Nyasaland and in the adjacent parts of north-eastern Rhodesia and Portuguese East Africa, were in uncomfortable proximity to two or three of the Angoni kingdoms. Farther north, the Angoni harassed and terrorised the Tonga tribe, which dwelt on the lake shore.

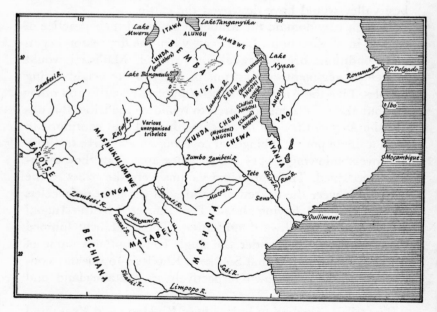

MAP 2. *Distribution of Tribes*

A Hundred Years Ago

In Northern Rhodesia there were two tribes of particular importance, besides the Angoni and Chewa already mentioned. These were the Barotse and the Bemba. Both were immigrants to the region, though of somewhat longer standing than the Angoni. They had come in the eighteenth century, probably about the middle of it. To what extent they had come by peaceful penetration, and to what extent by forcible extrusion of previous occupants, is unknown. The Bemba came from what became the Belgian Congo, and probably so did the Barotse, whose origin is to some extent in dispute. The Barotse established themselves on the upper Zambesi, in a plain which is about one hundred and twenty miles long with a maximum width of twenty-five miles; this plain is flooded every year when the river rises, and the alluvial deposit left by the floods constantly renews its fertility. By successful warfare and unusual administrative ability they established their rule over a very much wider area than the present Barotse Province, though even within the provincial boundaries they are an aristocratic minority among formerly subject tribes.

The Bemba took possession of the heart of the great plateau of north-eastern Rhodesia, spreading themselves extensively over a forested region with too poor a soil to support more than a sparse population, and planting their crops in beds of ash formed by burning piled-up branches lopped from the trees. They were, indeed, little interested in agriculture; they were warriors and hunters, capable of repelling an attack by the Angoni, and living to a large extent on the fruits of conquest. It was their boast that they did not know how to hoe, and that their only trade was war; they levied a regular tribute of produce from their neighbours. Unlike the Matabele and the Angoni, they were not interested in incorporating their captives into the tribe. If they thought about the matter at all, they may have realized that their poor soil and poorer agriculture could not support any great increase in numbers. Instead they enslaved the victims of their raids, and, when opportunity arose, sold them for export.

31

A Hundred Years Ago

The export trade in slaves was if possible an even greater curse to the weaker and less warlike peoples of eastern and south-central Africa than the ravages of the Zulus and their offshoots. The chief market for the slaves was in Arabia, where, indeed, there are still nearly half a million slaves at the present day. The Arab sultanate of Zanzibar, which more or less controlled the whole coast of Africa from the desert of Somaliland as far south as Cape Delgado, battened on the traffic, re-exporting some 20,000 slaves a year after retaining upwards of 2,000 for its own requirements. Arab caravans penetrated farther and farther into the interior of the continent, establishing an important trading centre at Ujiji on the shore of Lake Tanganyika, and pursuing their business far to the west of that lake. They were active from Uganda in the north to Nyasaland in the south; indeed Nyasaland seems to have provided them with more lucrative employment than anywhere else.

Many of the Arabs were half-castes, who were sometimes called 'black Arabs' as distinct from 'white Arabs'. The Arabs did not, as a rule, do their own raiding for slaves. They found it more convenient to buy the captives of tribes who were able to take them and willing to sell them, making payment in calico, cheap guns and ammunition. The guns and ammunition were useful in obtaining more slaves, and the demand for calico was passionate and unlimited, since the near-nakedness of the African was not due to preference but to lack of clothing. The victims of the slave trade were no better than its perpetrators: they were willing to engage in it themselves when they had the chance. In the 1880s it was a current saying among the British pioneers in Nyasaland that 'if you freed three slaves today, two of them, given the opportunity, would sell the third tomorrow'; and no less a man than Dr. Robert Laws affirmed that this was true.

The tribe most closely involved with the Arabs in the slave trade was the Yao, with whom they may well have been in contact for the previous two hundred years. When Livingstone visited the Yao Chief Mataka in 1866 he found the chief wearing Arab clothes and living in a square house, 'for the Arabs are

imitated in everything', useful as well as destructive. They had
even introduced the use of irrigation. He added that 'the low
coast Arabs', whom he and almost every British traveller regarded as a set of swaggering scoundrels, 'differ in nothing from
the Waiyau' (Yao).

Nearly thirty years later, when Major Edwards captured the
stronghold of Makanjira, he reported that 'many of the houses
were built in the coast style, and there was evidence everywhere
of the existence of a large Arab and coast population'.

About 1860 the Yao began to move southwards from their
homeland in the vicinity of the River Rovuma, which is now the
southern boundary of the state of Tanganyika. They entered the
Shiré Highlands in southern Nyasaland, murdering and enslaving the Lake people, burning their villages and looting their
grain so that those who escaped were faced with starvation.
Gradually, over a period of ten or fifteen years, devastation and
plunder were followed by conquest and settlement. The Yao
became the dominant tribe in the Shiré Highlands, along the
upper Shiré River, and around the south end of Lake Nyasa.
The survivors of the Lake people existed in subjection to them,
and were liable at any time to be sold to a passing Arab
caravan.

The Yao did not owe their victory to superior organisation,
for they were not, and apparently never had been, under the
rule of a single paramount chief; their chiefdoms were small and
the chiefs had not much more power or prestige than the village
headmen who ruled under them: sometimes they had even less.
They owed such cohesion as they had to the ties of kinship and
the cementing influence of customary law, much more than to
political institutions. Their overthrow of the Lake people is
sometimes attributed to their possession of firearms, and undoubtedly this was a contributory factor. But its importance
can easily be grossly exaggerated. No doubt the loud banging of
muskets struck terror into the hearts of the unwarlike people
who were being attacked; no doubt, too, even a Yao untrained
in the use of firearms could shoot to kill at point-blank range.
But in 1884 the Angoni of south-western Nyasaland, the group

C 33

ruled by Chief Chikusi, crossed the Shiré and swept across the highlands as far eastward as Lake Shirwa. The Angoni had only their spears and shields, but they knew how to handle them; the Yao had their guns, but were helpless before a disciplined and organised attack. The Angoni were able to scour the country at will, and to take home with them about eight hundred Yao captives.

The primary reason for the Yao conquest must be found in the fighting spirit and staying power of the people themselves. They were born soldiers, though they never learnt much about the art of war until, after being conquered by the British, they began to enlist in the King's African Rifles. They are also usually considered to be more intelligent than the Lake people, in addition to being incomparably tougher in character.

It would have seemed reasonable to expect that the harsh conditions of life in south-central Africa would have been mitigated by the influence of the Portuguese. The Portuguese were the heirs of a great imperial past. In the early sixteenth century they had controlled the trade routes of the Indian Ocean and monopolized Europe's developing commerce with the Far East. Their possessions in south-east and south-west Africa were all that remained to them of their former dominions, and of these possessions they were inordinately proud. But their very pride blinded them to present realities, and their Narcissus-like admiration of their own long-lost greatness was a poor substitute for administrative efficiency and commercial enterprise. The so-called province of Moçambique existed only in theory: the Governor had no control whatever over most of the coastline, still less over the interior. There were a few small coastal settlements: Moçambique itself, Ibo in the north, Inhambane in the south, and Quilimane at the mouth of the River Kwakwa close to the delta of the Zambesi. Along the Zambesi they had one place of some consequence, Tete, which, when Livingstone visited it in 1856, had a garrison of about eighty men besides a handful of civilians, less than twenty in number; there were about thirty European houses and 1,200 native huts. Lower down the river there was a mouldering settlement named Sena, on which one of the groups of marauders who had fled from Shaka, known locally as Landeens but usually called Shangaans, actually levied tribute. Zumbo, upstream from Tete, was merely a derelict ruin, though it was afterwards re-occupied.

Portuguese rule was as corrupt as it was ineffective. While the politicians in Lisbon affirmed their country's high-minded antipathy to the slave trade, and even enacted that the status of slavery itself should end throughout their possessions in 1878, they allowed their local representatives to connive at the slave trade and even to take a hand in it, and in 1881 they abruptly recalled the one official who had honestly and vigorously endeavoured to put it down. The Portuguese coast offered the Arabs an alternative outlet for their slaves after 1876, when, as a result of British pressure at Zanzibar, the coast farther north was to a large extent closed against them.

The Portuguese were in the habit of entrusting vast estates known as *prazos* to half-castes, to deal with as they liked. In the year 1890 Alfred Sharpe, an experienced and reliable observer, visited the huge domain of one of these half-castes, named Matakenya, who dominated the whole region of the lower Luangwa. He reported that those of the inhabitants who had not yet been sent away as slaves were living in such dread of the *prazo*-owner that they dared not call even their food their own: everything, they said with awe, was Matakenya's.

The slaves who reached their destination were no more than a fraction of the total number who were victims of the traffic. To them must be added all who were killed in the slave-raids, all who died of starvation after escaping from their pursuers, and all who fell by the wayside during the long, cruel march to the coast. The caravan-routes were strewn with the skulls and bones of slaves who had not been strong enough to complete their journey. To prevent escapes, the captives were made to carry wooden poles, forked at the end; their necks were secured in the forks, and the other end of the pole was carried by the next slave in the file. They had also to carry heavy loads of ivory when these could be obtained by their masters; they thus provided free transport for the ivory, and the profits of the trade were greatly increased. A slave who became too exhausted to go on was a financial loss to his purchaser, who would in all probability take revenge by murdering him in cold blood or leaving him tied to a tree to die of thirst or be eaten by hyenas. Livingstone repeatedly came upon slaves abandoned in this way; sometimes they were still alive, sometimes already dead. When a woman with a baby on her back was no longer able to carry both it and her load of ivory, she would be made to drop the baby.

'Athwart the path of progress', wrote Hubert Sheane in a book published in 1911, 'are the two stubborn barriers of superstition and sensuality.' Though the Bantu held that the world had been brought into being by a spiritual creator, the concept was far too hazy to lead to reverence and worship, and the spirits who were deemed important in practice were those who populated the forests and dwelt in wild beasts, who brought the rain, who gave fertility to the ground and victory to the tribe; the spirits of the dead who constantly interfered for good or ill in the affairs of the living. The spirits would assuredly be offended by any departure from the traditional customs of the tribe, and would severely punish such impiety. Therefore the most important lesson that children had to learn, and which was all too effectively impressed upon them, was to accept life as they found it without any attempt at critical questioning, any impious thought of innovation.

Any unusual occurrence was a source of dread. If a child's upper teeth were cut before the lower it was an ill omen, and, at least among the Bemba, the child must die or some terrible calamity would befall. 'Some time ago,' Sheane records, 'a full-grown native had to fly to the *boma* [the headquarters of the nearest British official] for protection, since his fellow-villagers, incited by the witch-doctor, were determined to drown him, and so correct the breach of customary law in the past committed by his parents in having suffered him to live' in spite of the fact that his upper teeth had been cut first.

The witch-doctor was the duly accredited representative of the tribe in negotiating with the spirits on its behalf. Anyone else who presumed to have dealings with them was guilty of witchcraft, a public enemy who must die. There was no such thing as death from natural causes (since there were no such things as cause and effect): when anyone died he must have been bewitched, and it behoved the witch-doctor to identify the criminal. The method of identification was ordeal by poison: to vomit the poison was to prove one's innocence. On the death of a chief the ordeal might be administered to very large numbers of his former subjects. To all the other causes of violent death must be added death by poisoning at the hands of the witch-doctor.

Undoubtedly the witch-doctors believed in their own mumbo-jumbo; they were as superstition-ridden as anyone else. But that did not prevent some of them from mixing an emetic with the poison when they wished or were bribed to spare the accused; just as the superstition of the layman (if we may use the term) did not prevent him from bringing an accusation of witch-craft against someone whom he hated, or of whom he was jealous.

Small wonder, then, that, as Sheane put it, 'the weight of witchcraft and the fear of magic has crushed any nascent critical faculty to death'. Yet, in the opinion of the same author, sensuality was an even greater barrier to progress than superstition. And here, of course, more recent opinion disagrees with him. It has become usual to justify the initiation rites to which both boys and girls were subjected on reaching the age of puberty, and the payment known as *lobola* which, in some tribes, was made to their prospective fathers-in-law by men arranging to marry. The early missionaries are censured or at best pitied for ignorance and narrow-mindedness in condemning the former as lascivious and the latter as implying that women were mer-chandise to be bought. It is pointed out that the lasciviousness which in greater or less degree attended the initiation rites was incidental to their primary purpose, which was to give useful instruction to the girls in the arts of the housewife and to the boys in the duties of the husband and warrior. Again, *lobola* was not an unconditional payment for a chattel, but was returnable to the husband if the wife gave him grounds for divorce; if, however, he ill-treated her so that she ran away to her parents, he could not claim repayment. Thus both he and his father-in-law had a financial stake (usually measured in head of cattle) in the success of the marriage, and in fact marriages were notably more stable among *lobola*-paying tribes than among others. *Lobola* may be called a sort of insurance payment, just as initiation rites were all that the Bantu had by way of a state educational system. And, to pursue the rather far-fetched analogy, polygamy served in lieu of national assistance payments to make provision for women, often elderly, who would otherwise have been destitute.

Undoubtedly there is much validity in this line of argument; though perhaps it may be mentioned that in recent years more than one politician in West Africa, haranguing a public meeting about the excellence of traditional African institutions in general and polygamy in particular, has been shouted down by a crowd of angry women. It is unfortunate that detailed anthropological knowledge, because of the very way in which it must be acquired, could not have been available at the time when it would have been most useful. Had the early missionaries been equipped with it, instead of having to find out for themselves what they could (and some of them found out a great deal), they might have been more careful not to drive out one devil from the house only to leave it 'swept and garnished' to be re-occupied by seven others worse than the first. In other words, a premature attack on a socially useful custom is likely to do more harm than good, however objectionable the custom may be on moral grounds. But to recognise this is a very different matter from imagining that one standard of morality is as good as another, provided only that it is equally suited to the environment of the people concerned.

'Marriage', as Lord Hailey points out, 'is seen as an institution for securing legitimate descendants for the lineage rather than for regulating sex relations' (*African Survey*, 1956 edition, p. 30).[1] It is also an arrangement for the division of labour, an

---

[1] Cf. Orde-Browne: 'Marriage, like murder, was regarded as the removal

unequal division in which the women raise the crops and pound the grain as well as cooking the food and rearing the children, while the men perform such occasional or seasonal tasks as hunting, fishing, cutting wood and building huts; at the period of which we are speaking their main occupation was to fight.

Marriage thus understood is a sexual and economic arrangement between a unit of one kinship-group and a unit of another. The pagan Bantu had no idea whatever of the dignity and sanctity of the human personality; all that mattered to him was his place in the web of kinship and the structure of tribal institutions. His relations with other people might be highly complex, but their very complexity was due to the fact that they were conventional and institutionalised, like those of the bee or the ant. Hence any weakening of traditional social bonds, as a result of alien educational and economic influences, has had the short-term result of demoralising the people and removing the basis of their self-respect. When sympathetic white man saw this happening a generation ago, they condemned their own people for 'cultural aggression' and attacked 'detribalisation' as an unmitigated evil. Indeed, as early as the 1890s, H. H. Johnston had remarked that the young men who were educated by the missions 'have lost the easy carriage and independent bearing of the unsophisticated native, and shuffle and slouch along in a lazy, loose-jointed manner', and that the mission girls were the worse for not undergoing 'the excellent native discipline which enforces amongst the women a modest bearing and a certain amount of deference towards people of the opposite sex' (*British Central Africa* (Methuen, 1897), pp. 195, 202). But Johnston had not drawn the conclusion that a European type of education was unnecessary or undesirable for Africans; on the contrary, he had concluded that at least three generations would be required to enable Africans fully to assimilate the civilising influences which the white man brought. Subsequent experience has shown that this assessment was substantially correct.

of a social unit from the group, thus requiring compensation.' (*The African Labourer* (O.U.P., 1933), p. 7.)

A Hundred Years Ago

In all this there is, of course, no justification whatever for feelings of moral or racial superiority on the part of people who, through no merit of their own, have inherited a loftier outlook and a richer culture than the nineteenth-century Bantu possessed. Nor should we forget the attractive and admirable qualities of which these impulsive children of nature frequently gave proof: their gay and boisterous good humour, and their devoted loyalty to a leader who could inspire their confidence. Although they were sometimes absurdly suspicious, they were also sometimes absurdly trusting, and, if they were lacking in prudence and forethought, it is not at all certain that that lack should be censured by people whose own religion bids them take no thought for the morrow.

But although it would be presumptuous to pass moral judgment upon the Africans themselves, it is both legitimate and necessary to make a historical assessment of the conditions under which they were living when the first British pioneers came into their midst. And only by a wilful disregard of abundant evidence is it possible to evade the conclusion that, on the whole, the picture was one of brutality, callousness, suffering and futility, and that the situation did not include any factors which offered hope of improvement in the future. No doubt it is wise to look with great scepticism at all claims, past or present, to a 'civilising mission', and to suspect those who have put forward such claims of being chiefly interested in gain for themselves or prestige for their own country, or in both combined. Nevertheless if it had not been for the coming of the British, or of some other people capable of playing a similar historic role, there is every reason to suppose that the tribes of the Rhodesias and Nyasaland would have remained, for centuries or perhaps millennia, sparsely scattered over a vast area, dominated by the immensity of the surrounding country and the capriciousness of nature, without the art of writing or the use of numbers, with scarcely the slightest idea of the relationship of cause and effect, with no ideals higher than the pride of bloodshed, with their whole environment and conditions of life promoting an attitude of apathy, improvidence, and fatalism.

CHAPTER 3

Christianity and Commerce

I t was while they were temporarily settled in the Transvaal that the Matabele first made contact with the British. Very occasionally a trader or big-game hunter ventured among them. In 1829 two of these traders were accompanied on their return by two of Mziligazi's indunas (headmen and military commanders), one of whom was his chief councillor, named Umnombate. For Mziligazi had heard of the mission station which Robert Moffat had established at Kuruman, among the southern Bechuana, and his curiosity had been aroused. With its well-built houses, its spacious brick church, its workshops, its fenced and irrigated garden producing an abundance of fruit and flowers and vegetables on the fringe of the Kalahari desert, it was an oasis of nineteenth-century civilisation as well as of Christian compassion, and was the halting-place of every British traveller on his way to or from the north.

In his journal Moffat gives the following account of the indunas' visit:

'On their arrival here with three attendants, everything astonished and interested them, and they themselves were the objects of still greater astonishment to our [Bechuana] people, who stared as though regarding another order of beings. They were shown every attention, and they in turn were full of gratitude. The order of worship and the singing arrested their attention, while the water-courses, gardens, houses, and blacksmith's forge kept their minds in constant exercise. Difficulties arose about their safe return to their own country. A report was spread that the tribes through which they had to pass intended to mur-

MAP 3. *Location of the Pioneer Missions*

der them as spies, and they were naturally in some alarm. In view of the warlike disposition and mighty power of the Matabele, who had already destroyed so many great tribes and deluged the Bakwena country with blood, I could not help fearing the dire results if anything should happen to these peaceful messengers.' He therefore himself accompanied them to the borders of their own country. But when he proposed to turn back, leaving them to complete their own return journey in safety, they pressed him to go on with them to visit their master, 'who, they declared, would be ready to kill them for allowing me to go back after coming so far. I at last consented.'

So Moffat came into the presence of Mziligazi, who welcomed him cordially, and marvelled at the ox-wagons which he had brought with him, especially the wheels on which they 'walked'. He remained eight days, 'during which I had many interviews with the chief and received many tokens of his friendship. . . . Laying his hand on my shoulder he said: "My heart is all white as milk; I am still wondering at the love of a stranger who never saw me. . . . I live today by you, a stranger." I replied that I was not aware of having rendered him such service. Pointing to the chiefs who had visited the Kuruman he instantly rejoined: "These are my great servants whom I love, they are my eyes and ears, and what you did to them you did to me." ' (Quoted by J. S. Moffat, *The Lives of Robert and Mary Moffat* (T. F. Unwin, London, 1885), pp. 158–64.)

Mziligazi urged him to prolong his visit, and made him promise to return and stay a year. It is hard to account for this display of gratitude and affection by a bloodthirsty despot in the fullness of his power and the prime of life, especially as Moffat not only explained that he, Moffat, was not a trader, but 'told him that though his cattle-posts were numerous they were lost in the immense and solitary region which was as a land that mourned, while innumerable bones that strewed the plains seemed to call to heaven for vengeance'. Perhaps he had some hope that Moffat might be able and willing to help him in fending off attacks by the Zulus: in 1833 one of Moffat's fellow missionaries suggested that this might be his motive. Then, too, it was of little avail for a missionary to protest that he was not a trader. This was indeed true in the sense that he did not seek financial profit by taking such exports as ivory to the markets of civilised men. But in another and perhaps more important sense every white man in the interior of Africa had no choice but to be a trader, since there was no currency, and all food and labour services had to be paid for in calico and other trade goods, such as beads and copper wire for use as ornaments; and the price often had to be settled by hard bargaining.

But it is improbable that Mziligazi was primarily seeking material or political advantages for himself in his dealings with Moffat, and it is not even certain that he was thinking of such things at all. He was a man of strong emotions, and seems to have felt a craving for the friendship and affection of one or two people as well as for the slavish obedience of the multitude. The death of his favourite wife in 1861, when he was growing old, upset him deeply, though he had upwards of two hundred others. It is quite possible that Moffat was the only other person to whom he was ever united by any real bond of human sympathy. In the extreme simplicity and intensity of his religious convictions, and in the domineering force of personality that burned behind an enormous black beard, Moffat must have been as impressive as an Old Testament patriarch reincarnate. His relations with Mziligazi were based on the mutual respect of two born leaders of men.

Though he could not abandon his life's work among the southern Bechuana to undertake a mission to the Matabele, Moffat was eager to prepare the way for others to do so. But it was not until 1835 that he had an opportunity to fulfil his promise to pay another visit to Mziligazi. In that year an expedition headed by Dr. (afterwards Sir) Andrew Smith was sent from Cape Colony to explore the country beyond the Vaal. It consisted of several explorers supported by a few soldiers, with seven wagons. When they reached Kuruman Moffat decided to accompany them, and his presence assured Smith of a friendly reception from Mziligazi, who received Moffat himself with great joy. 'At length he repeated my name two or three times, and said: "Now my eyes see you, my heart is white as milk." This he repeated again and again, laying hold of my hand and stroking my beard. . . . He seemed as if he could not help laying his hand first on one of my shoulders and then on the other, and sometimes taking a lock of my beard in his hand.' Moffat remained with Mziligazi for two months on this occasion, while the expedition pursued its work of scientific observation, or, as the Matabele might reasonably have suspected, of spying out the country for future settlement from the Cape. In fact, Moffat's son records that: 'The expedition was accorded full liberty to come and to go in any part of the wide extent of country then under the rule of Moselikatse [i.e. Mziligazi]; and it speaks well for its conduct and discipline that, during the long stay of this party of between twenty and thirty white men of very different grades in life, not a single serious misunderstanding or act of injury seems to have occurred.' (*Lives of Robert and Mary Moffat*, p. 194.)

Mziligazi on his side wished to learn more about the British, and sent Umnombate, his chief councillor, with a deputation to accompany Smith's expedition on its return journey to Cape Town, where it was to convey to Governor Sir Benjamin D'Urban an expression of goodwill from the Matabele king. A vague treaty of friendship was in fact concluded, and the indunas returned to tell their master of the marvels of the colonial capital.

Not long afterwards the Matabele were thrust out of the Transvaal by the combined pressure of Boer settlers and Zulu raiders, and when Mziligazi halted his northward march he was separated from Kuruman by a distance of about seven hundred miles. It was not until 1854, nineteen years after Moffat's second visit, that the two men met again.

In 1839, when Moffat was in England on leave, he made the acquaintance of David Livingstone, who was at that time a man of twenty-six, and was studying medicine with the intention of becoming a medical missionary. He had been accepted as a member of the London Missionary Society, to which Moffat himself belonged. Both men were Scots of humble origin— Moffat had worked as a gardener and Livingstone in a cotton-mill—and both were utterly dedicated men. Moffat spoke to him of the Kuruman mission, and of the vast extent of territory to the north where, he said, 'I had sometimes seen, in the morning sun, the smoke of a thousand villages, where no missionary had ever been.' It was a phrase to kindle the imagination, and Livingstone could not know that it was a gross exaggeration, for there were probably not a thousand villages in the whole of Bechuanaland, where even today the total population is a mere 300,000. Moffat was something of a romantic, and could not bear to sacrifice picturesqueness for the sake of accuracy. In this respect he differed entirely from Livingstone, who had a scientific turn of mind which his medical training developed, and who loved to collect precise information and record it in matter-of-fact prose. This is not to say that Moffat's integrity was less than Livingstone's: the difference between them was one of intellect and temperament rather than of moral worth. Both were great men, but Livingstone was the better educated as well as the greater.

In July 1841 Livingstone arrived at Kuruman, and almost immediately began a series of explorations of the more northerly parts of Bechuanaland with a view to founding a station of his own. For the next ten years he worked as a missionary among the Bakhatla and the Bakwena, between two and three hundred miles north of Kuruman. But the local population was too small to give adequate scope to a man of his energy and vision. The country to the west was desert, and to the east were the Transvaal Boers, who distrusted missionaries, desired to have no natives in their vicinity except as drudges to themselves, and in 1852 actually attacked and destroyed Livingstone's mission-station (fortunately in his absence), because they were enraged to find that the Bakwena had firearms, and jumped to the conclusion that Livingstone must have supplied them. But even before this misfortune befell him he had become convinced that his true sphere of work lay much farther to the north, away from both the desert and the Boers.

In 1849, accompanied by two big-game hunters who were wealthy and generous enough to bear all the expenses of the journey, he had gone far north across almost waterless country and discovered Lake Ngami. Two years later one of these friends, W. C. Oswell, again enabled him to proceed northwards, and this time he was able to visit Chief Sebituane, whose fame had already reached him, and whose headquarters were on the Chobe River, a tributary of the upper Zambesi.

Christianity and Commerce

Sebituane was the leader of a comparatively small body of Basuto marauders who came to be known as Makololo. A vigorous and able commander, he led his party northwards, murdering and plundering as barbarously as the Matabele, with whom for a time he disputed the possession of the western Transvaal. Worsted in this struggle, he continued northwards into Barotseland, where, in 1838, he and his followers were able to establish themselves in a position of dominance, because they happened to arrive at a time when the Barotse were paralysed by a dispute about the succession. His rule extended over the whole country between the upper Zambesi and the Kafue. But, because of the hostility of the Matabele, his former rivals, now established in their new domain south of the Zambesi, he thought it prudent to take refuge among the mosquito-infested swamps and islands of the Chobe River.

He received Livingstone and Oswell with great cordiality, and made a most favourable impression upon them both. Undoubtedly he had much intelligence and force of personality, and knew how to display a truly regal courtesy and generosity. But it is hard to see how a man with such a record could have won Livingstone's admiration and affection to such an extent as he did, especially as he admitted that he had recently sold two hundred young slaves to half-caste Portuguese traders from the west coast in return for guns to be used against the Matabele. Livingstone was even aware that the magnificent welcome given to himself was motivated by the desire to make use of him as a supplier of firearms. Yet he looked upon Sebituane as a model of all that an African chief should be, before conversion. And this intensity of affection and esteem is the more remarkable as the chief died scarcely more than a fortnight after their first meeting.

Not only was Sebituane Livingstone's ideal chief, but the Makololo were his ideal tribe. It appears to have been a case of almost wilful self-deception. As the years had passed he had more and more looked to the distant north as the region of his missionary vocation, and his hopes had been fixed on the famous chief long before they had met. Here, surely, in this land of

many rivers, was the place of opportunity to which he was being
guided by the hand of God Himself. And, once an idea pertain-
ing to his vocation became lodged in Livingstone's head, a formidable accumulation of evidence was required to remove it.

The ideal chief died, but the ideal mission-field remained.
The next task was to find some reasonably convenient means of
access to it. First he went south to Cape Town, and put his wife
—Moffat's daughter Mary—and children aboard ship for England. Then he returned to the Makololo country, where
Sekeletu, the eighteen-year-old son of Sebituane, now reigned.
He witnessed the treacherous seizure, by Sekeletu and his followers, of a dissident faction of the Makololo; he saw the
prisoners being thrown into the river as food for crocodiles.
And he had to admit that, 'though all, including the chief,
were as kind and attentive to me as possible, . . . yet to endure
the dancing, roaring, and singing, the jesting, anecdotes, grumbling, quarrelling, and murdering of these children of nature,
seemed more like a severe penance than anything I had before
met with in the course of my missionary duties. I took thence a
more intense disgust at heathenism than I had before, and
formed a greatly elevated opinion of the latent effects of missions in the south, among tribes which are reported to have
been as savage as the Makololo.' But, like his father before him,
Sekeletu thought Livingstone might be useful. For this was the
son-in-law of Moffat, who was known to have great influence
with the dreaded Mziligazi. The Makololo would be in less
danger from Matabele raids if they had Livingstone living in
their midst. Sekeletu took custody of Livingstone's ox-wagon,
since the country beyond was impassable for it, and kept it safe
with all its contents until his return several years later.

From the Makololo country Livingstone journeyed north-
westward, on foot, on ox-back, and sometimes by canoe, to the
Portuguese port of Loanda on the Atlantic coast. In the later
stages of his journey, weary, feverish and desperately short of
supplies, he was given valuable help by the Portuguese whom he
encountered. Indeed the friendliness shown towards him by
the Portuguese, in the Zambesi valley as well as in Angola, is

remarkable in view of the fact that they were opposed to every-thing he stood for, being deeply involved in the slave trade. Probably because of this trade, the tribes whom he encountered were inhospitable and aggressively exacting in their demands for payment for the privilege of passing through their country. Since the country itself was too difficult for regular use, Living-stone concluded that the route to his new mission-field must be by way of the east coast instead of the west.

So, having rested in Loanda and collected fresh supplies, he returned to the Makololo country and went on to complete the crossing of the African continent by way of the Zambesi. This was the greatest single achievement of his career, accomplished with scanty resources by unalterable tenacity of purpose and exceptional robustness of physique. The news of it made him a national hero, and assured him of an attentive hearing for all his subsequent pronouncements.

When he reached Quilimane in May 1856, it was four years since he had set out from Cape Town. By the following Decem-ber he was back in England, convinced that the Zambesi was 'God's highway' to the interior, and hoping that it might prove to be navigable as far upstream as the great Falls which he had discovered and named in honour of the Queen. He earnestly wished that it might be a highway not only for the gospel but also for commerce. 'Legitimate commerce', he wrote, 'breaks up the isolation engendered by heathenism and the slave trade, and surely if we take advantage of the very striking peculiarity of the African character (i.e. their fondness for barter and agri-culture) we shall eventually bring this people within the sphere of Christian sympathy and the scope of missionary operations.'[1]

Thus, though he was entirely a missionary at heart, his own projects and enterprises were far wider than the conventional idea of missionary work. To rescue Africa from degradation and the slave trade, secular as well as sacred influences must, he believed, be used. Christianity, commerce, and civilisation—that was his formula. He favoured white settlement in the vast

[1] Livingstone to Clarendon, 26th January 1857. Quoted in G. Seaver, *David Livingstone, His Life and Letters* (Lutterworth, London, 1957), p. 299.

unoccupied parts of the African interior, believing that the influence of civilised communities upon the Africans could not fail to be profoundly beneficial; besides, how much better it would be for the slum-dwellers of Britain's cities to make a new start in the open spaces of Africa! Then, too, he saw great agricultural prospects in the Zambesi valley. Might it not eventually produce enough cotton to make Lancashire independent of the slave-grown cotton of the American South?

Sir Roderick Murchison, the President of the Royal Geographical Society, put him in touch with the Foreign Secretary, Lord Clarendon, and suggested that Clarendon should initiate a Government expedition, under Livingstone's leadership, to explore the River Zambesi and its tributaries to ascertain what opportunities they offered to legitimate trade. Clarendon took up the idea, Livingstone resigned from the London Missionary Society, and in 1858 the Zambesi expedition began.

It had one notable achievement, the discovery of Lake Nyasa in September 1859. The lake itself is 350 miles long, and the River Shiré connects it with the lower Zambesi. Even though the Murchison Cataracts on the Shiré prevent continuous navigation from the Zambesi delta to the north end of Nyasa, they do not occur far enough down-river to impede access to the Shiré Highlands, a fertile and comparatively healthy region well suited to the establishment of a mission. The discovery of the lake and of the river which leads to it did far more to open up the interior of Africa than the exploration of the Zambesi itself. Here the results were merely negative. The Kebrabasa Rapids above Tete proved to be completely impassable for a distance of about fifty miles, and to run through such wild and rocky country that they could not be by-passed by overland porterage as, with some difficulty, the Murchison Cataracts could be. So, after all, the Zambesi was not 'God's highway'. As Professor Debenham has remarked, 'Africa leads the continents in her potential hydro-electric power, but pays for that lead in lack of water communications.'

When the expedition was recalled by the Government in 1863, it appeared a miserable failure. Its work had been handicapped by the poor engine and sieve-like hull of the steamer with which it had been provided. Its members had suffered much from fever and frustration, and Livingstone's wife, who had come out to join him in 1862, died of fever soon after her arrival. Livingstone himself had proved utterly unsuited to the leadership of a party of white men, who expected to be treated as colleagues and taken into his confidence. Though he was a fundamentally humble man, he often appeared insufferably arrogant. It was not that he had any petty-minded love of power; it was simply that he was obsessed with the task in hand, his God-appointed task, in which his fellow-mortals had no business to meddle. As his lifelong friend Oswell charitably put it: 'One trait in his character was to do exactly whatever he set his mind on. . . . It was not the *sic volo sic jubeo* style of imperiousness but a quiet determination to carry out his views in his own way without feeling himself bound to give any reason or explanation further than that he intended doing so and so. It was an immense help to him, for it made him supremely self-reliant and if it had not been, he never could have done half that he did' (quoted in J. I. Macnair, *Livingstone the Liberator*, p. 90). But it meant that he could do his best work and do it most happily when he walked alone, except for a dozen or two uncomprehending Africans who carried his belongings.

In 1864, about the time when Livingstone arrived back in England, the Barotse overthrew the Makololo and annihilated them. From then on, not only was the way to Barotseland barred by the Kebrabasa Rapids, but the place itself had lost its former attraction as a field for Christian enterprise. His interest was now focused on Nyasaland and on the still unexplored country west of the lake. In the valley of the Shiré he had been appalled to find the slave trade being conducted with far greater destructiveness and cruelty than in Angola. But the slave-traders, whether Arab or Portuguese, had fled from his presence, and this led him to underestimate the amount of force and effort that would be required to stop their activities. A single steamer on Lake Nyasa, he believed, would suffice to cut their communications. The recall of the Zambesi expedition was merely an interruption of his work, which must be resumed as soon as he could return.

In 1866 he began the series of wanderings which continued until his death in 1873. He went up the Rovuma valley, round the south end of Lake Nyasa, and then proceeded to and fro around Lake Tanganyika and the Bemba country, discovering Lakes Mweru and Bangweulu. But all the toil, privations, and illnesses which he had endured were beginning to wear him down. His strength of will remained unchanged, but his vitality was diminished, and so was his resistance to disease. No longer could he dominate and control a mob of truculent savages by simply looking at them and bringing them under the command of his personality. He was obstructed and thwarted, and spent long periods in futile meanderings. But what mattered was that he remained. His long isolation in the remote interior aroused speculation as to whether he was alive or dead, and attracted public attention to south-central Africa. His meeting with the journalist-explorer Stanley at Ujiji in 1871 became the most famous incident in both their lives, thanks to the nervousness which prompted Stanley to greet him formally with words ideally suited to become a standard music-hall joke. Two years later came the news of his death kneeling at his bedside near Lake Bangweulu, and of how his body and his journals had been brought all the way to the coast by his native companions.

His body was buried in Westminster Abbey; his *Last Journals*, in which he exposed the horrors of the slave trade more vividly than he had ever done before, were published by his friend Horace Waller. If that had been the end of the story, his life would have been a heroic failure. He had been looking for the source of the Nile, and had found instead the source of the Congo; he had given his utmost endeavours to bring liberty to the captives, and the slave trade flourished as never before. His Bakwena were forsaken, and his Makololo were slain. But it was not the end, it was rather the beginning. Livingstone triumphed in death as he had never done in life.

Already, by the fame of his great achievement in crossing the continent, he had inspired the launching of three new missions.

Christianity and Commerce

Early in 1857, about the time when he was giving up his own membership of the London Missionary Society, the Society resolved to send a mission to the Makololo. Such a mission could not, however, survive in the unhealthy swamps on the Chobe: if it were to establish itself successfully, Sekeletu and his people would have to move to the high ground near the lower Kafue. This, it seems, they would have been glad to do, for they themselves would have been healthier there; but they were deterred by fear of the Matabele. The Society hoped to overcome this fear by sending a mission to the Matabele themselves, and using the influence of the veteran Moffat to restrain them from carrying their raids beyond the Zambesi.

The third mission was undertaken by the English universities —Oxford, Cambridge, and Durham—in response to the famous appeal made by Livingstone at the end of his speech to the University of Cambridge towards the end of the same year (1857): 'I direct your attention to Africa. I know in a few years I shall be cut off in that country, which is now open. Do not let it be shut again. I go back to Africa to try to make an open path for commerce and Christianity. Do you carry out the work I have begun. I leave it with you.' The Universities' Mission to Central Africa was (and is) a High Church Anglican body, disowning the name of Protestant; whereas Livingstone was a Free Churchman. But, like the Apostle Paul before him, he did not care who preached the gospel so long as it was in fact preached. He himself, in the course of his Zambesi expedition, guided the missionaries to their destination in the Shiré Highlands. They arrived there in 1861, at the worst possible time, when the Lake people among whom they settled were being harried and enslaved by the Yao invaders. Bishop Mackenzie, their leader, was so distressed by the barbarities which he witnessed that he twice put himself at the head of a war party and succeeded in driving the Yao back. But the respite was only temporary. Mackenzie died of fever, and after his death the position of his clergy became increasingly precarious and miserable. When his successor, Bishop Tozer, arrived in 1863, it was obvious to everyone except Livingstone that the mission must be withdrawn. Tozer established his headquarters on the island of Zanzibar, and it is symbolic of the mission's achievement that a cathedral now stands on the site of the old slave market. From Zanzibar the mission penetrated inland, into what is now the state of Tanganyika, establishing stations as it proceeded, until eventually it reached the Nyasa country. But not until 1881–2 were the shores of the lake revisited by any member of the mission, and not until 1886 was regular work resumed there, with the launching of a mission-steamer on the lake. And by that time Livingstone had long been dead.

The other mission on which he had set his heart, the one sent by the L.M.S. to the Makololo, had been equally disappointing and even more disastrous. Two clergymen, Holloway Helmore and Roger Price, accompanied by their respective wives and their young children, arrived at Sekeletu's headquarters early in 1860, after suffering agonies from heat and thirst on the last stages of their journey to the fever-ridden Chobe. They expected to find Livingstone there, but he did not arrive until the following August. Sekeletu was not expecting their arrival, and would neither move with them to the healthy uplands nor permit them to go without him. Even if Roger Price was mistaken in believing that he poisoned an ox which he sent them as a present, the best that can be said for him is that he acted entirely in the spirit of the maxim:

> *Thou shalt not kill—but needst not strive*
> *Officiously to keep alive.*

Within a few weeks the only survivors were Price and two of Helmore's children, who, after Sekeletu had robbed them of almost all their belongings, struggled to escape to Kuruman, and were rescued on their way by a colleague who had been coming up-country to join them in their mission.

The second enterprise begun by the L.M.S. in 1857 was at least able to survive. Its survival was due in part to the healthiness of the high veld which the Matabele occupied, and in part to the influence which Robert Moffat had gained over the mind of Mziligazi. In 1854 Moffat had paid him a third visit, making the long and arduous journey at the age of almost sixty in the hope of being able to get in touch with Livingstone, from whom nothing had been heard since he had set out for the Makololo country at the beginning of the great journey which was to include the crossing of Africa. Though Moffat had not himself been able to reach the Makololo country on account of the tsetse fly, he had been able to send valuable supplies to await Livingstone's arrival. Mziligazi had provided a party of Matabele carriers to take the bundles to the Zambesi, where, however, the Makololo feared to approach them to accept delivery; they had therefore departed, leaving their bundles on the river bank to be collected by their enemies after they had gone. Yet when Livingstone arrived some months later on his return from Loanda, he found that the Makololo had kept everything safe for him.

On this visit Moffat had found Mziligazi growing old and so afflicted with dropsy that he could not walk. The old warrior wept for joy at their reunion. Moffat remained with him for three months, and was able to do much to relieve his dropsy.

When the Directors of the L.M.S. decided to send a mission to the Matabele, they instructed Moffat to accompany it, in order to assure it of a friendly reception and to help it to become established. But Moffat did not wait for the new missionaries. He at once set out and visited Mziligazi for the fourth time, to obtain his consent in advance. It was well that he did so, for the consent was given hesitantly and with reluctance. If his old friend were to be the missionary, he would be delighted, but: 'These new men, I do not know them. All men are not alike.' He was prevailed upon to admit them by the promise that one of them would be Moffat's son, John Smith Moffat. Nevertheless, when they arrived two years later, in 1859, they were far from welcome, and were denied permission to build themselves houses before the rains began, or to sow seed to provide their own future food supply. 'The king paid us a visit,' wrote Emily, the wife of J. S. Moffat. 'He eyed everything eagerly, and is not above begging for anything he fancies. There were some wild flowers on the table in a mug, and he asked if they were to be "eaten"! His Majesty wore a cap, great-coat, and a few beads round his ankles. . . . We cannot buy from him, for he always

asks for our useful things which we can ill spare. . . . We are
short of food and spend our days wondering what will come.
One of our greatest annoyances has been the rats. They have
tormented us sadly at night, scampering about our wagons,
eating away at our sacks of flour, and, worst of all, running over
us' (quoted by R. U. Moffat in *John Smith Moffat,* John Murray,
London, 1921, p. 93). After two whole months of frustration
and anxiety, the missionaries were at last allowed to establish
themselves. The elder Moffat remained with them for another
six months, during which, in his son's words, he 'smoothed a
hundred difficulties, such as must of necessity arise with a chief
and people so jealous and suspicious'; then he said farewell to
Mziligazi for the last time.

For the next five years J. S. Moffat with one or two colleagues
lived at Inyati, where Mziligazi usually dwelt, north of Bulawayo. 'Personally we were safe enough,' he wrote. 'The chief
had given my father his promise to take care of us, and this
promise was royally kept, and we never had one moment's un-
easiness on that score.' Mziligazi was willing enough to call his
people together for a religious service, and to be present himself. On only one of these occasions did he behave discourteously,
and his reason for doing so was significant. The younger Moffat
was preaching on the subject of prayer, explaining that every
one of the audience, whether man, woman, or child, could speak
to God Himself and be heard. Mziligazi rose, trembling with
rage, and shouted: 'You are a liar!' Twice he shouted it, and
each time there was a dutiful roar of applause from the audience.
Afterwards, however, some of them sent a message of apology
for having joined in the applause: 'We dare not be silent,' they
explained. 'but nevertheless your words about God were very
sweet to our hearts.'

A similar incident occurred in the time of Mziligazi's successor, Lobengula, who interrupted one of the missionaries,
William Sykes, when Sykes referred in a sermon to the King of
all the earth.

But the touchiness of the two successive Matabele despots on
the subject of their royal prerogative was not the main obstacle

to the mission's work. This, as J. S. Moffat reported to the
Directors, was 'the people themselves, in their habits, and in
their natural indifference to the truth'. J. B. Thomson, an outstanding missionary who served in Matabeleland from 1870 to
1876, expressed the matter more fully. 'The greatest hindrance
of all our work here', he declared, 'is to be found in the constitution and polity of the tribe. The Gospel goes dead against everything which distinguishes them as the Amantabele [i.e. Mata-
bele] Tribe—(1) It destroys all despotic power, makes men intelligent, thinking and responsible beings, who seek for judgement and justice. It takes from the King all Divine power
attributed to him, and attributes it to God alone. (2) It destroys
entirely all their military standing, whose sole object is bloodshed and death. . . . (3) It destroys all polygamy, and also that
honoured and much to be dreaded enemy of all life and liberty
—I mean witchcraft. These are the monuments of the nation,
in which they glory. . . . To receive the Gospel is to give them
all up. This the people know, and especially the king.'[1]

Not until the mission had been in the country for more than
thirty years did it make a single convert to the Christian faith.
It is scarcely surprising that in 1872 the Directors considered
withdrawing it from a field in which all its efforts appeared to
be thrown away.

Such were the fortunes of the three missions launched with
fervent enthusiasm on the morrow of the greatest feat of exploration in Livingstone's career. But when the news of his death
became known, and when his body was laid to rest in Westminster Abbey, the occasion seemed to be one for rededication
rather than for mourning. Among those who attended the funeral
was Dr. James Stewart, the head of the mission-college of Lovedale in Cape Colony. In 1860, when still a medical student,
Stewart had contrived to obtain enough support to go out to the
Zambesi and the Shiré at the time of Livingstone's expedition,

---

[1] L.M.S. Archives: Moffat to Tidman, 16th October 1865, and Thomson
to Mullens, 25th March 1873. For these and subsequent quotations from
the L.M.S. correspondence I am indebted to Mr. K. McWilliams, and for
permission to publish them to Miss I. Fletcher, the Librarian of the L.M.S.

to investigate the possibilities of beginning a mission there. The conditions which he had found were those in which the Universities' Mission was compelled to withdraw to Zanzibar, and he had been forced to admit that it was not practicable to put his project into effect. But now, in 1874, he thought the time had come to take it up again, and he proposed that the mission should be called Livingstonia, as 'a memorial of Livingstone, and the one of all others which I knew very well he would have himself preferred'.

Scottish Presbyterianism was at that time divided into three main bodies: the established Church of Scotland; the Free Church of Scotland, which had seceded from it in the famous 'Disruption' of 1843; and the United Presbyterians, whose church had been formed by the fusion of groups which had broken away from the established Church in earlier schisms. These churches were divided by the political and social conflicts of the past rather than by any differences in doctrine, and in the twentieth century they have been reunited—except for a small, rigidly fundamentalist remnant of the Free Church, commonly referred to as the 'Wee Frees'. In the 1870s they could already agree to co-operate, and this was particularly true of the non-established bodies. The Free Church, which made the shores of Lake Nyasa its sphere of work, was immeasurably strengthened by the presence of a medical missionary who was lent to it, at first on a temporary basis, by the United Presbyterians. This was Dr. Robert Laws. When Dr. Stewart, the first head of the Free Church mission, returned to Lovedale at the end of 1877, Laws became his deputy, and eventually became head of the mission in his own right. The history of Livingstonia is very largely the biography of this great man, who guided and inspired it from its earliest days until only a few years before his death in 1934.

The first site of Livingstonia was on Cape Maclear, at the south end of Lake Nyasa. In 1881 the mission was transferred to Bandawe, in the Tonga country on the western shore. The Tonga, harried and oppressed by the Angoni, were huddled in large, filthy villages on the edge of the lake or scattered on ledges and in caves on the face of the mountains, and the mission could do nothing to help them either materially or spiritually unless it could influence the tribe of marauders who were keeping them in abject terror. These were the northern Angoni, under Mombera. Dr. Laws visited Mombera in 1879, and won his respect to a degree comparable with Robert Moffat's influence over Mziligazi. From 1882 until 1887 two or three members of the mission resided at Mombera's village, existing on sufferance for the sake of what could be extracted from them by insistent, arrogant begging; they could only practise patience, which J. S. Moffat, who had long experience of similar conditions among the Matabele, described as 'a commodity without which little can be done in the interior of Africa'. But after 1887 the missionaries ceased to be in danger, and their work became increasingly fruitful. Mombera himself remained a pagan until his death in 1891, but because of his affection for Dr. Laws he forbade his warriors to make any further raids upon the Tonga at Bandawe. For a time his people continued to raid in other directions, but as the influence of the mission grew they became entirely peaceful; in 1897 they even elected a Christian to their chieftainship.

The conversion of the northern Angoni made it possible for the Tonga to acquire confidence and self-respect, and, under the influence of Dr. Laws and his staff, to develop into the most educated and enterprising people in Nyasaland.

When the Free Church mission was being organized early in 1875, the established Church of Scotland decided to start a mission of their own, though they had considerable difficulty in recruiting suitable staff, or indeed any staff at all. Those whom they did send out were mainly artisans, with an inexperienced young doctor and, after a two-years' delay, a clergyman who was to be in charge of the mission, but who, although scholarly and well-intentioned, lacked the intense moral conviction and force of character required to control the situation. The missionaries established themselves in the Shiré Highlands, and called the place Blantyre, after the town where Livingstone was born. Duff Macdonald, the clergyman, made a most thorough and valuable study of Yao customs. But in other respects the mission in its first phase was a disgrace to the church which sent it out, for its members, acting initially from worthy motives, assumed the power to punish crime, and, allowing themselves to be corrupted by the exercise of power in a savage environment, were guilty of several acts of extreme brutality, including the flogging of a man to death. The truth leaked out, and, when the ecclesiastical authorities in Scotland found that they could not hush it up, they made thorough enquiries which led to the dismissal of the entire staff, except one or two artisans.

The new head of the mission, appointed in 1881, was D. C. Scott, a man of great creative ability whose lasting monument is the majestic brick church which he himself designed without having had any architectural training, and caused to be erected without asking the permission of the Foreign Mission Committee at home, because he was sure that they would refuse to countenance a project which was so obviously impracticable. The church was opened in 1891. But the dominant figure at Blantyre was Alexander Hetherwick, who arrived in 1883, succeeded Scott as official head of the mission in 1898, and remained in its service until 1928. Craggy, ascetic, methodical and persevering, he was a born theocrat. His strength of purpose and practical effectiveness were accompanied by narrowness of mind, especially in the earlier years of his career. For example, he was opposed, with good reason, to the extreme drunkenness in which the natives indulged when their supplies of beer permitted it; but native beer consumed in moderation was a valuable anti-scorbutic for a people who did not have nearly enough fruit and vegetables. Hetherwick, however, forbade his converts to touch beer at all. 'Are you a Christian?' a High Court Judge asked a witness, in the days of the British Protectorate. 'No,' the man replied, 'I drink beer.'

While the two Scottish missions were laying the foundations of British influence in Nyasaland, the L.M.S. was beginning work in the even more remote African interior, on the shores of Lake Tanganyika. They reached their destination, Ujiji, by proceeding overland from Zanzibar, and for some years they

Christianity and Commerce

itinerated around the lake, using sailing boats and eventually a steamer. But, partly because of their heavy losses by death or by retirement on account of illness, they had not enough man-power to achieve any solid results by so much dispersal of effort. So, about ten years after the beginning of the mission in 1877, they settled down in two stations near the south end of the lake; other stations were afterwards opened in the same region. Here they were able to avail themselves of the water route by Lake Nyasa and the Shiré, with only a comparatively short porterage between the two lakes. Thus, by the late 1880s, there was a chain of British missions stretching from Blantyre in the Shiré Highlands by way of Livingstonia and the Universities' Mission (on Likoma Island near the eastern shore of Lake Nyasa) to the south end of Lake Tanganyika.

The central and southern parts of what was to become Northern Rhodesia were not yet the scene of any missionary settlement. A party of Jesuits did, indeed, attempt in 1880 to settle among the Tonga tribe—not to be confused with the Tonga of Nyasaland—on the Kafue highlands, the place to which Livingstone had hoped that the Makololo would move some twenty years previously; but this attempt ended in a disas-ter closely similar to that which had been sustained by Hel-more's mission to the Makololo themselves. Nor were mis-sionaries able to work in Mashonaland, where the Matabele made it clear that they would tolerate no European interfer-ence with their own routine of exploitation and murder.

In Barotseland many years passed after the departure of Roger Price before a renewed effort was made to introduce the gospel. During the interval the Barotse passed through a suc-cession of political upheavals. The overthrow and extermination of the Makololo in 1864 was followed by the reign of Sepopo, a son of the king who had died shortly before Sebituane's inva-sion. Sepopo's supreme pleasure was the thrill of watching other people dying in agony at his command, and after about five years his excesses of cruelty led to his own overthrow. His suc-cessor, his nephew Nganwina, was in turn overthrown after about six months by a revolt motivated by the ambition of

Nganwina's cousin Lewanika, who now, in 1870, assumed possession of the precarious throne.

The first white man to visit the Barotse after the collapse of the Makololo mission was an adventurous trader named George Westbeech, whose diary, recently published in the Robins Series (by Chatto and Windus), is a historical source of first-rate importance. After spending several years hunting and trading in Matabeleland, he proceeded to the Barotse valley, where he traded with such success that between 1871 and 1876 he exported no less than 30,000 lb. of ivory. Westbeech was an honourable man, and his dealings with the Barotse helped to make them disposed to be friendly to François Coillard, whom, when the time came, he did all he could to help.

The Paris Evangelical Society, which represented the missionary energies of French Protestantism, had become firmly established in Basutoland, and in 1878 Coillard, who had served it there for twenty years, made his way to the upper Zambesi and sent a message to Lewanika that he wished to begin a mission to the Barotse, who, because of their previous subjection to the Makololo, spoke the same language as the Basuto. But for various reasons Coillard was unable to remain, and six years elapsed before he could return. During the last two years of that interval a Scottish missionary, F. S. Arnot, representing a group of Plymouth Brethren, resided in the country, at Lewanika's request, before proceeding to his main work in Katanga—the country which afterwards formed part of the Congo state, projecting into the middle of Northern Rhodesia.

Arnot opened a school for such children as would come to him, and Lewanika then asked him what he had come to teach. He replied that his chief message was of divine grace, but that in addition he wished to teach the children to read and write, 'also all about the world they live in, and other things that the white men know, which are good for all people to know'. Lewanika then said: 'Yes, yes, that is good, to read, write, and to know numbers. But don't, don't teach them the Word of God; it's not nice. No, no, you must not teach that in this country.'

Christianity and Commerce

When Arnot left Barotseland in May 1884, he was aware that another revolution was imminent. When it occurred, Lewanika managed to escape with his fourteen-year-old son Letia (or Yeta), who afterwards succeeded him as king; the rebels murdered all his other children and all his wives, and put his ineffective cousin, Tatira Akafuna, on the throne in his place.

It was during this régime that Coillard arrived, in January 1885, to resume the work that Arnot had begun. Before the year was out, however, Lewanika had regained his throne and slaughtered his enemies. The witch-doctors were set to work to smell out treason, and the executioners to destroy it wherever it was found.

But although Coillard had sought and obtained the permission of Tatira Akafuna to build a mission-station at the capital, Lealui, there is no reason to suppose that Lewanika felt aggrieved because of his having had dealings with the *de facto* ruler.[1] On the contrary: 'Whatever his motives may be,' wrote Coillard, 'Lewanika has a great desire to see us established in his kingdom.' One reason for his friendliness was that he was influenced by the example of Khama, chief of the Bamangwato in northern Bechuanaland, the most worthy and enlightened ruler in the whole of south-central Africa. A further reason was his personal respect for Coillard, who was one of the greatest of the missionaries, a man of the calibre of Robert Moffat and Robert Laws, who impressed Lewanika as they impressed the savage autocrats with whom they for their part had dealings. It is true that Lewanika's attitude was variable, and at times dangerously hostile. 'What good are you all?' he burst out on one occasion. 'What do I want with a gospel that gives neither guns nor powder nor coffee nor tea nor sugar nor workmen to work for me?' But his vacillations are not difficult to account for,

[1] Professor Gluckman has, it is true, written: 'I am sure he distrusted Coillard because Coillard had negotiated with his usurper.' But on his own admission he has no evidence whatever to justify his being sure of it. And, if we must indulge in this sort of speculation, is it likely that Lewanika, himself a usurper, would have been a conscientious believer in the Bourbon doctrine of legitimacy? Or again, is it probable that such a highly intelligent realist would have cherished the American doctrine of non-recognition?

quite apart from the fickleness that seems to have been a Barotse characteristic. Some of his courtiers were opposed to the mission and all it stood for, and intrigued against it. The Mokwai, or 'Queen'—Lewanika's sister, whose position in the constitution of the tribe was second only to his, and who had been the rallying-point of his supporters at the time of his overthrow—was unfriendly. (Colonel Stevenson-Hamilton, who visited the country in 1899, found that her 'judicial murders, chiefly of women, had become so bad that Letia, her nephew, who is by way of being a Christian, was sent . . . a year or two ago to exercise a restrictive effect upon her'.) Coillard described his own place at court as above all that of 'a Micaiah[1] to this autocrat, who is incessantly befooled by the servile adulations surrounding him. . . . I see too much and at too close quarters.'

But the work went on, and increasingly bore fruit not only in conversions to the Christian faith but also in its humanising effect upon many, including Lewanika himself, who were not converted.

The cost was high, for the Barotse flood plain was so fever-ridden that white men could not expect to survive in it for long. Coillard himself outlived most of his colleagues, including his wife, who died in 1891; but he died of blackwater-fever in 1904. Indeed all these missions north of the Zambesi suffered a terribly high proportion of losses. By 1894, there were eleven dead among the thirty-six missionaries sent out by the L.M.S. to the Tanganyika mission since its inception in 1877, and at least an equal number had been invalided home. In the Universities' Mission, fifty-seven out of two hundred died in Africa in the first thirty years after an average service of little more than five years. So it was with the Scots in Nyasaland. But their spirit was expressed by Robert Laws in his reply to the suggestion that he should transfer his mission to a healthier place than Bandawe. 'Christ', he replied, 'chose to work in unhealthy malaria-stricken Capernaum, so that it came to be called His own city. It is enough that the servant be as his Master.'

'We have five stations', said Coillard in 1897, 'five places

[1] The reference is to 1 Kings, chap. 22.

like light-houses amid the darkness. . . . We have not only stations, but we have—graves. We have taken possession of the country by our graves.'

Yet these men were not quixotic fools. They knew that their duty was to remain alive if they could, for the work's sake, and to die only if and when they must. As far as possible they provided themselves with dry, airy houses, solidly built of brick, and with an adequate and properly balanced diet supplied as far as possible from their own mission gardens. With the exception of Arnot and the two colleagues who joined him in Katanga, they did not think it a necessary part of Christian humility to live like natives in mud huts, on a diet of porridge made from maize. On the contrary, they had what some people would nowadays call a 'prejudice' in favour of a civilised life, and thought they ought to set an example of it as well as of obedience to the gospel precepts.

What appears more questionable was the normal practice among Protestant missionaries of marrying and taking their wives with them, even at the start of the enterprise before any amenities had been created. And, quite as a matter of course, they begot the usual enormous Victorian families, only to mourn the death of one child after another in infancy or early youth. But the wives were fully as dedicated to the work as their husbands, and their presence contributed to the life and influence of the mission-stations a graciousness which would otherwise have been lacking. Moreover, the African found celibacy incomprehensible: it was the mark of a boy, and a boy (of whatever age) would not be listened to with the respect due to a man. The Roman Catholic White Fathers, who came to Northern Rhodesia in 1891, found that their celibacy was, in the words of their own Bishop Dupont, the 'heel of Achilles' of their system from the native standpoint.

To maintain a civilised life, especially a civilised family life, in the remote wilds of Africa necessarily involved a great burden of secular tasks and cares. They had to be their own gardeners, brick-makers, carpenters, builders, cooks, housekeepers and medical attendants, except in so far as they could persuade

E   65

exceedingly raw natives to enter their employment and learn how to do some of these jobs. But indeed they considered that the giving of such 'industrial training' was an essential part of their task: they held that habits of regular work must be among the aims of a sound moral training, and that a sound moral training was a necessary part of Christian teaching. Among different missions, it is true, the emphasis varied, and within some missions it changed with the passing of time. The Livingstonia mission, guided by Stewart and Laws, attached very great importance to it from the beginning. Does this mean that they can properly be labelled, in the sly phrase of one anthropologist, 'professional purveyors of white culture'? It does not. Dr. Laws, it is true, instructed his pupils not only in Christian doctrine, the 'three Rs', and various manual skills which he had himself mastered, but also in such things as the importance of public order, the necessity for taxation, the usefulness of sanitation, and the virtue of thrift. But he did so not from a prejudice in favour of 'white' culture, but from the considered conviction that these things ought to have a place in any culture. He also said this: 'I have always held very strongly that in the foreign field the native churches should grow up on their own lines and in their own surroundings if they are to be strong and healthy, and should not be presbyteries of any of our home churches'; and he went on to speak of 'the hindrance to the life and growth of the church brought about by trying to clothe an infant with the adult garments of the growth of centuries instead of the swaddling bands corresponding to its life history' (quoted in W. P. Livingstone, *Laws of Livingstonia*, p. 308). Those are the words of a man who had the wisdom to discriminate between the essential values of Western civilisation and the non-essential, imperfect, historically conditioned forms in which they were embodied and expressed in his own generation by his own fellow countrymen.

The most onerous of their secular tasks was the provision of transport. It was a problem which vexed every European traveller, but for the missionaries it was worse than for passing explorers and traders, since they required the means of con-

tinuous support on a permanent basis. In addition to such things
as clothes, tools, tea, coffee, sugar, and salt for their own use,
they needed an enormous supply of calico, beads, blankets and
other trade goods: a baggage train to serve as both purse and
bank account. And the more transport they required for their
impedimenta, the more impedimenta they required to pay for
their transport, especially where it could only be on the heads
of a file of porters, as at the Murchison Cataracts on the Shiré
or on the plateau between Lakes Nyasa and Tanganyika. It is
scarcely surprising that, when they were seen to be bringing so
much wealth into the country, they should have been as welcome in south-central Africa as holiday-makers are welcome in
a British seaside resort.

Dr. Laws had gone out to Africa for other purposes than to
act as storekeeper. This was a different matter from manual
labour, which he accepted as an integral part of his missionary
work: 'I have hauled ropes, driven an engine, sawed wood,
while a medical missionary at home or in India would have been
making pills or writing sermons. The nature of the case not only
justifies but renders such conduct necessary.' But when, in a
single year, he had expended a total of fifteen miles of calico,
something had to be done to relieve him of the burden. Besides,
his experience had convinced him of the soundness of Livingstone's opinion that the development of legitimate trade offered
the best prospect of eliminating the slave trade, and he would
even have felt morally justified in extending the Livingstonia
mission's trading activities beyond what was necessary for its
own requirements. But Dr. Stewart, who was still head of the
mission, was profoundly anxious to free its hands for its own
work. He therefore wrote to James Stevenson, a wealthy and
generous Glasgow merchant who was its chief sponsor in Scotland, urging how desirable it was in every way that a regular
store should be opened at Livingstonia. Stevenson took the matter up, and the outcome was that in 1878 a limited company was
formed. Known at first as the Livingstonia Central Africa Company, it soon took the name of the African Lakes Company. In
1879 it began operations in Africa.

Christianity and Commerce

It took over the little steamer, the *Ilala*, which the Livingstonia mission had, with most arduous toil, conveyed in sections past the Murchison Cataracts and put together for use on the upper Shiré and the lake. Afterwards, in 1890, it brought out to the lake another and larger vessel, the *Domira*. It operated a paddle-steamer, and later a second one, between the Murchison Cataracts and the Zambesi delta. It erected a store at Mandala, close to the mission at Blantyre, and roughly constructed a road to by-pass the cataracts. In 1881 Stevenson himself contributed £4,000 (worth several times as much in today's currency) for the construction of a road between the north end of Lake Nyasa and the south end of Lake Tanganyika, and in 1884 a permanent station was established at Karonga, the Nyasa terminus of this road. The company served not only the Scottish missions but the L.M.S. and the U.M.C.A. as well.

All this was valuable, and the Scottish missions were well pleased. Their pleasure, however, was shared by no one else. The other two missions both found the company's charges extortionate and its service exasperatingly poor. The correspondence of the L.M.S., in particular, abounds in detailed information and blistering comments on its offhand, grossly negligent treatment of the mission's property. It was equally indifferent to the comfort of its passengers. Everyone admitted that it had good intentions; but, as the explorer Joseph Thomson wrote to Cecil Rhodes in 1890: 'It is entirely made up of good intentions, good aims, great schemes for the benefit of the natives, and lives in a perfect atmosphere of philanthropy and religion, while they utterly fail to carry out their commercial engagements, and do things which would ruin the reputation of any third-rate house, while giving their employees starvation wages and housing them in the most miserable fashion, having at places boxes to do for chairs and tables, their jack-knives for their cutlery, etc. . . . That so much has been accomplished under the circumstances is a marvel' (quoted in Hanna, *The Beginnings of Nyasaland and North-Eastern Rhodesia*, p. 87).

The company was only partially to blame for its shortcomings, for it was crippled by lack of capital: the prevailing conditions in its sphere of operations were of course discouraging to financial investment. In addition, however, it was incompetently managed. John Moir, the senior of the two brothers who were its joint managers, was an enthusiastic blunderer. He did not even take the obvious precaution of putting a white man in charge of caravans of porters, no doubt wishing to save money; the result was that carriers frequently ran away with their loads, so that the net effect of the economy was to heighten the cost of transport.

The company seems to have achieved very little by way of developing legitimate commerce with the African population so as to enable them to buy calico without selling each other to the Arabs in payment. In 1890, when German action in East Africa had at last completely blocked the outlet for slaves to Zanzibar, the Arabs at Ujiji were at a loss to know how to export their ivory, and the company was presented with a wonderful commercial opportunity; this, however, it lacked the capacity, and apparently also the will, to seize. Yet the Board of Directors in Glasgow sourly resented the intrusion of any competitor into the region where for a dozen years or more they had enjoyed what amounted to a monopoly. Their attitude was due in part to the honest and not wholly unjustified fear that other traders' standards of dealing with the natives might not be as high as their own; in particular they were opposed to the introduction of cheap, potent European spirits. Still, if they could not adequately meet the needs of the country themselves they ought not to have tried to keep others out. It is not to their credit, for example, that in 1893 they told a new company which was about to start a steamer service on the Zambesi–Shiré route that they intended to run it out of business. In the end their monopoly broke down, but not before the coming of British rule had created a prospect of greater security and thus made the country more attractive to commercial enterprise.

Before 1889, therefore, there was not much commerce north of the Zambesi, though there was considerable missionary activity. South of the Zambesi this position was reversed. The L.M.S. mission continued to drag out its existence at Inyati, and even opened a second station, which it called Hope Fountain; but so far as the human eye could see it was achieving nothing. A Jesuit mission entered Matabeleland in 1880, and settled down to a life of equal frustration. But the influx of traders and hunters steadily grew. The hunters came first, some of them being Boers like the notable Jan Viljoen, and the early traders were for the most part those hunters—such as Thomas Leask, whose journals have been published as a volume in the Oppenheimer Series—who had to cover their expenses by the proceeds of the ivory obtained from the elephants they shot. By the time of Mziligazi's death in 1868 the route from Bulawayo to the Hartley Hills was already known as the Hunters' Road: for hunters were permitted to travel in Mashonaland even though missionaries were forbidden to settle there. The most famous of the hunters was F. C. Selous, who travelled widely in Matabeleland and Mashonaland in the 1870s, and whose published writings did much to reveal a country which had previously been largely unknown.

Gold, however, soon became a much more important lure than elephant tusks. A veteran elephant-hunter, Henry Hartley, pointed out evident traces of it to Karl Mauch, a German geologist, in 1864, and it soon became well known how widespread were the 'ancient workings' of Mashonaland. For a time attention was diverted by the diamonds of Kimberley, and Thomas Baines, who obtained from Lobengula in 1871 a concession authorising the mining of gold between the Rivers Gwelo and Hunyani, was unable to raise the necessary capital to develop it. Baines was an explorer and artist of some distinction, whose journals and water-colours combine to give the best and fullest picture we have of conditions in the early years of Lobengula's reign. He was a worthy man, who deserved better treatment than he received from the unscrupulous London financiers who sent him out and then repudiated all obligations to him. But most of the concession-hunters who increasingly plagued Lobengula as his reign proceeded were men without scruple or dignity. During the 1880s the missionaries became increasingly troubled by the new impediment to their work

Christianity and Commerce

which the presence of such whites involved. When J. S. Moffat visited the country in 1888—no longer in the service of the L.M.S., but still deeply interested in the success of its work— he found that 'seekers of gold concessions are as plentiful as blackberries'; they were, he said, 'a blight upon missionary influence—their lives are a practical contradiction of all Christian teaching'. A few months later one of the Society's own missionaries summed the matter up: 'Gold and the gospel are fighting for the mastery, and I fear that gold will win.'[1]

[1] L.M.S. Archives: Moffat to Thompson, 11th September 1888, and Carnegie to Thompson, 15th January 1889.

CHAPTER 4

Right of Conquest

The death of Mziligazi was followed by an interregnum of about eighteen months (1868–70), because most of the Matabele hesitated to accept the fact that his heir, whom he had called Kuruman in honour of Robert Moffat, had long previously been murdered at his command. During the interregnum the tribe was saved from disintegration by the able leadership of the aged Umnombate, who acted as regent. Lobengula, the next in succession, was extremely reluctant to allow his claim to be put forward, since he did not wish to die a usurper's death if his brother Kuruman should return from exile. In the end he was, as the Americans say, 'drafted' into the vacant office.

Lobengula differed from his father as much as Napoleon III differed from Napoleon I. He was no general, and, except on one occasion at the beginning of his reign, he did not lead his army in person. He lacked the demonic energy and force of will of Mziligazi in his prime. His supreme ambition was to live in comfort—that is, with a surfeit of beef, beer, and wives. Yet he was a shrewd politician, and at the beginning of his reign the white men in the country thought he was enlightened in comparison with his father. When a section of the tribe refused to believe that Kuruman was dead and to accept him as king, he took the field against it with reluctance—it was the one occasion when he took the field at all—and, after its defeat in a hard-fought battle, he showed a surprising amount of clemency to the vanquished, except their leaders. He had for some years been friendly with the L.M.S. missionaries, and at his accession he is said to have made them promises too good to be true: there would be no more raiding expeditions, and no more killing of people smelt out by witch-doctors. Baines and Leask, both worthy men who were in the country on secular business, were favourably impressed by him; Leask said he was 'a fine sensible native and in civilisation far in advance of his late father'. But the office shaped the man into its own mould. Though he had despotic power over every individual in the tribe, he could not safely deny an outlet to the arrogant restlessness of his younger warriors, eager to prove themselves worthy of marriage and of the head-ring won by the married men—and for this purpose, it seems, killing prisoners and infants in cold blood served as well as killing warriors in the heat of battle. So the raids on the Mashona continued unabated during his reign. Had he wished it to be otherwise, he would have encouraged the efforts of the missionaries to influence the young, and then the history of the Matabele might have been like that of Mombera's Angoni, among whom it was the younger men who rejected the old ways in favour of the ways of peace. Instead, the opposite happened: the younger Matabele clung to their tradition of slaughter and plunder even when the older indunas, for reasons of prudence, saw that it could not much longer continue unchanged. For this failure of mission work in his kingdom Lobengula himself must bear the primary responsibility. After his overthrow, the missionary Carnegie wrote: 'The people now will not point any more to Bulawayo with their fingers as their final argument to silence the tongue from confessing Christ; they will be no longer in fear and dread of that heathen monarch's tyrannical power to crush their ambition, enterprise and desire for knowledge' (*Among the Matabele*, Religious Tract Society, 1894, p. 106).

Tall, stately and enormously fat, Lobengula was an impressive potentate, especially when he refrained from wearing his greasy shirt and baggy trousers and allowed his vast corporation to bulk naked above a sporran of monkey-skins. All his subjects, and the lower type of European too, approached him in a cringing posture, shouting such terms of respect as 'Thunderer', 'Stabber of Heaven', 'Eater of men', and—also a compliment

—'Black Pig'. It seems that he was never as great a killer as his father had been, but he made full use of his witch-doctors to destroy anyone whom he considered potentially dangerous, and inflicted savage mutilations, sometimes with his own hand, for such an offence as stealing some of his beer or allowing one or two of his cattle to stray. In 1889 J. S. Moffat wrote from his headquarters:

'The Matabele are a miserable people, and have made myriads of other people miserable too. One daughter of the chief hung herself last week; this makes three of his children who have committed suicide. Another also tried to do so last week, but was prevented in time. One of the old wives of the late chief Mosilikatze cut her throat a month ago. The induna of a kraal near Hope Fountain died lately. Two of the wives are daily expecting to be murdered on the charge of having bewitched him. These things are what may be called the upper circle. Meanwhile the common people are awfully oppressed and there is no court of appeal for them—not in this world at least' (R. U. Moffat, *John Smith Moffat*, pp. 223–4).

When Lobengula wished to add another wife to the eighty or so he had already, he ordered the girls whom he considered eligible to parade before him, and selected the one he preferred. Then, according to Bishop Knight-Bruce, 'her friends come and condole with her, which indeed they may well do; but still it is a strange though general custom, and the stranger because uncomplimentary to Lobengula, while the whole tendency of the nation is to imbecile adulation of him' (*Gold and the Gospel in Mashonaland*, p. 109).

Like his father, Lobengula spent much of his time in travelling about the country, the better to keep his subjects under his eye. But he established his main headquarters at a place called Bulawayo, near the site of the present town; here as elsewhere he usually lived in an ox-wagon which he had obtained. He received his visitors in his cattle-kraal, a stinking, shadeless place which swarmed with flies; to impress them with his importance he kept them waiting there for some time before deigning to appear.

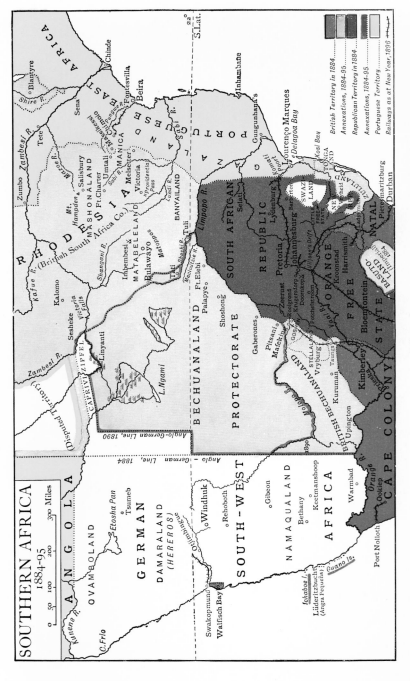

MAP 4

Right of Conquest

But the time was at hand when he would have to reckon with more formidable dangers than the intrigues of the concession-hunters who waited upon him in the dung of the cattle-kraal. In 1885 Britain annexed southern Bechuanaland, south of the River Molopo—an area which included Kuruman, and, more important for the future, Vryburg and Mafeking.[1] In addition, she declared a protectorate over the remainder of Bechuanaland, extending to the south-western limit of Lobengula's own territory. By these actions Britain prevented the Transvaal republic from expanding westward beyond the boundary recognised by the London Convention of 1884, and kept open what was called the 'Missionaries' Road', the strip of country between the Transvaal and the Kalahari where there was enough water to permit travel by men and oxen.

In the very next year, 1886, gold was discovered in the Transvaal itself, on the Witwatersrand; there was a gold rush, Johannesburg sprang into being, and, as Professor Walker puts it, 'the Transvaal, which had hitherto been the Cinderella of the South African family, suddenly blossomed forth as the Rich Relation'. For although the stolid, anachronistic Boers despised the cosmopolitan mob of Mammon-worshippers who rushed into their midst, they appreciated and made use of their taxable capacity.

Thus immeasurably strengthened, the Transvaal became a factor of far greater importance in South African affairs. The long-standing ascendancy of Cape Colony was challenged. British action in Bechuanaland had indeed kept open the road from the Cape to the north, but in 1887 President Kruger of the Transvaal made a bid to render that action almost valueless by forestalling the Cape Colonists and the British in the north itself. He sent a trader named Piet Grobler, who had already made several visits to Bulawayo, to arrange a treaty with Lobengula.

Lobengula, who was of course unable to read or write, afterwards explained that when, in July 1887, he scrawled his cross

[1] Ten years later this territory was incorporated in Cape Colony, and ceased to be considered part of Bechuanaland.

by way of signature on the document which Grobler presented to him, he understood it to mean no more than an assurance of general friendship. In fact, however, the terms of the treaty bound him to accept a resident consul and to throw his country open to Boer settlers. If that treaty had been allowed to stand, it would not have been long before Kruger's and his people's avowed ambition would have been realised: the Vierkleur would have flown as far north as the Zambesi. Today, instead of Southern Rhodesia, there would have been a fifth province of the Republic of South Africa, possibly known as Krugerland.

The Transvaal was within its legal rights in making this treaty, for the London Convention of 1884, which required it to obtain British consent to any treaties with tribes to the east or west, by implication left open the north to Boer expansion. And the Boers were by long tradition a land-hungry people.

When Sir Hercules Robinson, the High Commissioner for South Africa, heard of Grobler's mission, he sent an agent of his own to try to look after British interests in Matabeleland. This agent was J. S. Moffat, who had first visited that country nearly thirty years previously at the commencement of the L.M.S. mission, and had remained there for six weary years, during which he had become a personal friend of Lobengula, before withdrawing on account of his wife's ill health. In 1879 he had finally abandoned his career—though never his vocation—as a missionary, for reasons which were entirely to his credit, and had entered Government service. In June 1887 he had been appointed Assistant Commissioner for the Bechuanaland Protectorate. But no sooner had he completed a preliminary tour of the Protectorate than he was ordered to proceed to Lobengula's headquarters, where he arrived on 27th November, and where, as it turned out, he was to spend the greater part of the next five years.

Moffat's instructions were worded with deliberate vagueness, so that whatever he might do could be disowned by the Imperial authorities if they found it inconvenient. That anything was accomplished in spite of the caution of prudent officials was due to one man, Cecil John Rhodes.

Right of Conquest

Rhodes was an Englishman by birth and upbringing, the son of a country parson. In 1870, at the age of seventeen, he had gone out to South Africa for reasons of health, and since then he had come to identify himself with the interests of Cape Colony. After a short and unremunerative spell of farming, he had made his way to the new diamond fields at Kimberley, where, with the help of his German-Jewish partner, Alfred Beit, he had by 1888 acquired a complete monopoly in the diamond fields for his De Beers Consolidated Mines; he had also acquired a huge stake in the new goldfields on the Rand. 'How rich he actually was it is impossible to tell', writes Basil Williams, his biographer; 'and, probably, he himself hardly knew.' At least he was in a position to finance the great enterprise on which he now embarked; yet in 1888 he was still only thirty-five years old.

Money, for Rhodes, was not an end in itself, but a means to political influence and power. These he does seem to have enjoyed possessing for their own sake, but even these he valued chiefly as instruments in the service of an ideal. That ideal was the extension of the British Empire over as much of the world as possible; more immediately, over as much as possible of the African plateau, though he would 'let who will have the swamps which skirt the coast'. Such an ideal, it might be thought, merely adds the domineering arrogance of the *Herrenvolk* to the soulless ambitions of the fortune-builder. But this is to do Rhodes grave injustice. He was indeed naïve in outlook, crude in manner, and sometimes grossly insolent; yet he was an essentially magnanimous man. If he wished to see the Anglo-Saxon race predominant throughout the world, it was because he thought the Anglo-Saxon race cared more than other races for justice, freedom, and peace, and showed more competence in pursuing them. Towards the end of his career, indeed, he freed himself entirely from racialism, and laid down his famous principle of 'equal rights for all civilised men, irrespective of races, south of the Zambesi'.

One has only to look at his big, clumsy signature to sense the thrusting force of his ponderous personality. Charm of manner he had none, yet the infectiousness of his sincerity and childlike

simplicity of purpose was such that few could resist his persua-
sions. Barney Barnato, his chief rival for the control of the diamond fields, confessed, after admitting defeat in that contest,
that 'when you have been with him half an hour you not only
agree with him, but come to believe you have always held his
opinion. . . . Rhodes has an extraordinary ascendancy over
men. . . . You can't resist him: you must be with him.'

It was at Rhodes's prompting that Sir Hercules Robinson had
declared a protectorate over Bechuanaland, not for its own sake,
but because the 'Missionaries' Road' was what he called 'the
Suez Canal into the interior'. When he heard, in December
1887, that the Grobler treaty had been made, he rushed from
Kimberley to Grahamstown, where Robinson was occupied
with ceremonial duties in connection with Queen Victoria's
Jubilee, and urged him to take instant action to prevent the
Transvaal from frustrating all his hopes by bringing Matabeleland under its own control. What was therefore necessary, he
urged, was to take Matabeleland, and Mashonaland as well,
under British protection. This was more than Robinson could
do, for he knew that the British Government would not consent
to an extension of its existing commitments in South Africa, and
would disown such action if he took it. But he went as far as he
could. Fresh instructions were sent to Moffat, and reached him
before the end of January 1888.

When Moffat, acting on these instructions, asked Lobengula
about the Grobler treaty, Lobengula laughed at the suggestion
that he had given the Transvaal any control over his policy or
possessions. In effect, therefore, he repudiated the treaty, as he
was morally though not legally entitled to do, since he had not
understood its true purport when he signed it. And, after patient
discussions, Moffat obtained his signature to a new treaty, on
11th February.

Apart from assurances that peace and amity should continue
for ever between the British and the Matabele, the treaty contained only one provision; but this was of the utmost importance.
It was an undertaking by Lobengula that he would have no
dealings with any foreign power without the previous knowledge

78

and sanction of the High Commissioner. There were bitter protests from the Transvaal, but to no avail. There was also indignation in Lisbon, for the Moffat treaty referred to Lobengula as
ruler of the Mashona as well as the Matabele, euphemistically
describing them as 'tributaries' of the latter. The Portuguese, in
reply, resurrected a treaty which they had made in the early
seventeenth century with the Emperor Monomotapa, to prove
that Mashonaland belonged to them. Since the Mashona did
not remember so much as the name Monomotapa, this claim
was merely ridiculous. But it led Lord Salisbury, who was
Foreign Secretary as well as Prime Minister, to commit his
Government to the following position:

'Her Majesty's Government have satisfied themselves that
Lo Bengula, with whom they have concluded a treaty, is the
undisputed ruler over Matabeleland and Mashonaland.' He
justified this statement by pointing out that no person of any
nationality could enter Mashonaland without Lobengula's permission: this was perfectly true, but it meant that the criterion
of political authority was the physical power to exclude
foreigners. It implied that the capacity to devastate, plunder,
and depopulate a countryside was sufficient to convey political
sovereignty over that countryside. Lobengula did not govern
the Mashona, did not trouble to intervene in their internal disputes, did not protect them in the enjoyment of any rights whatever. If a village was left unmolested for a time, it was 'only
being kept to fatten, much as a pig is kept, before it may be
thought time to raid' (Knight-Bruce). To regard marauding
as equivalent to jurisdiction may have been diplomatically convenient, but it was morally reprehensible. Yet everyone seems to
have been blind to this fact. And the blindness continues to the
present day, when historians sympathise with poor Lobengula,
that tragic specimen of the noble savage, for having had his
authority over Mashonaland effectively usurped by Rhodes's
Chartered Company.

It was precisely to exclude the Boers and the Portuguese that
the Moffat treaty had been concluded: this, as Moffat perceived
and persuaded Lobengula, was an interest common to both

parties. But the treaty had a further effect, which neither Moffat nor Lobengula had foreseen or desired. It greatly encouraged concession-hunting, by seeming to imply that Matabeleland and with it Mashonaland were being drawn into the British orbit. There followed what Moffat described as 'a perfect avalanche of present-giving', not only to the king but to anyone who might have influence, in the hope of obtaining favours; so much so that Lobengula asked Moffat why people with so much money wanted to come to his country to seek gold. In the intrigues caused by so much competition for the favour of Lobengula, there were those who did not scruple to try to advance their own interests by spreading rumours and sowing suspicions about the intentions of their rivals. The hot-blooded young unmarried warriors, fearing with good reason that their country would be reduced to a chaos of competing interests if their king were prevailed upon to grant too much, began to agitate for a drastic remedy: to massacre all the white men in the country. But Lobenlula knew that such a course would not go unpunished: he knew that the British had broken the Zulus, and were well able to break the Matabele if sufficiently provoked. All he could do was to try to keep peace with the white men, send his young warriors out of the way to hunt Mashona, and use his diplomacy as best he could, by procrastinating and playing off one suitor against another.

In September 1888 an embassy from Rhodes himself arrived at Bulawayo. It was led by C. D. Rudd, who had been a business associate of Rhodes for sixteen years; its task was to obtain the assent of Lobengula and his council of indunas to an arrangement which would obtain for Rhodes an exclusive right to mine gold throughout the whole of Mashonaland, and would also authorise him to put an end to the plague of concession-hunting. Moffat, representing the Crown, was not directly involved, but he knew that the High Commissioner favoured the scheme and he himself thought it was the best thing that could happen in the circumstances. When Lobengula told him how much trouble and perplexity such large numbers of white people were causing, he 'took the chance of putting in a good word for us', as

Rudd recorded in his diary. Rudd and his colleagues also attempted to enlist the good offices of the members of the L.M.S., whose Society, however, had a strict rule of non-interference in such matters. Acting, no doubt, in accordance with Rhodes's well-tried maxim that every man has his price, they offered payment at the rate of £200 a year for a 'friendly intermediary and adviser between ourselves and the chief Lobengula'; the offer was refused, but the Rev. C. D. Helm reluctantly consented to help them to the extent of acting as interpreter, without payment.

While the negotiations were in progress, Sir Sidney Shippard, the Administrator of Bechuanaland and Moffat's immediate superior, paid a visit to Bulawayo, accompanied by a force of troopers, who were given such an unfriendly reception by the Matabele that a shooting incident which would have precipitated a general massacre was narrowly averted. Sir Sidney wrote to the High Commissioner on 29th October that 'Lo Bengula's present position is most difficult and dangerous. . . . He knows all about Majuba and the retrocession of the Transvaal . . . he knows how England, after the fairest promises, handed over 750,000 natives to the Boers whom they dread and detest. . . . He is sharp enough and farsighted enough to understand that the English alliance might be his best card if only he could trust the English, but there's the rub. England has a bad name in South Africa for breaking faith with natives.'

Shippard then reported a striking remark which Lobengula had made to Helm:

'Did you ever see a chameleon catch a fly? The chameleon gets behind the fly and remains motionless for some time, then he advances very slowly and gently, first putting forward one leg and then another. At last, when well within reach, he darts his tongue and the fly disappears. England is the chameleon and I am that fly.'

On 30th October, the day after this dispatch was written, Lobengula put his mark on the Rudd Concession.

By its terms he gave Rudd and Rudd's associates 'complete and exclusive charge' over all minerals located within his entire dominions, 'together with full power to do all things that they may deem necessary to win and procure the same'—a vague phrase which might refer to such things as the making of a road and the importation of mining machinery, but which might possibly be stretched to cover the enforcement of public order within the area of operations. Then followed the statement that whereas Lobengula had been 'much molested of late' by persons seeking grants and concessions of land and mining rights, he authorised 'the said grantees . . . to take all necessary and lawful steps' to exclude all such persons from his dominions, and undertook to give them 'such needful assistance as they may from time to time require for the exclusion of such persons, and to grant no concessions of land or mining rights from and after this date without their consent and concurrence'. In return, he was to receive a payment of £100 each lunar month (i.e. £1,300 a year), and was to be supplied with 1,000 Martini-Henry breechloading rifles—not ordinary cheap muzzle-loading trade guns—together with 100,000 rounds of cartridges to fit them. And, perhaps the strangest provision of this strange document, they were to 'deliver on the Zambesi river a steamboat with guns suitable for defensive purposes upon the said river, or in lieu of the said steamboat, should I [Lobengula] so elect, to pay to me the sum of five hundred pounds sterling'. One wonders what sort of armed steamboat could be taken out to the Zambesi and put in service above the Kebrabasa Rapids for a sum of £500, and what the Matabele would do in the engine-room after accepting delivery. Perhaps Lobengula was induced to opt for his £500 in cash.

A year later, on 29th October 1889, the British South Africa Company received its royal charter. To obtain it, Rhodes had gone into association with the holders of other concessions obtained from Lobengula, notably George Cawston, whose agent, Maund, had been perhaps the most prominent of the white courtiers at Bulawayo. The Board of Directors was adorned with two royal dukes, Abercorn and Fife. The petition asking for the charter had referred not only to concessions already obtained but also to concessions which might be obtained in the future, and accordingly Clause III of the charter authorised the Company to exercise such powers of jurisdiction and government as it might 'from time to time' in future acquire 'by any concession, agreement, grant, or treaty'. This meant that the Company was authorised by the Crown to administer its sphere of operations provided it was also authorised by Lobengula to do so. It had obtained no such authority as yet.

Not only so, but Lobengula, influenced by Maund and other frustrated concession-seekers as well as by his own misgivings, had repudiated the Rudd Concession itself; he had even sent two of his indunas to accompany Maund to England for the purpose of laying his troubles at the feet of Queen Victoria. Desiring a scapegoat to bear the guilt of responsibility for the Rudd Concession, he directed his witch-doctors to smell out his induna Lotje, its chief advocate, and sent a detachment of warriors to butcher him and all his family.

Mr. Philip Mason, in his recent admirable account of these events, seeks to excuse Lobengula from the charge of vacillation by asserting that 'he was like a hooked salmon trying to take out as much line as he could whenever the chance came'. True; but why did the salmon swallow the hook? Not because, poor fish, he could not see it, nor yet because the wicked British chameleon thrust it down his throat, but quite simply because he could not resist the bait. He did not like concession-hunters, and dreaded the consequences of yielding to their entreaties— but he did like their presents.[1] He could not bring himself to sacrifice today's

---

[1] The Matabele, like their kindred spirits the Angoni, were a nation of barefaced beggars, who accosted every white man in their midst with the persistent cry of 'Toosa, Toosa' ('Present, Present'), at the same time being careful to explain how very closely related they were to the king. The trader Leask found that the best way to receive the salutation of 'Toosa' was to treat it as equivalent to 'Good morning'. For the missionaries, who had to endure this for years on end, it was one of the severest trials. There was comparatively little to be had from them by way of actual presents, but the Matabele were glad to come to them for medical treatment, and to bring cattle to be doctored too. They were also from time to time employed to write letters for the king. Their disinterestedness was recognized, but they seem to have been regarded as slightly mad, or as we should say, as 'oddities', on account of it.

presents for the sake of tomorrow's independence. That was
why, in the end, he agreed that Rudd, acting for Rhodes,
should do on his behalf what he lacked the will-power to do on
his own. For he lacked no necessary power except power over
his own will. No white man could enter his territory until he
'gave him the road'; no white man could long remain in it if
he ceased to make any food available and forbade his subjects
to trade with the intruder. There was no need for a massacre
which would have provoked a British punitive expedition; all
that was required was a firm but courteous policy of exclusion.
The Moffat treaty could have been his salvation, for it kept out
everyone except the British, and the British would not have
come in without some figment of legality provided by himself.
If Lobengula is a tragic figure, the tragedy consisted in his inability to control his own appetite, including, in his later phase,
his appetite for champagne.

Having obtained his charter, Rhodes began to organise the
occupation of Mashonaland. Possession is nine points of the law,
and he did not believe that to send in a few prospectors would
be sufficient to secure possession. No doubts were felt as to the
financial prospects of the enterprise, for Karl Mauch had reported that the goldfields of Mashonaland were richer than those
of California or Australia, and subsequent visitors, as they ob-
served how numerous were the 'ancient workings' and as they
brooded on the mighty ruins of Zimbabwe, were confirmed in
the belief that there was enormous wealth waiting to be developed. There had, indeed, been an initial disappointment. In
1869 Sir John Swinburne, a man of aristocratic birth and dubious
character, had contrived to obtain a concession to mine gold in
the Tati area, on the Bechuana border of Matabeleland. Tati,
being much more accessible than Mashonaland, had attracted
the immediate rush, and when it proved a disappointment the
speculators had transferred their attention from the gold of
Lobengula's country to the diamonds of Kimberley—as Thomas
Baines had found to his cost. But the interest in gold had been
revived by the opening up of the Rand, only a couple of years
before the granting of the Rudd Concession. It was taken to be

virtually certain that the gold reef at Johannesburg, incomparably the richest in the world, cropped up again somewhere in Mashonaland. Such was the magnet which drew the Pioneers.

For Rhodes himself there was a further consideration. Until the gold rush to the Rand took place in 1886 the Cape had enjoyed an unquestioned ascendancy in the affairs of South Africa. Now the economic balance, and potentially the political balance, had been upset in favour of the morose and unfriendly Boer Republic. The development of Mashona gold, however, offered the prospect of restoring that balance in favour of the Cape. Rhodes would have desired the northward extension of the British Empire from the Cape, gold or no gold; but the presumed existence of the gold made the enterprise more attractive to himself as well as to those whose help he needed.

The occupation of Mashonaland took place during the dry season of 1890. The Pioneer column, a body of civilians who accepted military discipline for the duration of the march, consisted of just under 200 men carefully selected from ten times that number who volunteered. Most of them came from the Cape, including Cape Dutch as well as British; others came from the United Kingdom, Canada, and the United States. They were of diverse occupations and social origins, but all had to be resourceful and self-reliant. For their protection the Company provided a force of soldiers enlisted by itself, and tactfully called police. 'It is safe to say', writes H. M. Hole, 'that no finer *corps d'élite* than the British South African Company's Police and the Mashonaland Pioneers has ever been raised.' Hole was admittedly a partisan of the Company, but the statement is probably none the less true.

It was obvious that if a body of several hundred men with a hundred wagons arrived on the border of Matabeleland and asked Lobengula to 'give them the road', he would refuse. Even if he could be held to the terms of the Rudd Concession, those terms authorised only mining, not the effective occupation of Mashonaland. So, to minimise the danger of a collision with his army, it was decided to by-pass Matabeleland entirely and advance into Mashonaland in a north-easterly direction. Selous,

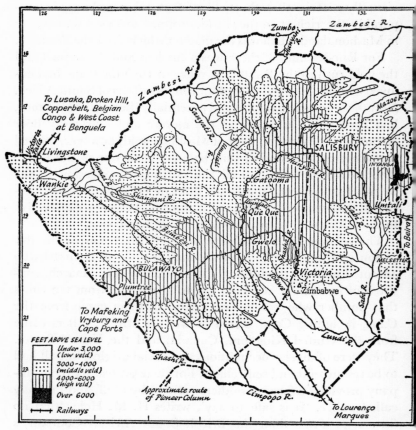

MAP 5. *Southern Rhodesia showing physical features*

who knew the country better than any other man, acted as
guide and gave invaluable service. The route was much more
difficult than the direct approach across the high veld from
Bulawayo: it involved making a road passable for the wagons
through a long stretch of low-lying country covered in dense
bush, and crossing a succession of rivers. It was also a dangerous
route, offering excellent opportunities for an ambush by the
Matabele. Lobengula's attitude was uncertain, though in the
end his prudence and his habit of procrastination prevailed.

86

Twice he sent messages of protest; on the second occasion
Colonel Pennefather, commanding the column, replied: 'In
obedience to the Queen's orders I must go on, but I will remain
on the high veld, and then, if the Queen orders me back, I will
go.' The implication was clear enough: the Company and the
settlers would take no notice of Lobengula's supposed authority
in Mashonaland (as distinct from Matabeleland) except in so
far as they might receive direct instructions from their own
Government. And, one may fairly ask, why should they?

So they marched on, taking all possible precautions against
a surprise attack, and at length emerged on to the open veld by
the approach which Selous, in his relief at finding it, named
Providential Pass. In September 1890 they stopped just south
of Mount Hampden, hoisted the Union Jack, and built a fort
which they named in honour of Lord Salisbury, the Prime
Minister. Thus began the capital of Mashonaland, and afterwards of Southern Rhodesia.

In accordance with the conditions under which they had
enlisted, the Pioneers were now disbanded, and each man was
given 15 gold claims and 1,500 morgen of land (the morgen is
a unit of land originated by the Boers in the Cape: it is
2·11 acres). The Rudd Concession justified the grants of gold
claims, but what of the land? Much of the best land had been
completely depopulated by successive raids and could properly
be regarded as no-man's-land, awaiting the first claimant, provided that sufficient consideration was shown to the needs of the
Mashona, who dwelt in barren and inaccessible places from
fear and not from choice. According to the theory of legality
held in London, however, Lobengula enjoyed sovereignty over
this land, and consequently the Pioneers could have no more
than squatters' rights until Lobengula could be induced to
grant a concession of authority to dispose of land, as distinct
from the mineral rights already conveyed by the Rudd Concession.

It was virtually certain that Lobengula would concede nothing further to the Chartered Company, whose power had increased, was increasing, and ought—in his opinion—to be

diminished. His policy was once more what it had been before the granting of the Rudd Concession: to play off one white man against another. True, he had expressly renounced the right to make any new grant without the consent of Rudd and his associates, and no doubt any grant made without such consent would have been declared invalid if disputed in a British court of law. Nevertheless, in October 1891 he bestowed upon a German named E. A. Lippert the exclusive right for one hundred years to make grants of land to Europeans both in Matabeleland and in Mashonaland.

By so doing he merely tightened the noose which was already lying loosely around his neck. For Lippert had come not as a rival to Rhodes, but as his agent. J. S. Moffat, who was still at Bulawayo, had been distressed to receive from Sir Henry Loch, who was now High Commissioner, a letter dated 12th September informing him of this fact and instructing him not to oppose Lippert's activities. Moffat was a man of complete integrity and most sensitive conscience, who cared little for his own advancement and would not swerve a hair's breadth from the path of righteousness as he saw it. 'I hope', he replied, 'nothing will occur to bring me into any closer contact with the proceedings. If I did not feel that the chief is quite as deceitful as those who are going to try conclusions with him, I do not know if I could sit still and let this go on.' To Rhodes himself he wrote even more bluntly (9th October):

'I feel bound to tell you that I look on the whole plan as detestable, whether viewed in the light of policy or morality. . . . When Lobengula finds it all out, as he is sure to do sooner or later, what faith will he have in you? I am thankful that my orders do not require me to take part personally in this transaction; it is bad enough to have to be cognisant of it, and I should fail in my duty if I did not tell you what I think of it' (quoted in R. U. Moffat: *John Smith Moffat*, p. 258).

So Rhodes was strengthened by the purchase of the Lippert Concession, while Moffat paid the price of his impolitic scruples by being transferred back to Bechuanaland at a reduced salary. The result was that in the crisis of 1893 he was no longer in

Bulawayo to advise Lobengula, and perhaps save him from the folly which brought the Matabele kingdom to an end.

For three years peace had been preserved between the Matabele and the British in Mashonaland. Lobengula had not attacked the Pioneer Column, and his verbal protests received scant attention. During the rainy season of 1890–1 the settlers had suffered great inconvenience and even hardship through lack of supplies, for the rains were exceptionally heavy, the rivers flooded, and the road impassable. But with the coming of the dry season in 1891 the road was re-opened, supplies were brought in, and perhaps as many as 150 new settlers arrived to join the Pioneers. Some machinery of administration and jurisdiction was urgently required, since the British could scarcely be expected to leave these matters to be dealt with as occasion arose by any Matabele induna who happened to be passing their settlements in the course of a raid against the Mashona. And by May 1891 the occupation of Mashonaland had continued undisturbed for a long enough time to enable the British Government to pretend that it existed with Lobengula's consent; relying on this pretence, it had issued an Order in Council (on 9th May) authorising the High Commissioner to issue proclamations making provision 'for the administration of justice, the raising of revenue, and generally for the peace, order and good government of all persons' within the Chartered Company's sphere. The High Commissioner had proceeded to appoint a Resident Commissioner, whose title was shortly afterwards changed to Chief Magistrate; from the beginning, however, the Company itself referred to this official as its Administrator. Although the Administrator received his power from the High Commissioner, on behalf of the Crown, and therefore had to enjoy the High Commissioner's confidence, he was a servant of the Company and was nominated by it.

The first Administrator, A. R. Colquhoun, was a former member of the Indian Civil Service who was not well suited to working in conditions where all the public institutions had yet to be created, and created on the basis of a legal fiction. He resigned within a few weeks, and was succeeded by Dr. L. S.

Jameson, who—in the words of H. M. Hole, who served as his secretary—'was unversed in official routine, impatient of formality and always prone to take short cuts to achieve his purpose—defects which were nevertheless an advantage in enabling him to deal expeditiously with the daily problems of the Pioneer community'. It is sad that this gifted and gallant man should be remembered not for his services in the making of Southern Rhodesia and afterwards as Prime Minister of Cape Colony, not for his frankness, charm, and buoyancy of spirit, but almost solely for the disastrous raid whose irresponsibility and folly can now be dutifully pointed out by the average schoolboy and the dullest undergraduate; it is all the sadder because if the raid had succeeded he would have been honoured in the textbooks as the liberator of his oppressed fellow countrymen, the British Garibaldi.

Jameson knew that the only way to preserve peace between the British and the Matabele was to establish a frontier between them, to limit British activities to the eastern side of it, and to bring Lobengula and his people to accept in practice if not in theory the fact that the substance—if not yet the full legal form —of sovereignty over Mashonaland now rested with the Company acting by authority of the Crown.

He therefore informed Lobengula that prospectors would not be allowed to operate west of the Umniati and Shasha Rivers, and called upon him not to let his warriors make any raids beyond those rivers. Two small-scale but typically brutal raids did in fact occur east of Jameson's line in 1891; Jameson protested to Lobengula, who replied that the matter was one between himself and his own subjects, and that he had given orders that the white men were not to be molested. But eighteen months elapsed before there was any further raid across the boundary, so that on the whole Lobengula appears to have tacitly accepted it, though he gave it no explicit recognition. White prospectors on their side were not always scrupulous in observing the line.

Thus peace was continued until 1893. Lobengula still considered that the Mashona were his property, and that he was entitled to do what he would with his own; when the Company, requiring peaceful conditions in which the development of the country could proceed, intervened in disputes between one group of Mashona and another, he protested against such interference. Moreover it had been his practice in the past to allow some Mashona villages to remain unmolested on condition that their cattle were recognized as his, so that the villagers could consume the milk but must not kill a single beast without his express permission. Thus there were numbers of what were acknowledged to be Lobengula's cattle in the keeping of Mashona east of the Umniati-Shasha line; and with the passing of time the Mashona began to treat some of these cattle as their own. This was more than Lobengula would tolerate.

In July 1893 a force of 2,500 Matabele appeared in the vicinity of Fort Victoria, in southern Mashonaland, just above Providential Pass. This time, whatever may have been their orders from Lobengula, they did not trouble to avoid British farms, but looted the farmers' livestock and murdered the Mashona farm-workers. Their commander even presumed to enter Victoria itself and demand from the magistrate, Captain Lendy, the surrender of a number of Mashona who had taken refuge there; he considerately promised that they would be killed far enough from the river to ensure that their corpses did not pollute its water. Captain Lendy, who was not a particularly patient man, kept his temper as best he could.

By this time the telegraph had been constructed as far north as Salisbury, so that Lendy could communicate at once with Dr. Jameson at his headquarters, and Jameson could keep in touch with Rhodes himself in far-away Cape Town. Jameson was at first disposed to make light of the incident: 'The Victoria people have naturally got the jumps,' he telegraphed to Cape Town, and added, 'I hope to get rid of the Matabele without trouble.' But he proceeded in person to Victoria, and as he approached it he began to change his mind as he saw villages blazing on both sides of the road, and bands of Matabele driving mules stolen from European farms and loaded with plunder. He sent out a party of police to summon the induna to meet him; the meeting was held on 18th July, nine days after the raiders had first appeared in the vicinity. Jameson pointed to the sun, and then to a position lower in the west, where it would be in about two hours' time. 'If you have not gone when the sun is there,' he said, 'we shall drive you.' When the time limit had expired, he sent Lendy with a force of mounted police to hasten their withdrawal. Lendy found that they had set light to another village, and opened fire, killing at least a dozen of them, including their insolent young second-in-command. The Matabele then withdrew.

Public meetings were now held at Victoria and also at Salisbury, to demand that the Company take steps to put an end to the Matabele menace once and for all. The threat was even expressed that the settlers would themselves avenge their losses if the Company did not give them the leadership they expected. By this time Jameson was inclined to agree, though Rhodes at first advised caution, in a telegram which simply bade him 'Read Luke xiv, 31'. Jameson had recently, as a measure of economy, reduced the numbers of the armed police from 650 to 150 men, and it was obvious after what had just happened that this force was inadequate to ensure the safety of the white population. If, however, it was built up to such a strength that it could take the field against the Matabele, it might as well do so and establish peace as remain indefinitely in idleness, drawing pay and rations which the Company could ill afford. For about half the original capital of £1,000,000 had already been spent, and the value of the Company's shares had fallen alarmingly.

Lobengula on his side was at first inclined to apologise for the incident and to send back the white men's cattle. His warriors, however, seem to have deliberately misinformed him about the sequence of events by garbling together their account of the meeting with Jameson in Victoria and of the subsequent shooting by Lendy's patrol, so that he was left with the belief that his men had been treacherously shot down during a parley. He now not only rejected the Company's demand for compensation but himself renewed the demand for the surrender of the refugees in Fort Victoria. Lord Ripon, the Secretary of State for the Colonies, compelled the Company to waive its claim to compensation, but reluctantly admitted that it must be allowed to build up its forces for the protection of its own people. This it proceeded to do, Rhodes himself energetically taking the lead. By blustering, by recalling an army of 6,000 men which he had sent to raid Barotseland, and by sending large forces to cover the approaches from Salisbury, Victoria, and Bechuanaland, Lobengula once more contributed to his own destruction, for he afforded the fullest justification for the military preparations made by the Company. Yet he did not want war, and made last-minute efforts to avoid it; his diplomacy miscarried through a succession of misunderstandings which were as trivial in their causes as fatal in their consequences. At last, in October, the Matabele were said to have fired not only on some of the Company's police, but also on a patrol of the Bechuanaland Border Police: they were thus deemed to have involved themselves in conflict with the Crown itself as well as with the Company. Sir Henry Loch now authorised Jameson to enter Matabeleland.

The advance was made by two columns: one, from the south, consisted of 225 Bechuanaland Border Police and a like number of Company's volunteers; the other, which bore almost the whole of the brunt of the fighting, comprised 414 men from Victoria and 258 from Salisbury, who joined forces and advanced, under the command of Major Patrick Forbes, along the watershed of the high veld. This force had a few machine-guns and a couple of 7-pounders, and two-thirds of the men were mounted.

The strength of the enemy was believed to be about 15,000 men, no longer entirely dependent on their traditional stabbing-spears, for they had the thousand rifles supplied by the Company itself under the terms of the Rudd Concession, together with whatever other firearms they may from time to time have acquired from traders. If the Matabele had reformed their tactics and training methods to suit the new weapons they would have been a formidable adversary. But so far were they from adapting themselves to changing conditions that in 1885 one of their armies had been severely mauled by a tribe which it had previously ravaged with impunity, but which had in the meantime taken refuge in the Okavango marshes, obtained rifles, and acquired sufficient competence in the use of them. In their war with the British a large part of their ammunition was left in store in Bulawayo, and blew up with a mighty bang when the place was burnt down by Lobengula's orders. What shooting they did was almost entirely harmless. In the two main battles of the campaign, on the Shangani River and later on the Bembesi, the British lost a total of five white men killed, together with a few friendly natives; the Matabele losses ran into many hundreds. The ruins of Bulawayo were occupied on 4th November. Lobengula withdrew towards the Zambesi, and the difficulties of the terrain and of the rainy season prevented Forbes from catching him up; but the hardships of his journey and the demoralisation of defeat were too much for him, and he died of smallpox at some time in January 1894. Some of his indunas had already surrendered, and his death brought the war to a close.

The course of the pursuit had given rise to the most famous single incident in Rhodesian history. A patrol commanded by Captain Allan Wilson crossed the Shangani River as it was rising with the floods, and made contact with the main Matabele force, which included Lobengula himself. Instead of withdrawing in accordance with his orders, Wilson committed the heroic folly of trying to capture the king with a force which was utterly inadequate. His party was surrounded, and Forbes, with the main force, was cut off from coming to his help by the rising waters of the river. The thirty-three troopers formed their horses in a ring, and, as the animals were killed by the Matabele, took cover behind their bodies and for several hours inflicted heavy losses upon the attackers; then, when their ammunition was exhausted, they died shoulder to shoulder, to the last man. The last stand of the Shangani patrol was one of those incidents which, like Bannockburn or the fall of the Bastille, become, with whatever degree of justification, the symbols of a people's pride in their own national identity. More than anything else this incident made the settlers feel that they were no longer Cape Colonists or emigrants from the United Kingdom, but Rhodesians.

Right of Conquest

After Lobengula's death the Company, representing the Crown, possessed all his dominions by the same right as he had himself possessed them, the right of conquest.

'The great Rhodes is prancing around,' wrote J. S. Moffat from Cape Town in May 1894. '. . . The popular tide is with him. Great is success! I wonder the old Greeks and Romans never had a God of Success—that is the sort of god which would be popular nowadays. I suppose there will be a crash some day.' What distressed Moffat was not the ending of the Matabele domination, about which he knew too much to have any romantic illusions, but the hypocrisy of the Company and the High Commissioner in pretending that they were trying to preserve peace after they had made up their minds that they must resort to war. On 23rd October 1893 he had sent a letter of protest to the High Commissioner. 'Had a plain and straightforward ultimatum been sent to Lobengula', he had then written, 'with the alternative of war, I should not have had a word to say' (quoted in R. U. Moffat, *John Smith Moffat*, pp. 278–9).

But would Lord Ripon have authorised 'a plain and straightforward ultimatum'? Would it, indeed, have been politically possible for him to do so if he had wished? And if not, ought the Matabele to have been allowed to continue indefinitely to harry all who were exposed to their attacks, and to retard the development of the white settlements in Mashonaland by keeping them under constant threat?

When Colonel Stevenson-Hamilton was in Barotseland in 1899, he was told by one of Coillard's colleagues some of the things the Matabele had done there in August 1893, during their last raid. The missionary had himself seen the bodies of forty babies and small children who had been hung up by the heels in a row and slowly roasted to death by a long fire lighted underneath them, for the amusement of the Matabele warriors as they sat by their camp fires. 'And yet', the Colonel noted, 'ignorant people at home cried out at our "brutality" in conquering these fiends of hell' (*Barotseland Journal*, p. 99).

95

CHAPTER 5

The Queen's Protection

Twenty years elapsed after the withdrawal of Livingstone's Zambesi expedition before the British Government again sent a representative to Nyasaland. The difficulties of transport and the deplorable political conditions which the expedition had encountered discouraged the Government from taking any further interest in the hinterland of the Portuguese settlements in south-east Africa; it therefore limited its activities to attempting to suppress the export of slaves by sea.

It had been making this attempt since the 1840s, but, owing to the vastness of the ocean, the ships of the Royal Navy could achieve little without access to Portuguese territorial waters, and, except for the few years from 1847 to 1853, this was denied to them. In 1857 a British consul had been appointed to reside at Moçambique and try to enlist the co-operation of the Portuguese authorities there; but he was a tactless man, and after little more than a year the local Portuguese managed to make life so unbearable for him that he had to take a passage home aboard a British warship. Not until 1875 did the Foreign Office venture to send out a successor.

Captain Frederic Elton, who was then appointed to the post, was an ideal choice. He was zealous in collecting information about the slave trade and in bringing it to the notice of the Governor-General, but he was also aware that the reluctance of the Portuguese to accept British co-operation arose at least as much from hyper-sensitiveness on the subject of their own utter weakness and inefficiency as from the influence of those who were directly implicated in the slave trade. But, having succeeded in establishing relations of genuine friendliness and mutual confidence with the Governor-General, he found to his disgust that the latter had to reckon not only with local interests and prejudices but also with the touchiness of nationalist demagogues in the Cortes in Lisbon. The Portuguese Government, in order to survive, had to pretend that it was fully in control of the coastal waters over which its nominal sovereignty extended; it had therefore also to pretend that the slave trade in those waters was, in the words of the British Minister in Lisbon, 'a mere hallucination of Her Majesty's Consuls'.

Frustrated and angry, Elton left Moçambique after two years to visit Nyasaland, where the Scottish missionaries had recently established themselves. He did not live to return from this journey, but his journals, which were published posthumously, contained a recommendation that the Government should extend its struggle against the slave trade to the source of supply in the interior, and should appoint 'a commissioner, whose aim should be to detach the chiefs from the Arab Slave Trade influences, and attach them to a policy of legitimate trade and progress'.

Elton's successor, Lieutenant H. E. O'Neill, was equally eager to work with the Portuguese and equally frustrated by their evasiveness. He too became convinced that the only way to stop the slave trade was to take action at its source, and he reminded the Foreign Office of Elton's proposal that a 'slave trade commissioner' should be sent to Nyasaland. His discovery, in 1880, that a large proportion of the captives were being retained on the mainland near Ibo for use on the estates producing oil-seeds was an additional reason for his conviction that the slave trade must be stopped at the source or not at all. He himself paid a visit to the country around Lake Shirwa, south-east of Lake Nyasa, in 1883, and was disturbed to find that the Portuguese were gaining a great influence in that region by selling guns and gunpowder to the Yao slave-raiders.

The Livingstonia Mission for its part had made repeated requests to the Foreign Office that a consul should be sent out, so that their mission-field should be brought under what they called 'a kind of British protectorate'. As Dr. Stewart explained, it was not from the natives that they desired protection, but from 'our Portuguese friends'. Their fear, which Elton considered fully justified, was that if Portuguese rule was established in Nyasaland their work would be rendered impossible by bureaucratic restrictions and religious bigotry; they therefore looked to their own Government to keep the Portuguese out, and if necessary to fill the vacuum itself.

As long as the Portuguese did not attempt to make good their tentative claims to Nyasaland by effective occupation, there was no need for Britain to engage in a controversy with them as to the limits of their possessions. Of more immediate concern was the question of access to Nyasaland. The Portuguese had, as a matter of courtesy, permitted Livingstone to import all the supplies and equipment of his Zambesi expedition free of duty, and in 1875 they granted a similar favour to the Livingstonia Mission when it was taking its initial supplies and the sections of its steamer to Lake Nyasa. But such permission was not to be counted upon as a general rule, and if the Portuguese subjected the missionaries to the almost prohibitive tariff in force at their own ports they would make the continuance of the mission extremely difficult.

It was not the British Cabinet or Foreign Office which first worked out a policy towards Nyasaland, but the British Minister in Lisbon, R. B. D. (afterwards Sir Robert) Morier. Morier was a man of exceptional ability, determination, and persuasiveness, a convinced free trader, and a firm believer in the possibilities of Anglo-Portuguese co-operation for the mutual benefit of the two countries and of south-east Africa, if only the Portuguese could be educated, cajoled or browbeaten to walk in the paths of common sense.

When he took up his duties at Lisbon in August 1876 he found that the Portuguese Government had just given an exclusive right to place steamers on the Shiré as well as the Zambesi to two of its own citizens, thereby clearly implying that the entire Shiré valley lay within the Portuguese dominions. The Church of Scotland Mission had not yet established itself in the Shiré Highlands in preference to the shore of Lake Nyasa, so neither the British Government nor even Morier himself as yet saw any reason to dispute this implied claim; and it was obviously significant that the Portuguese monopoly stopped short of Lake Nyasa. The Portuguese Foreign Minister, Corvo—who stood out among the politicians of Lisbon for intelligence, vigour and enlightenment, though he cared as much as any man for his country's national interests—informed Morier that he was willing to make an agreement with Britain concerning rights of transit to the lake, but at the same time he reaffirmed Portuguese sovereignty 'over all the territories of Eastern Africa comprised within the limits fixed by the Treaty of the 28th July 1817'.

By this treaty Britain had recognized that Portugal's possessions in East Africa consisted of 'le Territoire compris entre le Cap Delgado et la Baie de Lourence Marques'; Corvo was clearly interpreting this phrase as covering an unlimited extent of the interior. Morier's reply was to point out that the British Government had never disputed the fact of Portuguese sovereignty 'over the coastal territory' within the limits stated in the treaty; 'but', he continued, 'with regard to the vast interior of the African continent, respecting which no Treaties exist, they do not admit that the idea of sovereignty can be dissociated from that of *bona fide* occupation and *de facto* jurisdiction of a continuous and non-intermittent kind'.

The doctrine thus laid down, in his Note dated 14th January 1877, became the basis of the British position in the ensuing dispute with Portugal, the ground on which Lord Salisbury took his stand in the late 1880s.

In negotiating on the subject of transit rights to Lake Nyasa, Morier was greatly assisted by the fact that at this very time an attempt was being made—sponsored by Sir William Mackinnon, who was afterwards the founder of the chartered company which began the administration of Uganda and Kenya—to construct a road to the north end of Lake Nyasa from Dar-es-Salaam, on the Zanzibar coast. The project was ill-considered and eventually proved a waste of money, but while it lasted it pricked the Portuguese with an invaluable spur of threatened competition. Morier believed, and was able to convince them, that if their transit rates were higher than those of Zanzibar they would lose traffic to the rival northern route. The outcome was that they contented themselves with transit dues of only 3 per cent. At Morier's suggestion, they erected a customs house at the confluence of the Shiré and Zambesi for the clearance of goods leaving their possessions; thus for the time being they allowed the Shiré valley and Highlands to remain outside their control. Morier had the further satisfaction, after two years of persistent negotiation, of obtaining the cancellation of the obnoxious monopoly of steam navigation on the Zambesi and Shiré.

But he well knew that if these achievements were to have any permanence they would have to be embodied in a treaty, to which the British Government could appeal in the years to come when both Corvo and himself would have passed from the scene. His opportunity to obtain such a treaty came when the Colonial Office sought Portuguese co-operation in the building of a railway from the Transvaal—then a British possession—to Delagoa Bay (Lourenço Marques). Morier was able to convince the Portuguese that they were being offered a valuable commercial opportunity instead of being asked for a favour, and to obtain from them in return a draft treaty which recognised the right of unrestricted navigation on the Zambesi, and also provided for Portuguese acceptance of British naval co-operation in suppressing the slave trade. This treaty was the crowning achievement of Morier's work at Lisbon. For five months, from the end of January to the end of May 1879, he wrestled with his own Government to secure its acceptance. But the Colonial Office had had second thoughts about the railway, and so had Lord Salisbury. When at last he overcame their hesitations it was too late: the Portuguese Government fell, and was succeeded by a group of the most narrow-minded ultra-nationalists, who refused to ratify the treaty.

Five years later, in 1884, the British Government made an attempt to resurrect the clauses of the defunct treaty concerning free navigation on the Zambesi and the suppression of the slave trade. On this occasion they made these clauses their price for recognising the northward extension of Angola to the lower Congo. But the Congo treaty, like its predecessor, was never ratified. One reason for its collapse was opposition in Britain to any extension of Portuguese territory, but the main reason was the intervention of Bismarck, which made it necessary for the whole question of the Congo Basin to be referred to an international congress at Berlin.

By this time the presence of the British missions and of the African Lakes Company in Nyasaland had aroused bitter resentment among the Portuguese colonists and officials, many of whom became convinced that there was a British scheme afoot to take possession of the interior and then push them right out of Africa. Hence, as O'Neill reported in November 1881, 'the cry . . . that the Portuguese standard be raised on the shores of the Nyassa' was 'strengthening every day'. And in August 1882 an important step was taken in this direction, when the Governor of Quilimane proceeded with an armed force to the lower Shiré and formally took possession of the country on both its banks, as far north as the River Ruo.

This river, which comes cascading down from the heights of Mlanje to join the Shiré some distance below the Murchison Cataracts, became the boundary between the Portuguese and what was then known as the Makololo country. A few members of that tribe who had accompanied Livingstone down the Zambesi had remained on the lower Shiré instead of returning to their homeland; taking advantage of the confused situation caused by the Yao invasions, they had established themselves as chiefs over the local people, who were glad to find anyone self-confident enough to offer leadership. Their well-stockaded villages became cities of refuge for fugitives from the Yao, and they refused to have anything to do with the slave trade, recognising that to tolerate it would destroy their whole position. They were well-disposed, on the whole, to the fellow countrymen of Livingstone, but they were bitterly anti-Portuguese. Thus the approach to the Scottish mission-field in the Shiré Highlands was in the hands of men who were determined to oppose with all their strength the extension of Portuguese rule into their own country.

By the terms of the treaty of 1884 Portugal accepted the Ruo as the boundary of her possessions; but the non-ratification of the treaty left her free to renew her claim to the country north of it. About the same time the customs house at the confluence of the Shiré with the Zambesi was destroyed in a native revolt, and the Portuguese did not rebuild it. Relations between Britain and Portugal deteriorated as the attitude of each country hardened. The question of jurisdiction over Nyasaland could not much longer remain an open question, now that a general partition of the African continent was being precipitated by the action of the Belgian king in carving out a vast personal domain in the Congo Basin, and, even more important, the sudden irruption of Bismarckian Germany into South-West Africa and what had until then been regarded as the dominions of the Sultan of Zanzibar, as well as into the Cameroons and Togoland. From 1884 onwards the Portuguese officials in south-east Africa did all they could to impose their authority on the British in Nyasaland; they insisted that anyone proceeding to Lake Nyasa must buy a 'ticket of residence' in the province of Moçambique; they taxed the African Lakes Company, and in 1888 seized a new steamer which that company had brought out for use on the Zambesi and lower Shiré and held it until, as a result of British diplomatic representations, the Lisbon Government sent them instructions to desist. It was becoming increasingly apparent that the only alternative to the recognition of Portuguese rule in Nyasaland was the establishment of British rule.

When officials of the British Foreign Office contemplated this alternative, they vacillated. Might it not be possible to make a bargain with the Portuguese, obtaining treaty safeguards for British evangelical and commercial interests in Nyasaland in return for recognition of their sovereignty? No doubt British rule would be preferable, but it would require a substantial grant-in-aid from the Treasury, which would see no possible advantage in such expenditure. It would also require a line of communications with which the Portuguese could not interfere, but so far as was known there was no navigable mouth of the

Zambesi, and although Britain insisted that the Zambesi itself was a natural highway open to the commerce of all nations, she could not apply this principle to the port of Quilimane and the short overland journey to the Zambesi from the River Kwakwa, at the mouth of which Quilimane stands.

One step had, indeed, been taken to establish an official British connection with the interior. In October 1883 Captain C. E. Foot, R.N., had been appointed consul 'in the territories of the African Kings and Chiefs in the districts adjacent to Lake Nyasa'; the geographical scope of his work was not otherwise defined. His main duty was to win the confidence of the chiefs and persuade them that the slave trade was ruinous to their own interests; he was also to give all the support he could to the missionaries, and to report on whatever possibilities he might perceive for the introduction of legitimate commerce. Thus the pleas of Elton, O'Neill and the Livingstonia Mission had at last been heeded. It is probably significant that the appointment came not very long after the Portuguese action in advancing their frontier to the Ruo. But the consul had no jurisdiction, even over British subjects, and no armed force to support his diplomacy.

Consul Foot appears to have been well fitted for his exceptionally difficult task. On arriving at Blantyre in January 1884 he found that an alarming situation had been created by a dispute between the Lakes Company and the Makololo, and he rendered a most valuable service by negotiating a satisfactory settlement. In August of the same year, however, he died of fever, and his successor, A. G. S. Hawes, was little more than a pompous mediocrity. But the increasing frustrations which Hawes suffered were not primarily due to his own limitations, and although his masters at the Foreign Office found his reports depressing, they never suggested that he was himself in any way at fault. He was placed in an impossible predicament as soon as it dawned upon the slave-raiding Yao chiefs that the Government which he represented lacked either the means or the will to give him the slightest military backing. At first he was received with much courtesy and with assurances of friendship, but within a couple of years the attitude of the Yao had changed to one of unconcealed contempt. In 1887 a petty chief asked him, face to face, what he could do if the chief took part in the slave trade. When he enquired from the Foreign Office what he was to do if one of his own servants was kidnapped by a slave trader, all that he was told was that he was to use his tact and 'keep clear of any unnecessary embarrassments'. He asked to be provided with a dozen rifles and 5,000 rounds of ammunition: this request inspired a senior Foreign Office official to observe: 'How is all this to be paid for? . . . Hawes will be conquering Africa if we don't take care.'

When Hawes first arrived in Nyasaland, in 1885, he found that John Moir, on behalf of the Lakes Company, had been collecting the signatures of Makololo, Tonga and even Yao chiefs to documents purporting to cede their territory and jurisdiction to the company, which aspired to a royal charter authorising it to administer Nyasaland. But as soon as Hawes told the Makololo that Moir had not been acting on instructions from the Queen, their suspicions were aroused and they firmly denied that they had had the slightest intention of placing themselves in the hands of the company. Hawes himself reported to the Foreign Office that the company was totally unfit to carry out such an undertaking; no honest man could have reported otherwise. Whatever the Livingstonia Mission may have thought of the scheme—and it is hard to believe that Dr. Laws, much as he favoured the company, could have considered its political ambitions justified—the Blantyre Mission strongly opposed it. The grant of a charter to such a body offered the British Government no escape from its dilemma; so, without rejecting the alleged treaties outright, it deferred indefinitely allowing them to come into operation.

In July 1887 Hawes reported that he did not see much hope for an improvement in 'the present deplorable state of affairs' unless the British Government intervened by force to stop the export of slaves, by placing armed steamers on Lake Nyasa to intercept the dhows which ferried them across, and by despatching a small armed force to control the Yao of the Shiré Highlands. A few weeks later he applied for leave of absence, which was granted; when it expired he was given other employment, and the Nyasa consulate was allowed to remain vacant. But before his departure events occurred which made the situation much worse than it had been before.

The Arabs who traded in slaves and ivory east and west of Lake Tanganyika were beginning to feel the pressure of the Belgians in the service of King Leopold and of the Germans who were vigorously taking possession of what is now the state of Tanganyika. Their response to this pressure was to try to consolidate their own position in the remote interior by setting themselves up as 'sultans' over the tribes among whom they had previously been content to trade. To this end they greatly increased their importation of firearms. In 1888 Colonel Euan Smith, the British Consul-General at Zanzibar, asserted that firearms were passing into Africa at the rate of between 80,000 and 100,000 a year, and that these now included a large proportion of good breech-loading rifles. The Sultan of Zanzibar, who had a local monopoly of gunpowder, bought it from German merchants for 13 dollars per hundred pounds and sold it at 30 dollars to Indian traders, who supplied it to the Arabs.

Nyasaland and the country to the west of it were on the southern fringe of the region affected by this Arab activity. South of Lake Nyasa the Arabs were content to continue their long-established practice of doing business with the Yao. On the western shore of the lake, at a place called Kota-Kota some distance south of Bandawe, a dynasty of Arabs known as Jumbe—Prince—had already been established for three generations, and operated one of the chief slave-ferries to the eastern shore; but the ruling Jumbe was a cautious, shrewd old man, who would hold aloof from any adventurous enterprise until he was quite sure it would succeed. It was at the north end of the lake that the trouble developed.

The establishment of the Lakes Company's trading station at Karonga in 1884 attracted Arabs who wished to sell ivory, and some of these soon settled with their followers a few miles inland, assuring the local natives, the Wankonde, of their goodwill. The foremost among them was a half-caste named Mlozi; his chief associates were two other black Arabs named Kopa-Kopa and Msalema. Each of these established a stockaded village and built up a substantial following of armed robbers. In October 1887 they attacked the almost defenceless Wankonde, massacring large numbers and enslaving as many of the survivors as they could catch.

L. M. Fotheringham, the manager at Karonga, was the one thoroughly competent man in the company's service. He hurriedly began to fortify his station, and sent for help. He did not shrink from giving refuge to Wankonde fugitives. By the time the expected Arab attack on Karonga began, at the end of November, he had been joined by five other white men, one of whom was Consul O'Neill, who had been on a visit to the Livingstonia mission when news arrived of the danger at Karonga, and had hastened to the scene aboard the *Ilala*. Another was Alfred Sharpe, a solicitor who had gone to Africa to hunt big game, little foreseeing that his adventures were to bring him eventually to the Governorship of Nyasaland.

Consul Hawes, while awaiting his leave of absence, had gone on a visit to the group of Angoni known as Gwangwara, settled east of Lake Nyasa; but he proceeded to the north end of the lake as soon as he could, accompanied by John Moir, and arrived on 9th December. He then took part in an attack on Mlozi's village, made possible by the help of a large mob of natives from the north end; the village was taken, but the natives were so interested in carrying off the loot that the Arabs were allowed to escape, and when they returned and re-established themselves they took care that their fortifications were far stronger than before.

Hawes now proposed that the company should avoid further conflict by withdrawing entirely from the north end of the lake; but Fotheringham strongly resisted this proposal, which involved leaving the African population to be destroyed by Mlozi. The company therefore committed itself to a war to the finish against Mlozi, Kopa-Kopa and Msalema, in spite of the increasingly bitter disapproval of Hawes, whose view of the situation was accepted by the Foreign Office because of its instinct for avoiding trouble. Almost all the missionaries in Nyasaland approved of the company's stand, except those of the U.M.C.A., whose policy was complacently described by one of its leading members as one of 'live and let live'. Consul O'Neill, unlike Hawes, believed that it was supremely important to check the growth of Arab power in the interior, and therefore to drive out Mlozi, whom he regarded as the leader of its southward advance. He wished to join in the fighting in a private capacity, if the Foreign Office would give him permission; Hawes, however, angrily accused him of 'interference', and he therefore reluctantly withdrew from the consular district of his petulant colleague. Then Hawes himself returned to England, having apparently succeeded in depriving the men who were fighting against Mlozi of any better leadership than could be provided by John Moir.

He entrusted his consular functions to John Buchanan, who had established an extensive coffee plantation on the slopes of Mount Zomba, and who was the only prominent layman in the country unconnected with the Lakes Company. Buchanan, a gardener by trade, had been one of the party of artisan missionaries who established the settlement at Blantyre; he had been implicated in the atrocities of which they were guilty, and had been among those dismissed. Since then, however, he had won the respect of everyone who knew him by hard work, enterprise, cool common sense, and complete trustworthiness.

Accompanied by W. P. Johnson, an experienced member of the Universities Mission, the acting-consul attempted to mediate between Mlozi and the company before fighting was resumed; but Mlozi was evasive, and Buchanan went away convinced that there could be no peace with the Arabs 'other than simply allowing them to remain in their stockaded villages, and thus be a continual menace to all peace-loving and law-abiding people'. On his way back to Zomba he called at the headquarters of Makanjira, the powerful Yao chief who controlled the south-eastern shores of the lake, and whose association with Arab traders was particularly close; he explained that Makanjira's neutrality would be respected if the fighting was renewed, but he seems to have added an incautious warning that if Makanjira's people gave help to Mlozi they might have cause to regret it. They thereupon attacked him, and Johnson who was still with him, stripped and flogged him, and would not allow him to return to the mission steamer until a supply of trade goods had been handed over as ransom. This incident marked the nadir of British prestige in Nyasaland.

Soon after his return to Zomba Buchanan received a letter from a young army officer who was as yet unknown, but who afterwards became the most illustrious of British administrators in tropical Africa. This was Captain F. D. Lugard, D.S.O., who had come out to Africa almost by chance on leave from his regiment, and had been asked by John Moir to take command of the men at Karonga, who were being reinforced in preparation for decisive action. All that he had heard had convinced him that he ought to accept the offer, but he was anxious if possible to obtain official approval. Buchanan, in reply, had to state that the Government accepted no responsibility for the hostilities undertaken by the company, but he ventured to add that he personally gave his 'strong, hearty approval' to Lugard's going. For, as he explained in a letter to Hawes, he 'trembled' at the thought of the disaster which would certainly befall a military expedition headed by John Moir, and, as he had no power to prevent the expedition from proceeding, he did the next best thing by approving of its having capable leadership.

Lugard remained at Karonga from May 1888 to March 1889. But before he arrived the enemy had been given time to erect defences which were impregnable to anything less than artillery, and Lugard himself was severely wounded in an unsuccessful attempt to storm Kopa-Kopa's village. After this attempt, on 15th June, he could wage only a desultory warfare until early in the following year, when he received a sevenpounder gun for which he had asked. The arrival of this gun had been delayed for two months by the Portuguese Government, which professed to be shocked by the request that it should permit a foreign company to use artillery within what it insisted on regarding as its own territory; its obstruction was eventually overcome by the despatch of an exceptionally sternly worded telegram drafted by Lord Salisbury in person. For although Salisbury was not in a position to give the company any material help, he was not prepared to tolerate the attempts of the Portuguese to strangle it.

When at last the long-awaited opportunity arrived to bring the gun into operation, the shells failed to explode on hitting the stockade, but passed through it and burst in the village. Though they did considerable damage, their failure to open the way for a storming party made victory unattainable with such resources as Lugard had at his disposal, and he decided that the best thing he could do was to return to England to try to arouse sufficient support for the cause to bring the struggle to a successful conclusion. After his departure the indomitable Fotheringham remained at Karonga, assisted by half a dozen white men and a force of natives on whom Lugard had imposed some measure of discipline; his aim was to starve out the enemy by cutting off their supplies, and it was an open question whether or not this could be achieved before the company was itself reduced to bankruptcy by the cost of the conflict.

While Lugard was confronting overwhelming difficulties at Karonga and the Portuguese were doing their worst to paralyse and ruin the Lakes Company in his rear, Lord Salisbury appointed Harry Johnston to the consulate at Moçambique, from which O'Neill had now been transferred owing to ill-health. Johnston, an outwardly unimpressive little man of thirty, had attracted Salisbury's personal interest by his brilliance of mind and his exuberant energy, already displayed in his work as vice-consul in the Niger delta. Taking a hint dropped by the Prime Minister in conversation, he had published—anonymously, since he was in Government service—a long article in *The Times* on 22nd August 1888, on 'Great Britain's Policy in Africa': its purpose was to advocate a policy of attempting to secure for the British Empire a continuous stretch of territory from Egypt in the north to Cape Colony in the south. He afterwards claimed—in a letter to Rhodes himself—that it was he and not Rhodes who had first used the phrase 'Cape to Cairo'. At the time when he wrote his article for *The Times* the Moffat Treaty had already been made with Lobengula, and the Portuguese had been stung by it into intensifying their efforts to possess themselves of as much as possible of the territory they claimed both north and south of the Zambesi. But the Rudd Concession had not yet been obtained, and as yet Rhodes was practically unknown both to Salisbury and to the Foreign Office. Nevertheless the choice of this ardent young empire-builder to deal on the spot with the Portuguese in south-east Africa was proof that Salisbury had at last decided to make a firm stand for British interests in the Nyasa country in face of the increasing provocations of the Portuguese.

In March 1889, just as he was about to sail for Moçambique, Salisbury suddenly decided to send him to Lisbon to try to negotiate the basis of a settlement. In these negotiations John-ston light-heartedly sacrificed the Shiré Highlands in order to obtain the consent of the Portuguese to the interruption of the continuous belt of territory which they claimed between Moçambique and Angola. It seemed to him that the probable ruin of the Blantyre mission and the African Lakes Company was a small price to pay for the right to paint the country be-tween the Zambesi and Lake Tanganyika pink on the map. But Salisbury disagreed. He left it to Johnston himself to attempt the impossible task of convincing the Church of Scotland's Foreign Mission Committee of the advantages of the proposed agreement, and he dropped a strong hint to a prominent Scot-tish peer, Lord Balfour of Burleigh, that he would welcome an agitation to demand that his attitude towards Portugal should be uncompromising. The Kirk took the hint, and set Scotland aflame with anger against the Portuguese and determination that they should advance no farther towards Lake Nyasa.

Just at this time, at the beginning of May, it became known in Britain that one mouth of the Zambesi, the Chinde, had recently been found to have a sufficient depth of water to enable it to be used as a regular means of communication between Nyasaland and the ocean; thus the Portuguese would no longer be able to use their stranglehold at Quilimane to impede British enterprise in the interior.

In the same month the other great obstacle to British political initiative in Nyasaland was removed: the problem of finance. Rhodes had come to England to seek the support of the Colonial Office in his application for a royal charter, and he met Johnston at a party. The two men were excited to discover how closely their most cherished dreams coincided, and they eagerly discussed how they could co-operate. Although Rhodes's immediate concern was to follow up his acquisition of the Rudd Concession, his aspirations did not stop at the Zambesi, and it was not by chance that the charter, when granted, fixed no northern limit to his company's sphere of operations. Pursuing his usual policy of amalgamating his own interests with those of any others in the field, he hoped to buy a controlling interest in the Lakes Company, which, owing to its struggle with Mlozi, desperately needed the money. But the most urgent problem was to keep out the Portuguese, who had at last resolved to take possession of the Shiré country whatever opposition the Makololo might offer, and had already set in motion an expedition consisting of 1,200 natives, mainly Zulus, armed with guns, with 2,000 followers, commanded by Major Serpa Pinto and three other Portuguese officers. The only way in which Britain could obtain the legal right to keep them out was to declare a protectorate of her own; a necessary preliminary was to obtain the assent of the chiefs whose country was to be protected, duly recorded on treaties bearing their mark. Before meeting Rhodes Johnston had intended to visit the Zambesi valley to see the situation for himself, but neither in writing nor in conversation had he suggested to the Foreign Office that he should try to collect treaties. Now, after telling them about his conversation with Rhodes, he submitted a confidential dispatch on 27th May, asking 'whether it would be convenient to Her Majesty's Government if I concluded preliminary Treaties with the Native Chiefs, of a character not necessarily committing the British Government to actually granting British protection, but still forestalling and precluding any subsequent attempts on the part of Portuguese emissaries to bring the same districts by Treaty under Portuguese sovereignty'. The treaties, he explained, could be repudiated if the Government found them 'inconvenient or inopportune'.

Lord Salisbury gave his approval. Early in August 1889 Johnston reached the Ruo, where he found the Portuguese expedition ready to force a passage but hesitating to do so, and awaiting reinforcements. He hastened northwards by way of Blantyre, leaving Buchanan to make treaties with the Makololo who were immediately threatened by the Portuguese on the other side of the Ruo, and to take the decisive step, on 19th August, of informing Serpa Pinto 'that the Makololo country and Shiré Hills, commencing at the Ruo river, have been placed under the protection of Her Majesty'.

Lord Salisbury did not disown his subordinates. When, at the end of the year, the Portuguese crossed the Ruo, he sent an ultimatum to Lisbon requiring their withdrawal (11th January 1890). By the time the Portuguese force received the instructions to withdraw which Lisbon was compelled to send out to it, it had already established itself at the foot of the Murchison Cataracts; on Buchanan's advice the Makololo had refrained from offering opposition, though Buchanan himself was convinced that 'were we to meet the Portuguese by active resistance, and raise the natives against them, we could drive them out of the country'.

In the meantime Johnston had continued his treaty-making journey up the western side of Lake Nyasa and across the Nyasa–Tanganyika plateau to the stations of the L.M.S. near the south end of Lake Tanganyika. He had almost reached Lake Mweru when news of the Portuguese advance across the Ruo made him decide to turn back. He had thus staked a claim to the country which included the Stevenson Road, and which would otherwise have been incorporated in German East Africa: the treaty defining the Anglo-German boundary was concluded on 1st July 1890. While he himself was busy in the north, he had entrusted the task of making treaties to contain the Portuguese in the south, in the country west of Nyasaland, between the

PLAIN ENGLISH!

ɴ Bull. "LOOK HERE, MY LITTLE FRIEND, I DON'T WANT TO HURT YOUR LITTLE FEELINGS,-
BUT, *COME OFF THAT FLAG!!!*"

Punch, 18th January 1890.

H

The Queen's Protection

Luangwa and the Zambesi, to Alfred Sharpe, to whom he had given his complete confidence after a chance meeting near the banks of the Shiré. Sharpe made two journeys towards the Luangwa, reaching it at the second attempt, in 1890, when he took it upon himself to declare the whole country west of the Luangwa and the north of Zambesi to be under British protection. In the making of treaties, however, he had only limited success, for Mpeseni, the powerful Angoni who ruled what is now the Fort Jameson area, saw no reason why he should avail himself of the Queen's protection, and west of his raiding-grounds the inhabitants dared not accept it for fear of Matakenya, the Portuguese half-caste who dominated the lower Luangwa.

Rhodes and Johnston were both anxious that the British sphere should include Katanga, already famous for its wealth in copper: they did not realise that by the end of 1889 Britain had already recognised the boundaries of the Congo Free State, which included Katanga. So, when Sharpe returned from the Luangwa, Johnston sent him by way of Karonga, the Stevenson Road and Lake Mweru to try to obtain a treaty from the ruler of Katanga, a powerful despot named Msidi. His visit was in vain, but he had been able to supplement Johnston's collection of treaties by making two with relatively important chiefs in the country near Lake Mweru.

At the same time as Sharpe was setting out for Katanga on Johnston's orders, Joseph Thomson, an experienced traveller, was attempting to reach the same destination on direct instructions from Rhodes. Thomson proceeded westwards from Kota-Kota to the Luapula, south of Lake Bangweulu, and reached the upper Kafue. He thus traversed ground much of which had never previously been explored, and added considerably to the total stock of treaties; he did not, indeed, succeed in reaching Msidi's, but of course this failure to achieve his main object was of no practical importance. The treaties which he did make were drafted either by himself or by someone in the service of the South Africa Company; their wording was vague but comprehensive, and Johnston himself admitted that it was 'absurd'. The whole business of treaty-making with illiterate chiefs whose legal notions were far removed from those of a nineteenth-century white man was always open to misunderstandings, but whereas some of the white men tried to minimise these misunderstandings, others took advantage of them. The treaties made by Johnston and his agents Sharpe and Buchanan appear to have been made as far as possible in good faith, but the same can scarcely be said of the transactions between Thomson and chiefs who had never before had any dealings whatever with any white man. As a result of these transactions, Thomson claimed with pride that 'over an area of about 40,000 square miles the entire political, trading and mineral rights have been acquired at a very small expense and few future liabilities'. But the Thomson treaties were the only legal title which either the Crown or the South Africa Company ever obtained to the region of the upper Kafue, the economic heart of Northern Rhodesia.

Before this process of treaty-making with African chiefs was complete, the ultimatum delivered to Portugal in January 1890 had been followed by the signature of an Anglo-Portuguese Convention on the following 20th August. By its terms the Portuguese had recognized the right of free navigation on the Zambesi and Shiré, and had accepted a boundary which involved their renunciation of their claims both to the Shiré Highlands and to a continuous band of territory from Moçambique westwards to Angola. The boundary followed the Ruo to its confluence with the Shiré, and then proceeded in a straight line to a point on the Zambesi halfway between Tete and the Kebrabasa Rapids. The country north of this line, and north of the Zambesi above the point where it terminated, was British, except for a semicircle north of Zumbo whose radius was a mere ten miles.

South of the Zambesi Britain's claims were based on Lobengula's, and as the Matabele raiding-parties had not operated east of the Sabi River, the Sabi was taken to be the eastern limit of Lobengula's dominions. Accordingly, it was recognised as the Anglo-Portuguese boundary.

Rhodes was furious. East of the Sabi lay the country known as Manica, believed to be rich in gold, and if the Matabele had left it undisturbed so had the Portuguese. His anger at the inclusion of Manica in the Portuguese sphere was such that even his fellow directors of the South Africa Company were taken aback: the Duke of Abercorn made to George Cawston the delightful understatement that 'Rhodes is I fancy a little bit of an autocrat'. His horizon was for all practical purposes limited to southern Africa; he cared not in the least that British policy towards Portugal had to take account of the reactions of other Powers, especially Germany, or that Queen Victoria was worried in case the insecure Portuguese monarchy should be overthrown as a result of too severe a diplomatic defeat. But the Portuguese Cortes played into his hands by refusing to ratify the treaty. He promptly sent some of his Pioneers into Manica to establish squatters' rights to it, and when Captain Paiva d'Andrade and the influential half-caste Manoel Antonio de Souza tried to occupy the country for Portugal with a following of several hundred armed natives, Major Forbes with a small force of the Company's 'police' surprised them and put them under arrest (15th November 1890).

Lord Salisbury did not in any way associate the Government with these activities, but saw no reason to interfere with them. 'It is the business of the Portuguese to protect their own territory,' he told the Queen. He did, however, send two British gunboats to operate on the Zambesi and the lower Shiré, to dissuade the local Portuguese from any attempt to treat the freedom of navigation on those rivers as a dead letter because of the non-ratification of the Convention. So, in spite of recriminations, the Portuguese had to reconcile themselves to the necessity of making a new Convention less favourable than the one they had rejected; it was concluded on 11th June 1891. It established the boundary which still exists, giving Manica to Britain and therefore to the Chartered Company, while Portugal received, as a semblance of compensation, a tract of territory north of the Zambesi between Zumbo and Tete. To enable Britain to obtain full benefit from her right to use the Zambesi, she secured a 99-year lease of a piece of land at the Chinde mouth for the construction of warehouses and the transhipment of goods.

A few weeks before the long Anglo-Portuguese dispute was

thus finally settled, on 14th May, the British Government had formally proclaimed a protectorate over Nyasaland. It was almost two years since Buchanan had informed the Portuguese officers that the country immediately north of the Ruo had been taken under the Queen's protection—but 'protection' or 'protectorate' at first meant little or nothing beyond the exclusion of foreign Powers. Nevertheless it inevitably brought complications. By the very act of denying to others the right to annex south-central Africa Britain assumed a certain amount of responsibility for its future. However reluctant she might be to face the fact, she was now under an obligation to provide some kind of administration and police to bring slave-raiding to an end and to require that the white men who were arriving in growing though still not very large numbers should observe civilised standards of conduct in their dealings with the natives and with one another.

Since there was no possibility that this obligation would at once be accepted by the Treasury and the House of Commons, the obvious means of providing for the administration of the British sphere north of the Zambesi, including Nyasaland, was to leave it to the South Africa Company. Both the Scottish missions, however, distrusted the Company, and liked the idea of being brought under its rule almost as little as the idea of subjection to the Portuguese. Lord Salisbury's Government would get scant thanks in Scotland for having saved them from the one fate if it handed them over to the other. Besides, the Company had only just been formed, and in 1890 it had enough to do in arranging for the occupation of Mashonaland. As an interim arrangement, it paid the Lakes Company £9,000 a year, for eighteen months commencing on 1st January 1890, to maintain law and order; it had already invested £20,000 in that almost insolvent concern, and hoped to absorb it completely. The Lakes Company drew its £13,500, but took no steps whatever to maintain law and order. Adamant in its own self-righteousness, it played for its own hand and was able to resist absorption until August 1893; then at last it disappeared from the scene, being replaced by a much more businesslike organisation, the

African Lakes Corporation, with Fotheringham as its manager instead of the Moirs.

Towards the end of 1890 the Directors of the South Africa Company were well aware that they were wasting their money in giving it to the Lakes Company for purposes of administration, but that because of what the Duke of Abercorn called 'Scotch jealousies and cussedness' the Government would delay indefinitely authorising them to administer the country themselves. The best way out of the difficulty appeared to be to transfer the subsidy of £9,000 a year to the Government, to be spent by Johnston, whom Lord Salisbury had decided to send to Nyasaland with the status of Commissioner. The Treasury had with difficulty been prevailed upon to pay Johnston's salary and the salary of one assistant, but that was all: it would not finance the pacification of the country, so that, as Johnston put it, he and his assistant would be 'two lone men giving out a *vox et praetera nihil*'. With the help of the Company's modest subsidy he would be in a position to take some action. But he himself insisted that as a Government official he must not be in any way under the control of the Company, even if he were to receive its money.

Early in February 1891, when Rhodes was in London, Johnston had a long talk with him and obtained his approval for a scheme which, with some modification, was shortly afterwards incorporated in a formal agreement between the Crown and the Company. A boundary was to be drawn along the watershed which runs west of Lake Nyasa and roughly parallel to the lake; the country east of this boundary was to be the direct responsibility of the British Government, and thus the Scottish missions would be excluded from the field of the Company's administration, which was to extend northwards from the Zambesi over the whole of the British 'sphere of influence' west of the boundary—that is, over what was soon to be called Northern Rhodesia. Thus it came about that Nyasaland acquired a separate political existence from Northern Rhodesia, and the boundary within which, in the following May, it was declared to be a British Protectorate.

The Queen's Protection

The two territories were not, however, provided with separate administrations. Johnston's authority as Commissioner was to extend over them both, and although he was to receive the Company's subsidy at the increased figure of £10,000 a year, he was to be responsible only to the Foreign Office. He was to be free to employ the armed force which the subsidy was to finance wherever he pleased. The only effect of the boundary, at this stage, was that within the Protectorate the Company would be on the same footing as any other commercial undertaking, whereas the economic development of its own sphere would be under its own control. The agreement was to last until the end of 1893, and for a further two years if the British Government so desired.

In addition to the annual subsidy of £10,000 a year, the Company made a grant of £5,000 to cover initial expenses, and it made arrangements for Johnston's Administration to use the Lakes Company's steamers on Lake Nyasa free of charge. The whole transaction was a most generous one on the part of the Chartered Company, which received nothing at all in return for its expenditure in the Protectorate. Even if it had not paid a penny of the bills which ought properly to have been paid by the Treasury, the British Government would have had no valid reason for refusing to authorise it to extend its operations across the Zambesi to the country outside the Protectorate.

Unfortunately Rhodes repented of his generosity. For a time he left Johnston with a completely free hand, but early in 1893, when the Company's financial position had become difficult, he demanded to know what his shareholders were getting in return for the annual subsidy. Not only was much the greater part of the money being spent in the Protectorate, but the suppression of the Yao slave-traders was proving so difficult that Johnston had already an overdraft of nearly £5,600; a year later this had grown to £20,000. So now Johnston urgently needed more money, and Rhodes insisted that he must have value for it. The subsidy, it was agreed between them on 3rd May 1893, should be increased to £17,500 a year, but this increase was partly offset by the termination of the Administration's right to the free use of the Lakes Company's steamers, a service worth at least £2,500 a year. In return, the Crown was to transfer to the Company extensive areas of land within the Protectorate which Johnston had obtained from native chiefs the better to regulate its future disposal; it was also to transfer even more extensive rights of pre-emption. This proposed transfer was subject to important safeguards of native interests and of the interests of the Administration itself.

In one matter Rhodes showed that he could still be generous. The Yao chief Makanjira had successfully defied the Administration, and Captain Cecil Maguire, the officer in command of the British forces in Nyasaland, had been killed in the fighting. Maguire was the brother of Rhodes's friend, Rochfort Maguire, and Rhodes, determined that his death should not go unavenged, made available a fund of up to £10,000 to enable the Administration to strengthen its forces sufficiently to conquer Makanjira. This fund was quite unconnected with the proposed agreement, and Johnston successfully insisted on holding Rhodes to his undertaking even after the proposals collapsed.

The proposals themselves were thoroughly unsatisfactory—unsatisfactory from the point of view of the Administration, whose authority to govern would have been in some measure compromised in return for financial relief which would have been hopelessly inadequate, and which moreover was promised only for a five-year period; unsatisfactory even from the point of view of the Company, which would have increased its expenditure in return for an asset from which, as the subsequent history of Nyasaland has shown, it would have been most unlikely to draw any corresponding benefit, except perhaps by selling it back to the Crown sixty years later, at an inflated price, for occupation by land-hungry Africans.

Fortunately for everyone except the British taxpayer the agreement fell through, as a result of a misunderstanding between the Foreign Office and Rhodes which—through the malice borne towards Johnston by Dr. Rutherfoord Harris, the Company's secretary at Cape Town, and through Rhodes's own outrageous personal abuse of the Commissioner, that unhappily placed servant of two masters—made it impossible that the Nyasaland Administration should continue on any terms to be dependent on the Company's money.

By this time the Treasury had directly and indirectly contributed almost as much as the Chartered Company itself towards the costs of the Administration, beginning with the salaries of the Commissioner and his assistant, and continuing through a number of miscellaneous items—such as 'presents' to chiefs, compensation to the Makololo for their losses during the Portuguese invasion of 1889–90, and the erection and repair of Johnston's 'Residency' at Zomba[1]—to the supply of £9,200 worth of guns, rifles and ammunition by the War Office and the placing and maintenance of three gunboats on Lake Nyasa by the Admiralty. Before the end of 1893 the Treasury had grown so weary of repeated requests for money that it took the initiative in offering a fixed annual grant on condition that it was asked for nothing more. Thus in effect it accepted as an accomplished fact that Nyasaland was one more imperial burden which it would have to carry; and the Foreign Office, exasperated with Rhodes, lost no time in driving home the wedge. It prevailed upon the Treasury to assume responsibility for the debts of the Administration, and to take the Protectorate's finances under its own control. The way was now clear for the administrative separation of the Protectorate from the Company's sphere; within the Protectorate the Commissioner became quite unambiguously the servant of only one master, the home Government. Of course this change suited Rhodes at least as well as it suited Johnston, and on 24th November 1894 he signed an agreement with the Foreign Office which brought the operation of the 1891 agreement to an end on 30th June 1895.

The 1891 agreement had served its purpose: it had given time for Nyasaland to be brought within the Empire to such an extent that it had to be retained. The failure of the proposals of 3rd May 1893, and the termination of the whole arrangement, meant that Nyasaland was not, after all, to be drawn into the

---

[1] It had in fact been erected in the time of Hawes, to serve as his consulate. Buchanan was its builder.

orbit of the Chartered Company and of South African enterprise.

It would have been miraculous if such a peculiar arrangement, as embarrassing on the one side as it was unprofitable on the other, had worked better or lasted longer than it did, especially as Johnston himself was the hinge on which it turned. For Johnston was not a man to inspire confidence. His manner was effeminate, his tongue was glib, and he had the sort of ingratiating charm which arouses distrust. He was a man of whom it was easy to believe the worst, and he was in fact grossly maligned. Whereas Rhodes repeatedly accused him of 'disloyalty' because he was not an uncompromising partisan of the Company's interests, the Blantyre missionaries at the other political extreme saw in him the slippery little agnostic who had once proposed to hand them over to the Portuguese, and who now, they assumed, was lining his own pockets with the Company's money in return for advancing its commercial interests at the expense of the natives. Led by Hetherwick, they waged against him and his officials a campaign of misrepresentation and innuendo with that concentrated intensity of hatred of which only preachers of charity and reconciliation appear to be capable. In fact Johnston was as anxious as any man to protect native interests; but when, for this purpose, he prevented unscrupulous white adventurers from fraudently acquiring vast tracts of land, they joined with the Blantyre missionaries in denouncing his tyranny. He served Nyasaland too well to avoid unpopularity, and departed unhonoured and unloved. Yet the odium in which he was held was not entirely due to the difficulties of his position: this is shown by the fact that Alfred Sharpe, whom he appointed as his assistant and recommended as his successor, and who worked closely and loyally with him from beginning to end, was respected and liked. For Sharpe was masculine, straightforward and unsubtle, reassuringly capable but not disconcertingly brilliant.

The most difficult but the most necessary of the tasks which confronted Johnston's Adminstration was the pacification of the Yao, the necessary condition of any other achievement in southern Nyasaland and of safe access to the lake and the country west of it. It involved a succession of arduous little campaigns against chiefs who had abundant firearms and gunpowder, and who could in some cases withdraw with their followers to almost inaccessible mountain strongholds. At first Johnston's army, his so-called 'police', consisted of seventy-one Indians, more than half of whom were Sikhs and the rest Moslems, and a few Zanzibaris. Only the Sikhs proved entirely satisfactory, and from 1893 onwards Johnston relied entirely on Sikhs—he had a hundred of them early in that year and a further hundred, financed by Rhodes's 'Makanjira fund', later—and on a gradually increasing force of native troops, at first Makua recruited in Portuguese East Africa, then Tonga from within the Protectorate. This tiny force, commanded by a few British officers, had not only to take the field but to man the forts which were erected to consolidate the ground that was gained. From Maguire's death in December 1891 until the arrival of his successor, Captain C. E. Johnson, with a few fresh Sikhs in the following June, the understaffed Administration and the fifty-three Indian soldiers who were still alive and fit for service were in serious danger of being annihilated or driven out of the country. Not until November 1895 were the Yao finally subdued. That this was eventually accomplished at all with so small a force was due in part to the magnificent fighting quality of the Sikhs and to the ignorance of marksmanship and tactics shown by the Yao; it was due also to the disunity of the Yao, who had no common leadership, no sentiment of national or even tribal loyalty, merely a common interest in brigandage and kidnapping. And, as Johnston himself repeatedly pointed out, the Yao were only a minority of the population, and the original inhabitants who formed the majority not only were reluctant to help them but welcomed the British as liberators.

It was fortunate that the Angoni gave the Administration no trouble while it was still struggling to suppress the Yao. Indeed the formidable northern group of Angoni never did become troublesome, and eventually, in 1904, as a result of the influence of the Livingstonia Mission, they voluntarily placed themselves under the rule of the Protectorate Administration, which up to that date had prudently left them alone. The southern group of Angoni under Chikusi remained quiet until late in 1896, a few months after Johnston had ceased to be Commissioner; then, under an arrogant young chief who had recently come to power, they made raids which necessitated a punitive expedition. Farther west, on the Company's side of the boundary, Mpeseni's Angoni were roused to action in 1898 by the attempt of a body called the North Charterland Company to possess itself of several thousand square miles of their country in accordance with a fraudulent concession obtained or manufactured by a German named Karl Wiese; as a result they too were reduced to subjection by a punitive expedition from Nyasaland.

Towards the Arabs Johnston pursued a policy of appeasement, at first by choice but before long purely from necessity. In the course of his treaty-making journey in 1889 he had stopped at Karonga and negotiated with Mlozi to bring the long-drawn-out struggle to an end. It was about seven months since Lugard had left Karonga, and both sides were at the end of their resources: the Arabs were reduced to eating rats and were plagued with smallpox, while the Lakes Company had almost reached its last cartridge. Since neither side could still hope for a clear victory, Johnston was able to arrange a compromise peace which allowed the Arabs to remain where they were. To Lugard, when he heard of it, this peace was bitterly disappointing, for it seemed that all the hardship and losses endured in the conflict had been in vain. But Johnston could justly point out that the Arabs had had 'a most severe lesson', and would not be likely to 'attempt to tackle us again; at any rate, not for several years'.

With the other Arabs he encountered on his journey Johnston's relations were so good that he formed high hopes of co-operating with them in the future, believing that if they gave up the slave trade and settled down as rulers of the country they could exercise a valuable civilising influence. They had had their little wars, he remarked airily, 'but were not in so doing much wickeder than we have been in many of our acquirements of territory'—the sort of undergraduate pseudo-broad-mindedness which makes one dearly long for an opportunity to ask a few questions. His favourite Arab was Jumbe of Kota-Kota, who had always been profuse in his assurances of friendship to the British, but who had admitted in 1885 that the slave trade was an economic necessity. Now, in 1889, Johnston believed that Jumbe had almost given up the slave trade, finding it more profitable to keep his slaves on the land to grow rice for sale to passing caravans. Because of the strategic position of Kota-Kota and the prestige of being in a nebulous way the local representative of the Sultan of Zanzibar, Jumbe was regarded as a most important personage, whom it was necessary to conciliate. Johnston spared no pains to win him over, undertaking on behalf of the African Lakes Company to pay him a quarterly subsidy of 750 rupees, and arranging that a present and a letter should be sent to him in the name of Queen Victoria herself. And indeed the old man seems to have kept his undertakings remarkably well, in spite of the restlessness of his younger subordinates. But the hollowness of his apparent power was demonstrated in 1893 by a Yao chief named Chiwaura, an ally of Makanjira, who would have completely conquered him if a British force had not hastened to his rescue. There seem, indeed, to have been only two kinds of Arab in central Africa, the murderous and the decrepit; and the former were much the more numerous.

As for the Arabs in the vicinity of Lake Tanganyika, their cordiality towards Johnston in 1889 is easily accounted for. The only British with whom they had as yet had dealings were the members of the London Missionary Society, and to a lesser extent the agents of the Lakes Company; these, while expressing detestation of the slave trade, were in no position to interfere with it by force. At a time when the Germans and Belgians were making their traditional way of life increasingly difficult, they saw their best hope in the establishment of a British sphere of influence which, while excluding other and more troublesome white men, would directly affect them only slightly if at all. In 1891 Mlozi had the effrontery to ask for a subsidy, quoting Jumbe's as a precedent; the following year Sharpe received a similar request from Abdallah-bin-Suleiman, the Mlozi of the Mweru region. Sharpe wrote to Johnston:

'Abdallah said to me: "I'll govern the country for you, and you can give me a salary." This seems to be the idea now general among the Arabs in Central Africa, that they should get a salary and have a free hand. As the Arabs are themselves the only really serious disturbers of the peace in Itawa, it would suit them well.'

For several more years they did, in fact, have a free hand, though not a salary in addition. Until the Yao of southern Nyasaland had been brought under control and the line of communications secured, nothing could be done to chastise disturbers of the peace in the more remote interior. But as soon as the British were ready to cut off their supply of gunpowder and release the slaves they were trying to export, their pretence of friendliness disappeared, and in 1895 Mlozi openly defied the Administration. By that time, however, it was possible to bring overwhelming force against him. His village was bombarded into surrender, and he himself was hanged for some of his more recent atrocities. The other Arabs took note of his fate, and were brought under control with little trouble.

Johnston's own illusions concerning the Arabs had not lasted long. By the beginning of 1893 he was expressing the heartfelt wish 'that every Arab might disappear from Central Africa'.

Before handing over the administration of the country west of the Protectorate to Major Forbes, the Company's first Administrator there, Johnston had already taken some initial steps to bring it under control. As early as 1890, while the boundary with German East Africa was being discussed, the African Lakes Company had set up two trading-stations on the Stevenson Road between Lakes Nyasa and Tanganyika, and had called them Abercorn and Fife; this is said to have been done on the initiative of Rhodes, who afterwards gleefully explained that 'they' would not dare to hand over to the foreigner a place which was named after a member of the royal family. Johnston himself was doubtless following this example when, at the very beginning of his service as Commissioner, he gave the name 'Rhodesia' to an outpost on the eastern shore of Lake Mweru; for Rhodesia at first served merely to 'show the flag' for the purpose of preventing the southward extension of the Congo Free State, with which the boundary was not defined by treaty until 12th May 1894. But by 1894 this outpost had been sufficiently strengthened to afford some protection against the Arabs to the natives of the surrounding area, and towards the end of 1893 a fort had been built at Abercorn near the Lakes Company's station. When, in 1895, Forbes built a fort at Fife, and when Mlozi met his end about the same time, the British were in a position to put a stop to the export of slaves across their northern frontier into German East Africa, where the Germans for their part were already doing their utmost to bring the traffic to an end.

The powerful Bemba tribe, who inhabited an extensive tract of country south of the Stevenson Road, had been the chief agents of the Arabs in this region since the Arabs had first visited them a quarter of a century previously. Unlike the Yao, they formed a single despotically governed state, and it appeared likely that they would offer most formidable opposition to the British forces before they could be made to cease their raids upon their neighbours.

'From the moment of their accession to their burial', writes Sheane, 'the kings were hedged in by a ring-fence of sinister ceremonies and ruthless ritual, undoubtedly devised to strike terror into the hearts of the common people, and to pave the way for and render possible the stern and rigorous administrative system. . . . This system was . . . enforced [by] a scale of punishments and mutilations so ferocious that it is, perhaps, unparalleled except by the monstrous cruelties of King Chaka.[1] Like that of Chaka, it was extremely well organised, and disobedience to the orders of the king's deputies in the provinces, or refusal to supply men to do the king's work, or to contribute the customary dues, was checked by mutilation, devastation of gardens, seizure of cattle, and, finally—for the contumacious— enslavery of the whole village to the Arab merchants who

[1] Cf. the autobiographical story of one of the Bemba recorded by Miss Margery Perham in *Ten Africans* (Faber, 1936), pp. 29–31.

flocked around the capital.' (Gouldsbury and Sheane, *The Great Plateau of Northern Rhodesia*, pp. 17–21.)

Livingstone had visited the Bemba in 1867, and had been courteously and hospitably received; so had a French lieutenant named Giraud nearly twenty years later. Unfortunately the king had died so soon after Giraud's departure that Giraud was presumed to have bewitched him; for this reason, and perhaps also at the suggestion of the Arab traders, the Bemba adopted a strict policy of exclusion towards all white men, to whom they conveyed a clear hint of their attitude by adorning the stockade of their village nearest to the Stevenson Road with a long row of severed human heads. No treaty was made with them: Johnston and Sharpe skirted their country to the north and Thomson to the south. In July 1893, 5,000 of them clashed with and were defeated by a German force in the vicinity of the Stevenson Road; the German commander claimed that the conflict occurred on his side of the international boundary. This incident alarmed Johnston, who feared that the Bemba would not discriminate between Germans and British in their desire for vengeance, and it was in the hope of averting a collision which he could not at that time afford that he sent one of his officials with a handful of troops to found Fort Abercorn.

H. C. Marshall, the official entrusted with this duty, did succeed in establishing some amicable contact with the Bemba, and in 1894 Père Van Oost, of the White Fathers, took his life in his hands and ventured among them in the hope of preparing the way for mission work. The White Fathers, a French Roman Catholic missionary agency, had settled temporarily at the south end of Lake Nyasa in December 1889, and had proceeded to the Mambwe country near the Stevenson Road in 1891. There they had soon realized that little could be done among the raided unless they could convert or at least influence the raiders. Eventually, in 1898, they were invited to go to the village of Mwamba, a kind of sub-king of great importance and power, who was seriously ill and had heard that their medical skill might cure him. Mwamba, whose theory of incentives was evidently unusual, offered them half his kingdom if they saved

1. Slavers Revenging their Losses. An engraving from a 'rude sketch' by Dr. Livingstone

2. Mlozi. Photographed by Fred Moir

3. A corner of Mlozi's Stockade, drawn by H. H. Johnston

his life and the whole of it if he died—provided they would protect his people; there is however no reason to put a cynical interpretation on the fact that he died within a fortnight.

The death of a Bemba chief was the signal for wholesale slaughter inflicted by neighbouring chiefs upon his people, who were presumed to have caused his death. And by this time the reign of terror among the Bemba had been intensified to a point at which even they found it burdensome, as a result of frustrated anger at the action of a small British force in repelling them from raiding the Senga country in 1896, and thus shutting them in on the east as they had already been shut in on the north. On the day after Mwamba's death bands of avengers were reported to be coming from all directions, and his people in terror begged the priests to help them. By some combination of persuasion and bluff the priests were able to turn back all the approaching bands without any bloodshed. The official in charge of Fife hastened to the scene, took the people under his protection, and built a fort, near the present Kasama. Mwamba's heir, Ponde, whose arrival the people dreaded, was forbidden to approach; when he defied this warning and fortified himself in a strong position near the British fort, the British attacked him and drove him out. There was no further opposition: the whole Bemba country had been brought under control with incomparably less effort and loss of life than had appeared possible five years previously.

West of the Kafue, where the entire country as far as the undefined boundary with Angola was, or was assumed to be, comprised within the kingdom of Lewanika, the introduction of British influence and authority came from the south, and was entirely unconnected with that northward and westward penetration from Nyasaland which brought North-Eastern Rhodesia into existence.

Lewanika was troubled by the constant danger of a Matabele invasion, for though the Matabele do not seem to have in fact raided Barotseland proper, they threatened to do so, and from time to time they crossed the Zambesi lower down and raided the Tonga and the Mashukulumbwe, whom Lewanika regarded as his own on much the same grounds as Lobengula claimed sovereignty over the Mashona. He was in close and friendly relations with Khama of the Bamangwato, and asked him if he was happy under British protection. Khama replied that it had been a blessing to him, relieving him of all anxiety from both the Boers and the Matabele. Lewanika himself was not troubled by the Boers, but he was becoming worried about the designs of the Portuguese in seeking to extend their possessions inland from Angola.

So, in January 1889 at Lewanika's request, Coillard wrote to Shippard, the Administrator of Bechuanaland, to ask that Barotseland should become a British protectorate, and that the Matabele should be restrained from making further attacks. In due course the Colonial Office sent a reply which, though friendly, was non-committal: it could scarcely have done otherwise. And in the meantime, in June 1889, Lewanika put his mark on a document submitted to him by Henry Ware, a trader from Kimberley, granting to Ware exclusive mineral rights in the Tonga country, in return for £200 a year and a 4 per cent royalty.

Rhodes paid a high price to buy up the Ware Concession, but by itself it was not enough. It was purely economic and non-political, and it did not apply at all to the country occupied by the Barotse themselves. But Coillard's letter had been shown to Rhodes, who recognised the opportunity that it offered for imperial expansion, an opportunity which would have to be taken by his own Company if it was to be taken at all. In November 1889 he sent F. E. Lochner, an ex-officer of the Bechuanaland Police, on a mission to Lewanika. After a journey of 900 miles by ox-wagon and 300 by canoe in the worst of the wet season, Lochner reached his destination in March 1890, with two English companions, all of them suffering severely from fever. They were cared for by Coillard and his Scottish wife, but it was not until May that Lochner was well enough to begin his negotiations. He encountered strong opposition from some of the councillors and deep suspicion on the part of Lewanika himself, for during the interval since Ware's departure they had been told by other traders that far too much had been granted away already, and they were now told by the same not wholly disinterested informants that Lochner and his friends did not represent the Queen at all but were seeking their own private ends. Lochner, however, asserted the contrary, believing that it was his only hope of success, since it was hopeless to try to make clear to the chief and councillors the precise character of a chartered company. Because of this claim that he represented the royal authority he was afterwards accused of obtaining his ends by fraud, but although it is true that he did not directly represent the Crown, it is equally true and more relevant that he represented it indirectly, since the Company had been given a royal charter.

Lochner's diplomacy was supported, though cautiously, by Coillard, whose only interest in the matter was to do what appeared best for the Barotse themselves. He won popularity by organising sports, giving a feast of beef, and letting off fireworks in honour of the Queen's birthday (24th May). But when his proposals were debated by a great council of the nation, attended by representatives of the subject tribes, on 26th June, there was still strong opposition, until the timely arrival of a messenger from Khama. This messenger told the assembly that British protection was like a tasty dish which Khama had tasted and wished to share with his friends, and that the Company which Lochner represented was composed of 'Queen's men'. All opposition was now stilled, but it remained to arrange details, including the amount of the subsidy to be paid for a concession of mineral and commercial rights over the whole of Lewanika's dominions. During his exile Lewanika had acquired enough knowledge of the world to understand the value of money, and he refused to accept a penny less than £2,000 a year, a figure to which Lochner had perforce to agree. The concession was signed on 27th June. By its terms Lewanika accepted the Queen's protection, to be afforded by the Company, and after signing it he presented Lochner with two enormous tusks of ivory in token of submission. Presumably these were intended for the Queen herself, but the Company used them to adorn its own Board Room.

The Queen's Protection

The treaty with Portugal, concluded on 11th June 1891, stated that 'the territory of the Barotse Kingdom . . . shall remain within the British sphere; its limits to the westward . . . being decided by a Joint Anglo-Portuguese Commission'. Since it proved impossible to agree as to where the western limits of Lewanika's dominions lay, the two Governments made a provisional agreement, dated 31st May 1893, to regard it as following the line of the Zambesi and its tributary the Kabompo; thus the Portuguese provisional frontier was advanced to the very heart of the Barotse kingdom, and Lealui, the capital, became a frontier settlement. The Chartered Company not only refused, with good reason, to accept this line as a satisfactory permanent boundary; it proceeded to embarrass the Foreign Office by publishing in its annual report a map claiming the line of longitude 20 deg. E. as the true limit of Barotseland and therefore of its own sphere.

While the question remained unsettled, Portuguese half-caste slavers were coming in from the west coast to the Balovale country, which lies north and west of the Kabompo within the region allocated to Portugal. They encouraged the petty headmen to raid neighbouring villages, offering abundant supplies of guns and ammunition in exchange for captives. They seem to have had the approval of the Portuguese authorities, who were building forts and putting pressure upon the Balovale chiefs to recognise their authority in place of Lewanika's. 'Their occupation', wrote Major Colin Harding to Rhodes in 1900, 'is most pernicious and predatory'; he went so far as to call the slave trade 'a governing principle, or rather an ungovernable passion, of the Portuguese administration'.

The difficulty of reaching a satisfactory territorial settlement with Portugal was increased by the Boer War, which created a situation in which her friendship was of more than usual importance to the United Kingdom, especially in connection with the use of Delagoa Bay. Milner, the High Commissioner, wrote to Rhodes on 28th December 1900, that he believed 'if we were rather cleverer at a bargain, that we could keep Portugal's friendship and yet get our way about the Barotseland Boundary.

The Queen's Protection

But the F[oreign] O[ffice] seem to have great misgivings, and it is only the F.O. which can move in the matter. I do not like to press them too much' (Rhodes Papers).

In August 1903 the British and Portuguese Governments agreed to refer the question to the arbitration of the King of Italy. The award, given on 30th May 1905, recognised that the Barotse kingdom included the Balovale country,[1] and fixed the western boundary along the line of 22 deg. E.

By the terms of the Lochner concession it had been agreed that the Company would arrange for a British Resident to come to Lealui. It was left to Johnston to do what he could towards carrying out this undertaking, and Barotseland was included in the area for which he was responsible. He was in fact helpless to do anything whatever so far to the west, and in the end he had to tell Rhodes that Barotseland had better be approached from the south. It was not until 1897 that R. T. Coryndon arrived to represent the Company at Lealui, accompanied by a small party of white men who were to help him to lay the foundations of government. In the meantime the Matabele had raided across the Zambesi in 1893, the Portuguese were encroaching on Barotse territory, and it seems highly improbable that anything of Lewanika's £2,000 a year had been reaching him. His patience had been sorely tried, and he was inclined to wish he had never signed the Lochner Concession. But Coryndon was so tactful and efficient that he soon won Lewanika's complete confidence, and on 25th June 1898 he obtained his assent to a new agreement which defined more specifically the respective rights of the British and the Barotse. This agreement, formally executed more than two years later at a meeting between Coryndon and the full council of the Barotse notables on 17th October 1900, provided that prospectors should be excluded from Barotseland proper, and that in return the Company's annual payment should be reduced to £850, including the £200 and the royalty due under the Ware Concession. The willingness of Coryndon to agree to Lewanika's request that prospecting

[1] In 1941, however, at the request of its inhabitants, the Balovale district was removed from Barotse control. Of course it remained part of Northern Rhodesia.

should not be permitted except in the outlying parts of his kingdom was increased by the opinion that gold was most unlikely to be found in such sandy country as the Barotse occupied. All elephants (and therefore their ivory) were recognised to be Lewanika's. Lewanika also expressly reserved judicial rights in all cases in which white men were not involved, but he recognised the Company's right to deal with cases which concerned only white men and with those which concerned both white men and natives.

A further concession, dated 11th August 1909, transferred to the South Africa Company the ownership of the land outside the area reserved from prospecting, in return for the extension of that area westwards from the Zambesi to the Portuguese frontier as defined in 1905. There were provisions to safeguard the interests of Lewanika himself and of the native inhabitants. As long as Lewanika lived, his authority was recognised as extending over the whole of North-Western Rhodesia; but after his death in 1916 the Barotse and their chief ceased to have any residual authority outside their own country. The lasting effect of the agreements of 1900 and 1909 was to give the Company wide powers throughout North-Western Rhodesia, but to reserve for the inhabitants of the Barotse Province a security in relation to the interests of the white men which was unique in comparison with the rest of Northern Rhodesia, and still more strikingly so in comparison with Southern Rhodesia.

The ownership of slaves, as distinct from the export trade in them, was an integral part of the Barotse way of life, and the British authorities thought it unwise to make any direct attack on a custom so deeply rooted. But neither would they do anything to uphold the rights of the owner when a slave deserted, and by 1906 the Barotse were becoming disturbed by the gradual melting away of their labour force. Lewanika and his councillors therefore allowed themselves to be persuaded to accept a compromise, by which, in accordance with a proclamation issued in October 1906, the slaves were emancipated, although the chief and the aristocracy reserved the right to a limited amount of free labour service each year.

The Queen's Protection

Lewanika visited England for the coronation of Edward VII, and had a personal audience of the king. 'On entering the audience chamber,' writes H. M. Hole, 'he somewhat startled His late Majesty by falling on his knees and rubbing the ground with his forehead, loudly ejaculating "Yo-Zho" several times, in true ba-Rotse fashion.' But Lewanika was by no means a figure of fun amid the bewildering strangeness of London. Hole also records that 'he won good opinions by the natural dignity with which he conducted himself, and few who saw him in the quiet grey suit in which he went about England, or in the rich uniform which he donned for State functions, could have imagined that less than twenty years before he had been a naked savage fleeing for his life among the swamps of the Okavango, or presiding over strange rites and gory executions in the barbaric surroundings of a remote kraal in the heart of "Darkest Africa". . . . The Chartered Company was fortunate in having such a man to deal with, and happy in being able to place on the spot officials who were able to draw out his good qualities, and use him as a colleague without humiliating him.'
(*The Passing of the Black Kings*, pp. 300, 302.)

CHAPTER 6

The Rhodesias Under Company Rule

'You will be the first entitled to select land, and you will deal with it after provision has been made for the natives. . . . It is your right, for you have conquered the country.' Thus Rhodes addressed the assembled volunteers in the ruins of Lobengula's capital on 19th December 1893. So far as the Victoria men were concerned, he might equally well have said 'it is yours by contract', for before consenting to march they had required Jameson to sign an unskilfully and therefore somewhat ambiguously drafted document, commonly called the 'Victoria Agreement', by which each of them was promised 3,000 morgen (over 6,000 acres; twice the amount given to the Pioneers when they occupied Mashonaland) in Matabeleland, twenty gold claims, and an equal share of half the 'loot', i.e. cattle. They thus gave their critics the opportunity to assert that their real reason for fighting the Matabele was the desire to possess themselves by force of property to which they had no lawful right. In fact they were merely following the usual South African 'commando' practice of claiming a share in the fruits of victory in lieu of pay. Why, they would have asked, should they bear the toil and hazards of the campaign merely to enrich the Company's shareholders in London? Rhodes himself, in the speech just quoted, declared that their opponents were talking nonsense. 'Do they think', he asked, 'you have left everything, and run the risk that everyone said you were running—which was that you were all going to be slaughtered—for what? Let us say a farm. What is its present value? Say £40. Then am I to be told that you left your occupation and your employment and took the risk of being shot for the value of a farm worth £40? The thing is ridiculous. No, the reason you came was that you knew your property in Mashonaland was worthless unless the Matabele were crushed.'

But before the Company could legally give away anything in Matabeleland or exercise any kind of lawful authority there, it had to have its powers recognised by the Crown. Rhodes therefore hastened to Cape Town at the beginning of 1894, and by the middle of February he had reached agreement with Loch, the High Commissioner. Their agreement was approved by the Government and embodied in the Matabeleland Order in Council, issued on 18th July 1894. This Order clarified the legal position in Mashonaland at the same time as it made provision for Matabeleland: its scope was the whole of Southern Rhodesia. But the name 'Rhodesia' was not formally adopted, even by the Company, until May 1895.

The Administrator was to be nominated by the Company, with the approval of the Secretary of State for the Colonies; he was to be assisted by a Council consisting of four members appointed in like manner, one of whom was to be a judge. The Administrator was given power to legislate and levy taxes with the assent of at least two members of the Council; in other respects the functions of the Council were to be merely consultative. A Land Commission was to be set up, consisting of three members, with one nominated by the Secretary of State, one by the Company, and the judge who served on the Council acting as chairman. It was to assign to the Matabele 'land sufficient for their occupation . . . and suitable for their agricultural and pastoral requirements, including in all cases a fair and equitable proportion of springs and permanent water'.

Rhodes had told the volunteers that they would have first claim to the available land 'after provision has been made for the natives', but in fact, by the time the Land Commission set to work, they had already carved out their chosen farms. The Commission did its work in a hasty and perfunctory manner, setting up two huge native reserves, one of about 3,500 square miles on the Shangani River, and the other, nearly as large, west of the Gwaai. It paid a hasty visit to the former, but was content to rely on the evidence of native witnesses as to the suitability of the Gwaai reserve. The witnesses followed the usual practice of telling the white man what they presumed he wanted to hear: in this case, that the land was fertile and well watered. In fact it was almost useless, and the Shangani reserve was little better. Fortunately there was at this time no thought of confining the natives to the reserves. They were free to remain on unalienated land, though without security of tenure; there was also plenty of room for many of them on the vast European farms, where they were willingly retained as an indispensable labour force.

To the Land Commission also fell the task of executing a Solomon's judgment on the Matabele cattle. In theory all of them belonged to Lobengula, but there was a recognised distinction between those which were entirely his and those to which his subjects had qualified rights. The Company claimed Lobengula's cattle, and shared them with the settlers, but it left the others to their possessors. The difficulty was to identify those which were undoubtedly Lobengula's, since it was in the interest of the natives to make the number appear as small as possible. In the resulting settlement injustice was undoubtedly done to individuals, through unavoidable ignorance rather than carelessness or ill-will, and was made worse by the uncertainty caused by delay in making a final settlement. Still, these hardships were light in comparison with those which had been accepted without question in Lobengula's time. Far more serious was the attack of rinderpest in February 1896. The disease was as disastrous for the Europeans as for the Africans, destroying not only the livestock on the farms but the chief means of transport. In a desperate attempt to check it, the veterinary officers ordered the shooting of all wagon-teams and herds of cattle among which an infected beast was found, and thousands of healthy cattle were shot. It was of no interest to the Matabele that both the disease and the shooting were as disastrous for the white settlers as for themselves. Both, it seemed to them, had been brought upon them by the white man. So had the severe drought and the swarms of locusts which had recently afflicted them. Their witch-doctors consulted the Mlimo, an invisible deity who dwelt in the inaccessible fastnesses of the Matoppo Hills, whence he presided over the seasons and the crops. Until this time he had been entirely non-political, and for that reason the Matabele had readily adopted his worship from the Mashona, among whom it originated. Now that the rains had failed, the crops had been devoured by locusts, and, worst of all, most of the cattle had perished, it was for the Mlimo to reveal what had gone wrong. And, not surprisingly, he replied that all would be well when, but only when, the white men had been exterminated or driven from the land.

The Matabele had other grievances, which made them the more ready to respond to this propaganda. Sir Alfred Milner, who as High Commissioner visited the country towards the end of 1897, reported that 'a lot of unfit people were allowed to exercise power, or at any rate did exercise it, especially with regard to the natives, in a manner which cannot be defended'. He added that he was aware that the difficulties were enormous, and that Rhodes and the Company's chief officials now fully realised the need for a better administrative personnel, but, he continued: 'The number of competent men available is small, and the amount of riff-raff having some sort of claim on the Company, or its principal members, is considerable. This would not matter so much, if the worthless people were only appointed to small clerkships and sinecures, of which latter there are a certain number. The danger comes in, when they are sent to important administrative posts, especially Native Commissionerships. In the present state of the country the government of the natives must be largely personal government. They understand nothing else. In wide districts with a small, rather rough European population and thousands of natives, a great deal of power must be given and a great discretion left to the "head of the district"—to use an Indian phrase. But it is extremely difficult to get a sufficient number of men at all fitted to exercise such wide powers, liable as they are to abuse.' (Milner Papers.)

The Company had recruited a native police force, whose

members were largely drawn from former slaves of the Matabele. To be placed in a position of authority in relation to their former arrogant masters was for these men such an immense and undreamt-of rise in the world that they were strongly tempted to abuse the powers entrusted to them, and they were not given enough supervision by competent white men to check this tendency. The white miners urgently needed labour, which the Matabele were reluctant to provide; the black police were sent to the villages to arrange for it to come, and few questions were asked as to the methods they used. Thus the Matabele felt themselves injured not only in their interests but in their pride. Yet they still had large hidden supplies of arms, including firearms, because Lord Ripon as Secretary of State had compelled the Company to grant them peace without insisting on the surrender of their weapons—a humanitarian gesture which was destined to cost far more lives than it saved. And although a few of the Matabele regiments had been severely mauled in the fighting, most of them had scarcely been engaged at all, and had not been chastened by defeat.

Yet the Company did not expect trouble, and neither did the settlers. In January 1895 Rhodes gaily told the shareholders that 'there can be no more wars, for there are no more people to make the wars'. In the following October that very judicious scholar-statesman, James Bryce, travelled from Mafeking to Salisbury by the Bulawayo route, accompanied by his wife, with only his wagon-driver and one native 'Cape boy' for additional company, and, he remarked, 'no one of the friends we consulted as to our trip even suggested that I should carry so much as a revolver, or that the slightest risk was involved in taking a lady through the country. . . . It is easy to be wise after the event. . . . We travelled, unarmed and unconcerned, by night as well as by day, through villages where five months later the Kaffirs rose and murdered every European within reach.'

At the end of December of the same year, Dr. Jameson, who was Administrator of all Southern Rhodesia, led almost the whole of the Company's armed police into the Transvaal. His surrender at Doornkop was a disastrous blow to British prestige among the Matabele, and it came at a time when he had left the country denuded of troops.

Barely two months later came the rinderpest, and on 23rd March 1896 the Matabele rose.

It was an ill-concerted revolt, with no supreme leader among the rebel indunas and little attempt at a coherent strategy; yet it cost the Company and the settlers far heavier losses and far greater effort than the war of 1893. Isolated farmers and prospectors were stealthily approached and either stabbed with a spear or felled with an axe. It was well that few of them were married, or the numbers who were butchered would have been much higher. During the first fortnight 128 white men, eight women and eight children were killed; their bodies when found had usually been viciously mutilated. By the end of that fortnight the only Europeans still alive in Matabeleland were those who had managed to reach Bulawayo and the mining centre of Gwelo, and three or four parties large enough to defend themselves behind a laager. Relief parties were hastily despatched from Bulawayo, and sometimes reached small beleaguered groups in time to bring them back to relative safety.

The men at Bulawayo were sufficiently numerous and skilled in the use of weapons to protect the place itself and keep open communications, but they could undertake no adequate offensive operations, especially as they were short of horses. A relief force of about 200 volunteers hastened from Mashonaland. At Kimberley and Mafeking about 800 men were quickly recruited, equipped and mounted, and were on the road to Bulawayo by the end of April. Early in June a heavy defeat was inflicted on the Matabele, who then withdrew to the Matoppo Hills, which offered admirable cover for guerrilla operations.

No sooner did peace appear to be in sight than a new disaster befell. On 15th June the Mashona began a wave of murders similar to that with which the revolt of the Matabele had begun. In the first few days 119 Europeans, including several women and children, were massacred. There, as also in Matabeleland, any Africans from Cape Colony brought into the country as servants were murdered with their employers. For a time the position was desperate, for the relief force which had gone to Bulawayo had taken with it most of the rifles and the best of the horses in the country. But Salisbury and the other, smaller settlements, managed to hold out until help arrived, and by the beginning of August the Mashona had to retire to the kopjes which had in the past been their refuge from Lobengula's raiders.

The Europeans could understand the desire of the Matabele to revolt, but the action of the Mashona appeared incomprehensible. True, they disliked regular employment, especially underground in a mine, as much as did the Matabele; they disliked the annual hut tax of ten shillings which they had to earn by selling their labour, and methods of recruitment which sometimes savoured of the press gang. Still, it is scarcely credible that they were longing for the good old days of Lobengula's war-parties before the white men came among them—though a writer to whom one can normally look for sound judgment has recently, it seems, taken at its face value a remark by an old Mashona man to that effect.

Although the grievances of the Mashona doubtless contributed to the making of the revolt, their importance was altogether subsidiary, and by themselves they would not have led to violence. The Mashona rose because they were called upon to do so by the witch-doctors in the service of the Mlimo, notably by one Kagubi, who spread the news that the Matabele had wiped out the relief column from Mashonaland, had killed all the white people in Bulawayo, and were now advancing to resume the mastery of their old raiding-grounds. There were no white soldiers left, and the scattered settlers were an easy prey. Let the Mashona rise and share in their extermination! And let them consider what chastisement they would receive at the hands of the victorious Matabele if they failed to respond to this call to arms.

By August 1896 the Company faced the prospect of prolonged guerrilla operations against both the Matabele and the Mashona, desperate men with the courage of desperation, lurking in innumerable interconnected caves where they could inflict heavy losses on their pursuers, and from which even the use of dynamite could scarcely drive them out. In the case of the Mashona the prospect had to be accepted, for it was useless to try to parley with the fanatical Kagubi, and the numerous petty chiefs were merely his tools. The main stronghold was taken on 26th July 1897, and although Kagubi escaped from it his prestige was ruined and he became a hunted fugitive. By the end of September the campaign was over, and a month later Kagubi himself surrendered, to face trial and execution.

In Matabeleland, however, a prolonged struggle which would have been ruinous to the Company's finances as well as costly in lives was avoided by the happy accident which caused the mother of one of the leading rebel indunas to fall into the hands of the troops, and thus gave Rhodes the opportunity of using her as an intermediary to open negotiations. Rhodes no longer had any official position: he had resigned from the Board of Directors because of his involvement in the Jameson Raid. But the Directors continued to follow his advice in everything, and Milner found that it was still with Rhodes that he had to deal where the affairs of Southern Rhodesia were concerned. To the Matabele he was still the 'great white induna'. They were much too suspicious to venture into the open to negotiate, but they expressed willingness to talk with Rhodes if he would come into the hills. So, on 21st August 1896, accompanied only by three white men and two Africans from the Cape, he rode five miles into rebel-held country, dismounted, and waited for the Matabele indunas to approach. They did so, and a process of negotiation began which lasted until 13th October, when peace was concluded.

The Matabele were required to surrender all weapons, and to hand over all murderers for trial. But, the agreement stated, 'all rebels, whether chiefs or common people, who are guilty of rebellion alone, and who surrender themselves and lay down their arms, are permitted to return to their homes, except in the case of those whose homes are in the Matoppo Hills, who shall be permitted to proceed to some other spot or spots hereafter fixed upon and notified'. The reason for clearing the Matoppos was, of course, one of military security. The Company undertook to supply the tribe with food and seed to enable it to avoid starvation; it also undertook to give recognition to certain influential indunas, including three who had not taken part in the rebellion, and to pay them salaries. Thus the power of the Matabele was finally broken, and at the same time the tribe was in some measure conciliated. From then on, for over sixty years, the internal peace of Southern Rhodesia was undisturbed. And from then on one seldom heard of either Matabele or Mashona —one heard of 'natives' and 'the native problem'.

Even before the revolts began the Jameson Raid had made it imperative that the Government should take steps to curb the Company's freedom of action. In theory that freedom had always been qualified by the need to obtain the assent of the High Commissioner to all appointments, all ordinances and regulations, and the execution of any death sentence; but the High Commissioner, relying on such information as the Company's own Administrator provided, had of necessity to approve what he was in no position to question. Early in 1896, however, the Government appointed a Resident Commissioner to act as the High Commissioner's representative in Southern Rhodesia and to keep him properly informed. The control of the Company's armed police was removed from the hands of the Administrator —just in case he should wish to emulate Jameson—and placed in those of the Resident Commissioner.

This arrangement was abhorrent to Rhodes. 'Generally speaking,' wrote Milner, 'the Rhodes game is to get rid of Imperial control in the B.S.A. Co's territory. He hates it, as he hates all control.' But in Milner Rhodes encountered a man with whom he could indeed co-operate, but whom he could not use as a tool. 'Of course,' Milner admitted, 'all "duality" of administration, against which Rhodes rails, presents difficulties, requires tact and "give and take". But with these qualities there is absolutely no reason why the present system should not work for some time.' In fact it worked remarkably well for as long as the Company remained responsible for the administration of Southern Rhodesia.

4. Rhodes with Consul Johnston and others at Kimberley, May 1890.

Standing, left to right: J. Grant, J. W. Moir, Joseph Thomson
Seated, left to right: J. Rochfort Maguire, H. H. Johnston, C. J. Rhodes, A. R. Colquhoun

5. The statue of Cecil John Rhodes and Tanganyika House, Third

The Rhodesias Under Company Rule

On 20th October 1898 Southern Rhodesia received a new constitution by Order in Council. Provision was expressly made in it for the office of Resident Commissioner, but, at Milner's suggestion, this office became exclusively political in character, and a 'Commandant General' appointed and paid by the Imperial authorities was placed in charge of the military police forces. Thus the new constitution transferred some of the substance of power from the Company to the Crown. It also made a beginning with another and quite different transfer of power —from the Company to the settlers. Instead of the general-purpose Council set up in 1894—whose legislation, Milner discovered, had been 'apt to be rather harum-scarum and exceedingly drastic'—there were to be an Executive Council and a Legislative Council. The Administrator was to preside over both, and the Executive Council was to consist of the Resident Commissioner and at least four members nominated by the Company. In the Legislative Council, in addition to five nominated members, there were to be four elected members: in effect, four representatives of the settlers.

The introduction of a representative element into the Legislative Council was a development which Milner and the Colonial Office could scarcely oppose, and Rhodes himself pressed for it in the belief that it would not weaken but strengthen his own hand. Up to this time there had been little or no friction between the Company and the settlers. The Company had spent money lavishly on the opening up of the country, had quelled the Matabele, and had made prompt payments on a most generous scale to compensate the settlers for their losses in the rebellion—losses which had come on top of the destruction of their cattle, and would have completed their ruin. Rhodes was their inspiration, and Jameson their hero. As soon as they had heard that Jameson had invaded the Transvaal they had discussed with eager enthusiasm whether it might be possible for a force of volunteers drawn from their number to hasten after him as reinforcements. Milner, commenting on the proposal for a representative element in the new Legislative Council, wrote on 15th June 1897:

The Rhodesias Under Company Rule

'Rhodes is going for it "hot and strong", avowedly with the object of strengthening his own position in any differences with the Imperial Govt. . . . They may bully the Company, he says frankly, but they won't dare to bully a representative Council. At the same time it is quite obvious, that this representative Council will simply be Rhodes, even more completely than the Company is. That can't be helped. Only it should make us careful not to give the Council, even if representative, the control of anything—armed forces for instance—which for reasons of Imperial policy it is not safe to put absolutely into the hands of one strong-willed and hasty man.'

This belief that the settlers could be trusted to act as staunch 'Company's men' was soon shown to be a complete illusion. The very first session of the Legislative Council, in 1899, brought out a conflict of interests which was to provide the main theme of Southern Rhodesian politics for nearly a quarter of a century. The settlers had lost Jameson as a result of the raid, and Rhodes himself had not long to live. The Company began to seem impersonal and remote, and became an object of distrust.

With the departure of Jameson the era of debonair amateurism in Southern Rhodesian administration came to an end. Sir William Milton, who became Administrator soon after the rebellions and remained in that post until 1914, was a professional civil servant, able, dignified, public-spirited and hard-working, who provided the country with the machinery of government of a modern state and took care that it was properly staffed.

By the time Milton took office a great deal had already been done to equip the country with its railways, the essential condition of its development. When the Pioneers entered Mashonaland in 1890 the line had not yet been completed from Kimberley to Vryburg, and Vryburg was 1,000 miles from Salisbury. The journey from the railhead by ox-wagon took four months or more, and the cost of importing supplies was almost prohibitive. The breakdown of transport during the rainy season of 1890–1 demonstrated the urgent need for improved communications, and an attempt was made to open a road to the sea at Beira, less than 400 miles away. This route, however, soon proved use-

MAP 6. *Railway Development*

less for wagon-transport, since it was infested with tsetse fly; so in 1892 a railway was begun. But the difficulties of construction were enormous: the coastal belt consisted largely of marsh with neither shade from the tropical sun nor water to drink, but infested with mosquitoes and lions—the former much the more dangerous, though the latter also claimed their victims among the workers.[1] Beyond it there was the long ascent to Umtali, on

[1] 'It was not found possible to obtain a good supply of labourers from the local Natives. Five hundred Indians were imported, but practically all of

the high veld. It was not until early in 1898 that the line reached Umtali, though scarcely more than another year sufficed to carry it across the high veld to Salisbury.

In the meantime the Cape railway system had been extended from Vryburg to Mafeking, and, after the conquest of Matabeleland, towards Bulawayo.

It had been carried 100 miles north of Mafeking when the rinderpest paralysed the ox-drawn transport on which Matabeleland still depended; it had still 400 miles to go to reach Bulawayo, and the extreme difficulty of bringing in supplies was one of the greatest troubles which beset the Company and the settlers during the revolt. When the revolt had been suppressed the work of construction was pressed ahead with redoubled effort, and Bulawayo was reached before the end of 1897. Rhodes desired that its further extension should take it over the Zambesi and across North-Eastern Rhodesia to the southern shores of Lake Tanganyika, but Sir Charles Metcalfe, who was responsible for surveying the route, persuaded him that the difficulties of construction would be much less and the financial prospects of the line incomparably better if a more westerly direction were taken, by way of the rich coalfield which had been discovered at Wankie. Wankie was reached in 1903; then the line was carried across the Zambesi, by a bridge whose design is worthy of its majestic setting at the Victoria Falls, and on across the Kafue to Broken Hill, where important lead and zinc deposits had been found. From Broken Hill it was continued to the Katanga border, to link up with the railway system of the Belgian Congo. By 1909 it had been completed.

The rail connection between Salisbury and Bulawayo was built during the Boer War, when communications with the

them died. . . . So many people died that Pauling [the contractor] provided a stock of tombstones at Fontesvilla. A man could make his choice and have his name printed on the stone. As four hundred Europeans died during the five years of construction the need for tombstones can be understood. Even burials were difficult. When the graves were dug they filled with water; and as there were no stones it was most difficult to keep the coffin in the grave while the earth was thrown on to it.'—G. H. Tanser, *Founders of Rhodesia* (O.U.P., Cape Town, 1950), pp. 76–7.

south were cut and it was necessary to rely on the east coast route for all contact with Britain and even with the Cape. Then branch lines were built to tap the gold-producing areas.

Thus within the first twenty years of its existence the Chartered Company provided both Southern and Northern Rhodesia with their railway system, offering alternative outlets to the sea.[1] The Company did not itself build the lines, but, since the British Government refused a guarantee, it had to lend most of the money to the railway companies, which therefore became its subsidiaries. This investment was its most outstanding service to the development of the territories under its charge. It was a speculative investment, depending for its financial soundness on the value of the gold mines, which could not be properly assessed until heavy rock-crushing machinery was available—that is, not until the railway already existed to bring the machinery into the country.

'The great question therefore is', wrote Bryce after his visit in 1895, 'How will the gold-reefs turn out? There had been formed before the end of 1895 more than two hundred Development Companies, most of them gold-mining undertakings, and others were being started up till the eve of the native outbreak in March 1896. Very many reefs had been prospected and an immense number of claims registered. The places in which actual work had been done in the way of sinking shafts and opening adits were, of course, much fewer, yet pretty numerous. . . . No one of these workings was on a large scale, and at two or three only had stamping machinery been set up, owing, so I am told, to the practically prohibitive cost of transport from the sea' by ox-wagon, before the coming of the railway.

[1] The Cape route is quicker and much more convenient, but it involves a longer rail journey and is therefore more expensive for freight. But the port facilities at Beira, although much improved in recent years, have been inadequate to cope with the vastly increased volume of post-war trade, especially as Beira serves Moçambique and Nyasaland as well as the Rhodesias. A third railway connection with the sea has existed for many years, through the Belgian Congo and Angola to Lobito Bay; but for various reasons it has been comparatively little used. A railway has therefore been built from Southern Rhodesia to Delagoa Bay, the nearest really good harbour; it was completed in 1955.

The Rhodesias Under Company Rule

'It must be remembered', Bryce explained, 'that in these mining districts the gold occurs in quartz-reefs. Comparatively little is found in alluvial deposits, which in California and Australia and the Ural mountains have often been more important than the quartz-reefs. None at all is found diffused equally through a stratum of rock, as in the Transvaal. Now, quartz-reef mining is proverbially uncertain. The reefs vary not only in thickness but also in depth, and it is not yet certain that any go very far beneath the surface. So, too, even when the reef itself is persistent in width and in depth, its auriferous quality varies greatly. What is called the "shoot" of gold may be rich for some yards, and then become faint or wholly disappear, perhaps to reappear some yards farther. Thus there must be a good deal of quartz crushed at different points before it can be determined what number of pennyweights or ounces to the ton a given reef, or a given part of a reef, is likely to yield.'

It seems that the Company did not realize how risky was its investment in the railway: it was carried away by the prevailing optimism, as were the thousands of settlers who flocked into Southern Rhodesia. By 1898, the year in which the settlers were given representation in the legislature, their number had risen to about 13,000; this figure includes women and children, but there was still a marked preponderance of men. Yet until the end of March of that year the total production of gold since the beginnings of white settlement in 1890 had been worth no more than £20,700.

In the following year the output of gold began to give some solid grounds for hope: it was worth almost £126,000. From then on it gradually increased. But the Boer War (1899-1902) interrupted development, and so disrupted the whole South African economy that it was followed by a depression which only gradually came to an end, between 1905 and 1908. For nearly a decade, therefore, there was scarcely any further capital investment in Southern Rhodesian mining, and scarcely any immigration of new settlers. The output of gold continued gradually to increase, but only because earlier investment was bearing fruit. During these years it became apparent that although there was indeed enough gold in the country to be worth developing, Southern Rhodesia was no El Dorado, and the gold was so scattered and hard to win that no vast fortunes were likely to be built on it. Such as it was, however, it was the basis of the whole economy. It was the only export: it therefore paid for all imports except in so far as they were paid for out of capital. The gold miners and their African labourers provided the only reasonably accessible market for agricultural produce, so that European agriculture developed as a subsidiary of mining, and therefore only in the mining areas. Indeed, as late as 1914 Southern Rhodesia was, on balance, a food-importing country.

As the true facts concerning Southern Rhodesia's gold resources became increasingly apparent during the early years of the twentieth century, the Company's Directors had to redesign their whole policy to take account of them. They had previously assumed that the gold would be extracted by a few big mining companies, and they had claimed for the Chartered Company the right to receive up to half the vendor scrip of these companies. Rhodes could, indeed, point out, in his speech to the shareholders in 1898, that the Company encouraged prospectors by allowing each of them ten claims and charging them no licence fee, whereas in any other country they could have had only one claim and would have had to pay 10s. a month for it: on the 157,000 claims then registered such fees would have brought in nearly £1m. a year. He could also declare with justice that 'you will hear over and over again in the world of some man trudging along with his donkey and his pack, and finding something worth a million or two. It would be far better when he made that discovery, that he should give a portion to the government of the country, and you are the government of the country.' But what if they ceased to govern? The charter itself had provided (clause XXXIII) that after twenty-five years, and after every succeeding period of ten years, the Crown would be entitled to repeal the charter or to amend its provisions; it would have the right to take over any buildings or works used exclusively or mainly for public purposes, and the Treasury would have the last word in determining the amount of compensation to be paid for them. The Company had never intended to conduct the administration any longer than was necessary: Rhodes had from the beginning looked forward to a self-governing colony which would enter into a federation with the rest of South Africa. But he meant the Company to retain its commercial assets even when it had laid down its administrative burden. It was not really because it was the governing authority, that, in his opinion, it was entitled to half the proceeds of gold-mining, but because it held the Rudd Concession in its own right. So he cheerfully went on to assure the shareholders that 'when the government of the country becomes self-governing, I feel sure that they will make no objection to your retaining that interest'; though he added, as an afterthought, 'You might give them a certain share in your interest for managing the concern.' He thus added a political illusion to an economic one. If he had been more clear-sighted, how much less he would have achieved!

The economic illusion was the first to be disproved, very soon after his death in 1902. Many of the mines were too small to justify the flotation of a company, and must be worked by individual 'smallworkers' or not at all. Even when companies were formed they could not prosper if the Chartered Company held half their vendor scrip. In 1903–4 the Company grudgingly decided to tolerate smallworkers on payment of royalties, and to be content with 30 per cent of the vendor scrip of the companies. But even this burden was too great. If production was to expand so that the country could prosper, the Company would have to be content with much less.

In 1907 the Directors sent out a commission, headed by Jameson, to investigate the situation, and it was as a result of this visit that the Company embarked on its new policy. It now contented itself with a royalty, graduated from $7\frac{1}{2}$ per cent to nil according to the prosperity of the mine. Its hopes of gain had from then on to be placed elsewhere than in gold, and the only other possibility was agriculture.

It believed that it owned the land throughout Southern

Rhodesia—except such land as it had itself alienated—as surely as it owned the minerals. Its title rested on the Lippert Concession and on the fact of conquest. Rhodes had asserted the claim in 1895, and the Duke of Abercorn re-asserted it in 1904. In 1898 the Colonial Office had appeared to confirm this view by the terms in which it refused a request by the Company for permission to constitute a public debt to be serviced from the administrative revenue. The Colonial Office had replied that it could not allow a charge to be placed on the revenues of the territory as distinct from those of the Company, 'which has been placed in possession of all the assets of the country'. It reiterated this ruling in 1905. The Company therefore borrowed £3m. in addition to its existing capital, which had already been increased to £6m., and in all good faith it assured investors that its assets included the land of Southern Rhodesia.

The Directors' aim was now to raise the value of the unalienated land by stimulating the demand for it. This involved encouraging immigration, and providing farmers with technical assistance and with loans for such purposes as the construction of fences and dipping tanks. There would be a period of heavy financial outlay, on top of all that had been spent in the past, especially in the building of the railways; and this was unmistakably a long-term investment, which would not become profitable for many years.

This transformation of economic policy had political implications which were at least equally important. The Company would not be ready to relinquish the administration of Southern Rhodesia when the twenty-five-year period expired in 1914. It therefore had to conciliate the settlers, lest they should persuade the British Government to take the administration out of its hands before it was ready to make the transfer. Besides, it could scarcely hope to attract large numbers of fresh immigrants if the existing settlers were discontented. It was therefore compelled to yield more and more political power to the settlers, and by increasing their numbers for the sake of economic development it unavoidably increased their capacity to bring pressure to bear upon it. The census of 1911 showed that the number of Europeans in the country had risen to 23,700, an increase of over 10,000 in five years.

As early as 1903 the number of elected members of the Legislative Council had been made equal to the number of officials —there were to be seven of each—though the Administrator retained a casting vote. In 1907, as part of the general programme of reform, the settlers were given a majority in the Council by the withdrawal of two of the officials; from that date onwards the Administrator and his Executive Council confronted a potentially hostile majority in the legislature. Having once accepted this situation, the Company had not much more to lose by allowing the number of elected members to rise, and by 1914 there were twelve of them.

The settlers absolutely refused to accept the assumption on which the Company's whole policy after 1907 was based—that the Company owned the unalienated land. They were equally determined to take no responsibility for the accumulated administrative deficits. The Company held that, when Southern Rhodesia became self-governing, the new state would inherit all debts while it retained for itself all assets, or sold them at market value. The settlers replied that when that time came the Company must keep its own debts—even though they had been incurred in bringing the state into being—and hand over its assets to them. The more intelligent among them indeed realized that they could not divest the Company of its mineral rights, secure under the Rudd Concession; but in all other respects the disagreement was irreconcilable.

After 1907, however, it was allowed, for a time, to fall into the background. The Company's programme of renewed capital investment was directly in the settlers' own interests, and they were content to milk the Chartered cow as long as the milk supply continued abundant, especially as their own position in the Legislative Council was steadily being strengthened. In the general election of March 1914 eleven of the twelve successful candidates favoured the continuance of the Company's rule beyond the initial twenty-five-year term which was shortly to expire. But ten of the eleven attached conditions, the commonest being that responsible government should be established as soon as the European population was large enough and the revenue sound enough to justify it. The Colonial Office accepted this proviso: the Supplemental Charter which was issued in March 1915 held out the prospect of responsible government if an absolute majority of the whole Legislative Council should pass a resolution requesting it, and if the condition of the territory financially and in other respects justified the request.

By this time the First World War had already begun. The settlers were eager to participate to the full, and over 4,000 enlisted out of a total white population (including both sexes and all ages) of barely 34,000: a larger proportion than came from any other British territory overseas. But in Southern Rhodesia, just as in all the Dominions, the efforts and sacrifices of the war years stimulated the growth of national pride and self-confidence. The rule of the Company became increasingly irksome. One cause of friction, among several, was that the settlers were willing to accept considerable increases in the customs duties, which had previously been light, but only on condition that the whole of the increased revenue was spent on the war; the Company insisted that the first claim on the revenue was the ordinary cost of administration, on which there was almost invariably a substantial deficit.

The conflict of interests was sharpened by personal antagonism. Sir Charles Coghlan, the unchallenged leader of the elected members, was a man of Cromwellian temperament (and appearance),[1] vigorous, tenacious, and blunt, warm-hearted and generous towards individual opponents, and unswervingly devoted to whatever he believed to be right, but assuming as self-evident that the cause of righteousness was identical with the interests of the little community of white settlers in Southern Rhodesia, except in so far as those interests were transcended by the common cause of the whole Empire. He avowedly cared nothing for 'the legitimate demands of the shareholders', just as he cared nothing for the advancement of the African popula-

[1] But not Cromwellian in religious belief: he was a Roman Catholic of Irish ancestry.

tion who outnumbered the whites by at least twenty-five to one, but who were absent from his thoughts when he championed the interests of 'the people'—they remained almost forgotten in the background throughout this white men's controversy.

The Administrator with whom Coghlan had to deal after Milton's retirement in 1914 was Sir Drummond Chaplin, an able administrator but an inept politician, cold, ambitious, self-centred and aloof. Between the pushing plebeian and the super-cilious aristocrat there was little or none of the mutual respect which had existed between Coghlan and Milton, in spite of political differences.

In April 1914 the newly elected Legislative Council had re-iterated the settlers' denial that the unalienated land was the private property of the South Africa Company, and in the fol-lowing July the Government had referred the question to the Judicial Committee of the Privy Council. The ensuing litigation almost coincided with the entire duration of the war.

In opposing the Company's claim, based on the Lippert Con-cession and the right of conquest, counsel for the settlers de-clared that the land belonged to the Crown, which was holding it in trust for the settlers themselves, so that it would become theirs when they took over the administration. A counter-claim was submitted by certain philanthropists on behalf of the native inhabitants; their counsel claimed that the Matabele owned the land communally, so that Lobengula had no right to part with it, and after his defeat and death the Crown had merely in-herited his position, leaving the position of his people unchanged. This argument seems to imply that it was only Lobengula and not the Matabele tribe who had been conquered in 1893; it also offers doubtful comfort to the Mashona. But the Judicial Com-mittee rejected it, because the claim of the natives to continuous ownership of the unalienated lands could not be substantiated, and because the Crown had recognised Lobengula as fully sovereign and that was an end of the matter.

There was a fourth claimant, in addition to the Company, the settlers, and the natives. This was the Crown itself, repre-sented by the Attorney-General of the United Kingdom. And, when the Judicial Committee at last announced its decision in July 1918, it was the Crown which received the award. The Committee pointed out that the Lippert Concession was not a transfer of land-ownership, but merely authorised the concession-holder to act as the agent of the Matabele king, for a defined period of time, as his agent in the disposal of land. When the Matabele kingship was extinguished in 1893–4, so in effect was the Lippert Concession. Ownership of the land devolved upon the Crown by right of conquest, though the Company, as the agent of the Crown in the work of conquest and subsequent administration, was entitled to sell land as long as it remained the administering authority, using the proceeds to help to cover expenses. Thus the settlers' point of view had in the main been upheld, except that the Crown obtained freedom of action to make what provision it conveniently could make on behalf of native interests, when the time came to terminate the Company's administrative control.

To the Company the Judicial Committee's decision came as a bitter and completely unexpected blow; and indeed it is an interesting legal curiosity to find that for a quarter of a century the Crown had been owning the land in a territory which it had not yet formally annexed. But the Company could take con-siderable comfort in the fact that the Committee had upheld its claim to reimbursement of its administrative deficits. Its aim was now to rid itself of the burden of administration as soon as possible, in return for whatever compensation it could get; and it promptly announced that it would spend no more of the share-holders' money on the development of lands which were not its own.

The settlers, finding that there was no more money to be had from the Company, at once began to demand the termination of its rule. Their economic position was now much stronger than before the war, for war-time demands and shortages had stimu-lated exports and encouraged the diversification of the economy, which in the past had been over-dependent on that limited and wasting asset, gold. In 1914 the amount of gold produced was 854,500 fine ounces, but from 1916 onwards there was a falling off, and after the war production settled down to an annual output of about 600,000 fine ounces—though the rising price of gold made this output increasingly valuable. But there was a large increase, during and after the war, in the output of coal, asbestos, and chrome; for a time copper was important too. Whereas in 1914 the gold produced was worth £3,580,200 out of a total mineral output of £3,883,000, in 1920 it was worth £3,056,500 out of £4,451,000. Agricultural production and exports became important too, more important than any mineral other than gold. Between 1915 and 1920 agricultural exports increased more than fivefold, and in 1920 were worth £1,483,000. The main item consisted of beef cattle, which, although they were as yet of inferior quality, found a market on the Rand and in East Africa. The number of European-owned cattle in Southern Rhodesia rose steadily from 164,000 head in 1911 to 994,000 in 1923. Maize became an important export too. The growers of tobacco and citrus fruits gained some precarious foothold in the overseas market, and were assisted by the United Kingdom's adoption of Imperial preference in 1919. The total revenue in 1913–14 was £776,900, while expenditure was £836,500; in 1922–3 it was £1,326,500, and expenditure was £1,357,400. The settlers could reasonably claim that the country was now in a position to stand on its own feet. In the general election of 1920—which, owing to the war, was the first since 1914—twelve of the thirteen successful candidates were pledged to try to obtain responsible government. The Women's Franchise Ordinance, passed in 1919, made the result look twice as impressive by doubling the size of the electorate.

Coghlan and his adherents, however, were no more ready than they had been in the past to accept any responsibility for the repayment of the administrative deficits incurred by the Company. From their point of view it was perfectly obvious that the Crown's assets, that is the land, were the assets of Southern Rhodesia, while the Crown's liabilities were the liabilities of the United Kingdom Treasury and taxpayer. The British Government on its side saw no reason to accept the burden, and favoured the absorption of Southern Rhodesia by the Union of

South Africa. The Government of General Smuts was eager to consolidate all Africa south of the Zambesi in a single state, and to strengthen its own political position in relation to the Nationalist Opposition by bringing the Empire-minded Southern Rhodesians into the electorate of the Union. It was therefore prepared to offer generous terms both to the Company and to the settlers. But Coghlan and the majority of the settlers refused to contemplate entry into the Union, except perhaps as a distant prospect, when they would be much more numerous and influential than they had as yet become. They feared that instead of helping Smuts to swamp the Nationalist vote, they would themselves be swamped by it. They feared an influx of Afrikaner 'poor whites'. They preferred to look after their own economic interests, rather than merge them in those of a Union in which they would be merely an outlying province.

In the end the British taxpayer had to carry the burden, as the price of reaching any settlement at all. The Colonial Office appeared miserly in its bargaining with the Company, whose President, Rochfort Maguire, told the shareholders in March 1923 that he did not think any of the gentlemen who had been Secretary of State for the Colonies since the Privy Council judgment would have acted in their private affairs as they had done in those of the Crown. From the floor of the hall a resolution was proposed: 'That the shareholders present at this meeting protest against the cat and mouse policy which the Crown has systematically thought fit to adopt in its dealings with our Company, and its callous disregard of our Company's services to the Empire in doing a Government's work for over thirty-three years, and making a colony'—it was passed unanimously and with enthusiasm. After all, the shareholders had not received a penny of dividends at any time during those thirty-three years. In the following September, however, the Duke of Devonshire, as Secretary of State, gave his approval to the 'Devonshire Agreement', by which the British Treasury was to pay £3,750,000 to the Company.

By the time this agreement was reached between the Government and the Company, the political future of Southern Rhodesia had already been decided. In March 1921 a committee under Earl Buxton was appointed to report on the constitutional future of both Southern and Northern Rhodesia; it submitted both its reports in the following month. It recommended that a draft constitution should be prepared, giving Southern Rhodesia responsible government with certain limitations, particularly in the form of safeguards for native interests, and that the adoption or rejection of this constitution should be determined by referendum to the Southern Rhodesian electorate.

In the following October a deputation of elected members, headed by Coghlan, visited London and engaged in arduous negotiations with the Secretary of State, at that time Mr. Winston Churchill. Both as the friend of Smuts and as the man of wide Imperial vision, Mr. Churchill thought Coghlan and his supporters were being merely parochial in their refusal to enter the Union. But Coghlan was immovable in his stand on the principle of 'Rhodesia for the [white] Rhodesians', and when he went home in December he took with him draft Letters Patent providing for responsible government.

Mr. Churchill, however, had stipulated that in the coming referendum the electors must be offered the alternative of entry into the Union, and the Union cause was favoured by both the two daily newspapers of the territory and by the main financial interests, including the South Africa Company itself. Coghlan therefore had to overcome vigorous opposition backed by ample resources, and of course he made his appeal to 'the people' as the champion of their just rights against the sinister influence of big business with its headquarters in the Union. It was a rowdy, strenuous campaign that preceded the referendum, held on 27th October 1922. On the eve of the poll the 'R.G.s'—advocates of responsible government—smashed up a meeting held by the 'Unionists' in Bulawayo, shouting down the speakers and pelting them with rotten eggs. 'It was a grand night,' commented Lady Coghlan, after giving her daughter an ecstatic account of the incident. 'The heart of Rhodesia beats soundly here in Bulawayo,' declared Sir Charles himself when the poll closed the following day.

Of the votes cast, 8,774 were for responsible government and 5,989 for entering the Union.

On 12th September 1923, Southern Rhodesia was formally annexed to the Crown. It was the only one of the three territories in the former federation where this was ever done; but it was done merely as a preliminary to the introduction of responsible government by Letters Patent on the following 1st October. The constitution established a single-chamber legislature consisting of thirty elected members. It authorised the subsequent creation of an upper house, but, not surprisingly, the legislature did not choose to curtail its own authority by instituting any such body.

What was to be done with Northern Rhodesia? Here there had been no gold rush, since there was no gold, except for a small amount in the extreme south-east. Though the railway had been constructed to Broken Hill and the border of the Belgian Congo, there had been comparatively little investment in the country, and the total white population recorded at the 1921 census was only 3,634. When it is remembered that this figure included missionaries, administrative staff, and travellers, and also wives and families, the smallness of the settler population becomes even more conspicuous. At that time the African population was reckoned to be almost 1,000,000, outnumbering the whites by 270 to 1. With such a ratio, Northern Rhodesia could scarcely as yet be described as a plural society, except in the dreams of the more hopeful white settlers. It was an almost purely African territory. Such white settlement as existed was concentrated almost entirely in the vicinity of the railway, except for about 250 people in the vicinity of Fort Jameson, near the Nyasaland border, and an even smaller number in the Abercorn area. This concentration of the white population in the 'railway belt' persists to the present day, when the numbers are much larger; it may be contrasted with the widespread dispersal which has existed in Southern Rhodesia ever since the conquest—a very uneven dispersal, it is true, since the bulk of the white population has always congregated in the towns, especially Salisbury and Bulawayo, but sufficient to make the power of the white landowner directly felt throughout the length and breadth of that territory.

'If you look at the map,' wrote Sir Kenneth Bradley a few years ago, 'you will see that Northern Rhodesia has a very odd shape, like a lop-sided butterfly. . . . The Cape-to-Congo railway with its attendant towns and farming areas runs up from the Victoria Falls through the body of the butterfly to its head. The body is, realistically, the centre of nearly all the country's activities, and the two great wings have stayed, except for an occasional flutter, quiet, beautiful and changeless' (*Copper Venture*, 1952, p. 15).

An unusual characteristic of this butterfly was that it had developed out of two previously quite separate and distinct organisms, North-Western and North-Eastern Rhodesia. In 1894, when arrangements were being made for the separation of North-Eastern Rhodesia from Nyasaland and when the Matabeleland Order in Council was being issued, the Colonial Office had intended to extend the authority of the Administrator of Southern Rhodesia over both parts of the Company's domain north of the Zambesi; but the Jameson Raid had made such a consolidation of the Company's rule appear inadvisable. So, while Coryndon administered the north-west in collaboration with Lewanika, Forbes and later Robert Codrington administered the north-east in continuing close association with the Commissioner for Nyasaland. Forbes was invalided home in 1897, while conditions were still so primitive that a framework of administration scarcely yet existed; indeed the Administrator had to establish his headquarters at Blantyre, and it was not until 1899 that they could be moved to the newly founded Fort Jameson within North-Eastern Rhodesia's own boundaries. It was Codrington who created a regular administrative organisation in the territory, and although his financial resources were extremely meagre he did it so well that men said the meaning of 'B.C.' was 'Before Codrington'.

After years of hesitation, at the turn of the century, the British Government gave a proper legal basis to the existing mode of rule. By this time the Southern Rhodesia Order in Council of

The Rhodesias Under Company Rule

1898 had created a Legislative Council on which the representatives of the settlers occupied an influential position, but the Government wisely gave this council no voice in the affairs of the Company's northern possessions. Nor did it introduce the legal system of Cape Colony, as it had done in Southern Rhodesia, and as the Company would have liked it to do in the north. Instead, the law of England was to be applied there, as in Nyasaland, in so far as anything other than African customary law was required at all. In fact, South Africa, the land of white supremacy, was to stop at the Zambesi. For the northern territories, unlike Southern Rhodesia, were not, and did not seem likely to become, settler-dominated; it was significant that whereas in the south the armed 'police' force which maintained public order consisted of white men, in both the northern territories, especially the north-east, it consisted mainly of Africans recruited from the local tribes.

The Barotziland–North-Western Rhodesia Order in Council, issued on 28th November 1899, was concerned with all the territory west of the Kafue, and with as much of the country east of the lower Kafue as was occupied by the Mashukulumbwe. The North-Eastern Rhodesia Order in Council, of 29th January 1900, applied to the remainder of the Company's sphere north of the Zambesi. In the north-west, as in Southern Rhodesia, the Crown's control over the Company's Administrator was to be exercised by the High Commissioner for South Africa, whereas in the north-east it remained with the Commissioner for Nyasaland. This difference reflected the fact that North-Eastern Rhodesia's links with Nyasaland continued to be much closer than her links with North-Western Rhodesia; indeed to this day the Fort Jameson area is essentially an outlying part of Nyasaland, relying on the Nyasaland railway for the export of its produce.

When Northern Rhodesia's own railway was constructed in the early years of the twentieth century, the first part of its route lay through the north-western territory and the latter part through the north-eastern. Consequently it became administratively convenient to detach the country on the upper Kafue from the control of far-away Fort Jameson, and to place

The Rhodesias Under Company Rule

it in the hands of Coryndon's Administration. Thus, in 1904, the entire railway belt—the 'body' of the butterfly, to use Mr. Bradley's metaphor, as distinct from the 'wings'—became part of North-Western Rhodesia. North-Eastern Rhodesia, slightly reduced in size but greatly diminished in importance, from then on attracted little white settlement or investment, and the influences of civilisation were brought to it mainly by the missionary, the administrator, and the tribesman returning home from a period of employment in the mines or on the farms of white men hundreds of miles away. Cullen Gouldsbury, one of the Company's officials, described the country vividly if with rather uncritical affection a few years before the First World War:

'Here on the Plateau—rimmed about by the encircling lakes, overshadowed by the hills of old; exempt, the gods be praised! from the boisterous commercialism of twentieth-century civilisation—we lead a lotus-life of our own. Away in the dim distance, within hearing of those tourist hordes that flock to view the Victoria Falls, lie Broken Hill and the railway. But between us and that outpost of modernity there are many many miles of dim bushland, and swamps, and rugged hills. It is a six-weeks' walk from Tanganyika to the Zambesi, and, in a month and a half, one finds ample scope for a change of viewpoint. . . . Nowadays there is electric light at Zomba, and a photographer at Blantyre; Bulawayo possesses a Grand Hotel and a roller-skating rink, . . . but here upon the Plateau we still tread the old, primitive paths. . . . So far as the eye can reach there is naught but the exuberance of vegetation: tall, tangled grasses—tufted trees—fantastic antheaps, the primeval rock—these and nothing more. Here and there, a pin-point in the wilderness, lie clusters of thatched huts, wreathed in a mist of smoke—tiny patches of human life and human thought hedged about with gardens, wrested from the void.' But he added that 'day by day, or at least year by year, the increased inter-tribal communication is tending to break down the barriers of tribal reserve and hostility', and he remarked that although calico was still the main currency, the native was learning the difference in value between a shilling and a bright new penny.[1] Though the pace of change in North-Eastern Rhodesia was, and has continued to be, comparatively slow, it has been cumulatively important. And in North-Western Rhodesia, west of the railway belt, the pace and the general trend have been broadly the same.

Between 1907 and 1911 the Administration of North-Eastern Rhodesia was gradually absorbed into that of the north-west, and the long-standing political ties with Nyasaland were completely severed. In 1911 a united Northern Rhodesia was established by Order in Council. Two years previously, at the Company's request, the supervisory authority of the High Commissioner for South Africa had been extended to the whole country. In fact it was not until 1911 that Imperial control was of any practical importance, for it was not until that year that a Resident Commissioner was appointed to provide the High Commissioner with independent information, as had been done in Southern Rhodesia after the Jameson Raid. The Company itself had given its Administrators a free hand, and, since the Administrators were admirably suited to their work, this was probably the best course that could have been followed.

In 1917 the Company tried to enlist the co-operation of the small settler community by creating an Advisory Council consisting of five elected members. But this body possessed neither legislative nor executive powers, and the settlers, few though they were, desired something more than the right to give advice. In accordance with the invariable instinct which British colonists in all parts of the world have shown ever since the founding of Virginia, they held that no taxation could rightfully be imposed upon them without the consent of the elected representatives of the settler community. Indirect taxation was bad enough, but, when, in 1920, the Company proposed to introduce an income tax, with the High Commissioner's approval, a petition to the King was drawn up, signed by 175 of the settlers, and forwarded to London. The petitioners complained that 'the white population are allowed no share whatever in any kind of government in the Territory', and demanded that 'the expenditure and collection of all monies from the public of

¹ Gouldsbury and Sheane, *The Great Plateau of Northern Rhodesia*, pp. 1-15.

The Rhodesias Under Company Rule

Northern Rhodesia shall be subject to the approval of, and be controlled by, the Advisory Council'. In addition, the Council should have a veto over all future legislation. Finally, they asked for an enquiry to be made into the ownership of the minerals and the unalienated land, because: 'The British South Africa Company claims to own all the land and minerals in the country as a private commercial asset, and the people claim that both these belong to the Crown, and say that the country will be greatly impoverished if the greatest part of its wealth is thus taken from the Crown as custodian for the people of this Territory.'[1]

So, even more preposterously than in Southern Rhodesia, 'the white population' was synonymous with 'the public' and 'the people'.

Lord Milner, the Secretary of State, replied that the far-reaching constitutional demands submitted in this petition would require 'full consideration', and that in the meantime revenue must be raised, and the income tax must be paid. But, as a result of the petition, the affairs of Northern Rhodesia were included in the terms of reference of the Buxton Commission, appointed in the following March.

The Commission reported that in its opinion the Company 'should be asked at once to consider the creation of a Legislative Council on which the settlers would have adequate representation. In the circumstances of the Territory, and especially in view of the large annual deficits, it would, of course, be necessary to maintain a standing Official majority. But we are decidedly of opinion that the settlers ought to be allowed to take an effective share in the work of legislation.' Their report on Northern Rhodesia was mainly concerned, however, with the question of ownership of the land and minerals. They considered that this question was so complex, and affected so many interests—the settlers, the native population, and perhaps the Treasury, in addition to the Colonial Office and the Company itself—that the only satisfactory course was that suggested by the Advisory Council in a resolution passed in June 1920: to obtain

[1] The petition is printed as Appendix I in the Buxton Commission's Second Report (Cmd. 1471).

The Rhodesias Under Company Rule

a decision from the Judicial Committee of the Privy Council. This decision should also cover the large financial issues which, in Northern as in Southern Rhodesia, were in dispute between the Company and the Crown.

The Company, however, had no desire to embark upon a second lawsuit before the Judicial Committee, and chose to agree with its adversary quickly. The Devonshire Agreement of September 1923 applied to Northern as well as to Southern Rhodesia. The Company had claimed that the excess of administrative expenditure over revenue since the country passed under its jurisdiction, a sum amounting to £1,660,000, should be paid to it by the Crown; the Crown had put in a counter-claim for almost £2,000,000 which it had advanced during the First World War to promote the campaign in German East Africa. Both these claims were now abandoned. On the subject of land ownership a compromise was reached: the Company should receive, until 1965, half the net proceeds of all alienation of land in North-Western Rhodesia, and, in North-Eastern Rhodesia, it retained in freehold three estates which together covered an area of about 2,500,000 acres. Finally, it was left in perpetual enjoyment of the mineral royalties.[1]

Rochfort Maguire explained to the shareholders that the Board recommended the acceptance of these terms, 'not because we consider the terms generous or even just'—a remark which was greeted with 'Hear, hear', and applause—but because 'they are the best we could get', and the only alternative was endless litigation of which the outcome would have been far from certain. The Company could be excused for feeling aggrieved: it had obtained no compensation for its accumulated

[1] The Company's claims in North-Western Rhodesia rested, of course, on its agreements with Lewanika. In North-Eastern Rhodesia the mineral rights were deemed to have been secured by the Sharpe-Thomson treaties—which, since they were made on behalf of the Company, were concerned with economic interests as well as political. But those interests did not extend to land ownership. The three estates to which the Company made good its claim, all of them in the vicinity of the Stevenson Road (the Abercorn area), had been obtained by the African Lakes Company and had been transferred to the B.S.A. Company as part of the general settlement between the two companies in 1893.

administrative deficits, and the money spent on the East African campaign had brought no special advantage to the shareholders. Its land rights, except to some extent in the railway belt, were of little practical value, and its mineral royalties amounted to less than £13,000 a year and seemed unlikely to become much more valuable in the future. No one could foresee that within fifteen years their annual yield would have risen to over £300,000, and that, as a result of the Devonshire Agreement and the jettisoning of its whole administrative burden, the Company was destined to a future of most enviable prosperity.[1]

The Company's rule ended in Northern Rhodesia on 1st April 1924, six months later than in Southern Rhodesia. Northern Rhodesia now became, like Nyasaland, a Protectorate, administered by a Governor with the assistance of an Executive Council consisting of senior officials, and receiving its laws from a Legislative Council which, as the Buxton Report had suggested, included a minority of elected representatives of the settlers with an official majority to secure full Colonial Office control. There were five elected unofficials and nine officials.

By 1924, therefore, the settlers had achieved a political position comparable to that accorded to the white Southern Rhodesians in 1898. To that extent they had encroached upon the Colonial Office principle—or rather, had disproved the Colonial Office prediction—that the ascendancy of white settlers in southern Africa would stop at the line of the Zambesi. In the years ahead they were to advance a long way farther, but their advance was to be both slower and less sure than had been that of their fellow countrymen in Southern Rhodesia in the quarter-century after 1898.

[1] Indeed it became exposed to the charge that it was drawing far too much money from a territory which, in spite of the newly found prosperity of its copper-mining industry, was still, taken as a whole, poor and backward. In 1949, therefore, it agreed to pay one-fifth of the net revenue from its mineral royalties to the Government of Northern Rhodesia until 1st October 1986, and it further agreed that on that date the remaining minerals should become the property of that Government without payment. But in 1964, on the eve of the country's independence, the African nationalists who now formed the Government insisted on abrogating this agreement and terminating all royalty payments forthwith.

CHAPTER 7

European Progress and 'Native Policy'

In the first financial year after the ending of Company rule, the revenue of the Northern Rhodesian Government was £309,795. In 1952, on the eve of federation, it was £26,064,540. When due allowance has been made for inflation during and after the Second World War, the increase in real terms was at least thirty-fold.

Even more striking is the growth in exports. In 1924 they were worth less than £400,000; in 1952, more than £82,600,000. This vast expansion was due almost entirely to the development of the copper industry, and the growth of Government revenue was to a corresponding extent due to the taxation of that industry and of the men it employed.

The copperbelt lies on the Katanga border, at the northern end of the railway belt. It covers about 1,600 square miles—which, it should be remembered, is scarcely more than a two-hundredth part of the total area of Northern Rhodesia. Here half the entire European population of Northern Rhodesia now resides, together with more than a quarter of a million Africans. At the beginning of the century there were scarcely any Africans, and no Europeans except an occasional prospector.

The early prospectors on the Northern Rhodesian side of the Congo border found copper in a number of places, including Roan Antelope (1902) and Nkana (1910): the mines at these places, with two others and recently a further two, constitute the copperbelt in so far as it has yet been developed. Why were these discoveries so long neglected? The reason is that the oxide ores, lying near the surface, were not nearly as rich as those in

Katanga, and although some mining was in fact done, it proved to be such an unrewarding activity that by 1907 it was abandoned, except at one mine, named Bwana Mkubwa, where a certain amount of production continued until the late 1920s. Below the oxide ores, at a depth of 1,000 feet or more, lie sulphide ores, much more profitable to treat by modern industrial methods—by what is called the flotation process—but only if they were found in such very great quantities as would justify enormous capital expenditure. In Katanga the rich surface ores changed at depth to low-grade ores, not worth extracting; this discouraged investigation of what lay beneath the oxide ores in Northern Rhodesia.

In the early 1920s Chester Beatty, an American mining engineer of great experience who had become a British subject, began to take an interest in the possibilities of the copperbelt, and, in association with others, including Sir Ernest Oppenheimer's Anglo-American Corporation of South Africa, obtained from the South Africa Company an exclusive right to prospect in an area as large as England. The finance required for deep drilling in the remote wilds of Africa now became available, and so did the technical knowledge which made it possible to prove vast deposits of ore by making only a relatively small number of drill-holes. At the end of 1926 there were still few who believed that the copperbelt was worth developing; by the end of 1930, over 500,000,000 tons of ore containing more than 20,000,000 tons of copper were established. Further prospecting has revealed additional deposits, and in 1963 the known reserves have an estimated copper content of about 26,000,000 tons, the third largest in the world (after Peru and the United States).

Development work was begun in 1928. It involved making extensions to the railway, and importing thousands of tons of machinery, building materials, and supplies. By the end of 1931 the first copper was being sent overseas—just at the time when the great depression was cutting off demand. The price of copper fell from £72 to £27 a ton. Production was drastically curtailed, not only on the copperbelt but at Broken Hill, where for a time the mining of zinc ceased entirely. The European population, which had risen from 3,600 in 1924 to 13,300 in 1931, fell to 10,500 a year later. The general situation was summed up as follows by the Finance Commission in 1932: 'the price of base metals so low that the three producing companies are compelled to limit their output; the European population reduced by one quarter and experiencing great distress; the fields of employment for natives restricted and their markets stagnant; the Territory's trade suffering a severe set-back; the repatriation or the maintenance of European destitutes imposing a considerable drain on revenues; the proceeds from native taxation greatly diminished by the serious drop in native employment; the farming industry struggling against adverse conditions; . . . and, finally, the immense and incalculable potentialities of a heavy locust invasion.'

From 1933 onwards there was a gradual improvement. In that year 103,000 tons of copper were exported, amounting in value to over £3m.; in 1938, 220,000 tons, worth £10m. With the coming of war there was no longer any need to limit production to what the world market could absorb: the need was now to achieve the greatest possible output, in spite of shortage of manpower and of railway rolling-stock. For more than ten years after the war the demand for copper appeared unlimited: it was a dollar-saver and even a dollar-earner at a time when the sterling area had great difficulty in balancing its payments, and copper prices soared. In 1956 an output rather less than twice that of 1938 was worth the record total of £115m. In 1957 and 1958 there was a sharp fall in copper prices, but by 1963 the price per ton had recovered, and in addition there had been a substantial increase in output.

The pre-war increase in the European population was slow, amounting to scarcely more than the number who had left the territory during the depression. After the end of the war, however, there was a phase of far more rapid immigration than ever before. At the 1951 census the Europeans numbered 37,221—still only about as many as the inhabitants of a single English town the size of Dover, but fully as many as had been given self-government in Southern Rhodesia in 1923. Five years later, at the next census, they had increased to 64,810, and the increase was continuing.

In Southern Rhodesia the gradual expansion and diversification of the economy continued until the depression; then it was temporarily reversed. The prices of agricultural products fell disastrously, and so did those of coal and base metals, of which the output in 1929 had been worth more than the output of gold. It was not until about 1937 that the products of farm and mine had fully regained, both in quantity and in value, the level reached before the slump. Yet Southern Rhodesia did not suffer as severely as Northern Rhodesia, because, when all other prices were falling, the price of gold went up, as a result of the abandonment of the gold standard late in 1931. Production was stimulated on marginal workings, and in 1937 the yield was 804,000 fine ounces, the highest since 1917. In 1939 it was almost as large, but by the end of the war it had again dropped to 550,000 ounces or less; since then it has been almost static, reaching its lowest level (487,000 ounces) in 1951, and subsequently making a full recovery. In the meantime, from the end of the depression until about 1960, there was a continuous and rapid advance in production other than gold. In 1961 the total mineral output was worth over £27m., of which gold amounted to just over £7m. But the main strength of the territory's postwar economy has not lain in mineral production at all. The development of agriculture was much more significant, especially the cultivation of tobacco for export. From its beginnings just before the First World War tobacco production expanded, mainly since the Second World War, until the amount exported annually was worth at least £30m. In addition, an important manufacturing industry has developed.

The growth of the European population was continuous until 1960; even during the years of depression the immigrants slightly outnumbered the emigrants, and from 1945 to the late 1950s they poured into the country so fast that it had great difficulty in providing them with the housing and services which they expected—for the immigrant of recent years was no longer the 'frontiersman' type of pioneer, prepared to 'rough it' in a new country. By 1951 the number of Europeans was about 138,000; by 1961 it was 221,000. Since 1961, however, the number of emigrants has slightly exceeded the number of immigrants.

Having achieved self-government, the settlers felt increasingly irritated by the South Africa Company's continuing right to receive royalties on all minerals produced in the Colony, and in 1933 the Government of Southern Rhodesia offered to buy the mineral rights for the sum of £2m. Since the Southern Rhodesian royalties for the previous ten years had averaged a little under £100,000 a year, it was a fair offer, and the Company accepted it. In fact the arrangement proved highly advantageous to the Colony, because of the increasing value of mineral production; but it also suited the Company, which was enabled to invest heavily in the new companies which were developing the Northern Rhodesian copperbelt.

In 1947 the Government further extended its effective authority by buying the Rhodesia Railways. Since, however, the railways involved in this transaction run from Vryburg in the south to the copperbelt in the north, it concerned Northern as well as Southern Rhodesia, and also Bechuanaland. These territories were therefore associated with the new arrangement, Northern Rhodesia's part being to underwrite up to 20 per cent of any losses on the working of the railway—most improbable losses, since the railway was no longer under-employed as it was in the early days, but required a great extension of its facilities and a great increase in its equipment to enable it to meet the requirements of a rapidly expanding economy, in a part of the world where road transport had scarcely yet begun to compete with transport by rail. The management of the railway system was made responsible to a 'Higher Authority' consisting of representatives of the Governments of both the Rhodesias, the Federation, and Bechuanaland.

The self-government achieved by Southern Rhodesia in 1923 was not the full 'Dominion status' which was soon afterwards defined in the Balfour Report of 1926 and was given legal form by the Statute of Westminster five years later. The limitations on her autonomy laid down in the Letters Patent of 1923 remained in force, apart from certain modifications made in 1937, until 1962, and although in practice she came to be treated almost as if she were a full member of the Commonwealth, her formal status remained that of a 'self-governing colony'. The most important of the Imperial controls were those which nominally preserved a principle laid down a quarter of a century previously in the Southern Rhodesia Order in Council of 1898, stipulating that no law or regulation 'whereby natives may be subjected or made liable to any conditions, disabilities or restrictions to which persons of European descent are not also subjected or made liable' should be valid without the express approval of the British Government—except, indeed, in connection with the supply of arms, ammunition or alcohol, where racial discrimination was considered necessary for the safety of the whole community, including the African population itself.

Why, it was sometimes asked, should an outside authority with no direct stake in the country suppose itself to be competent to interfere with the elected representatives of the settlers themselves in governing their own country as they thought best? It could scarcely be because they were better informed than the 'man on the spot'. Could it, then, be on the ground of moral superiority, of a more just and humane attitude? By what right—so the argument ran—did people in Britain consider themselves better than their 'kinsmen overseas'; especially in view of the fact that recent immigrants from the United Kingdom were not a whit more liberal than life-long Rhodesians in their attitude to the Africans?

The answer to this question was given once and for all by the Commission on Closer Union of the Dependencies in Eastern and Central Africa, in its Report (Cmd. 3234), published in 1929. The following passage (from pp. 90–2), though specifically concerned with Kenya, applied with equal force to both the Rhodesias:

'There are few matters about which European opinion in Africa is more sensitive, and rightly so, than any suggestion that

British residents on the spot are less fitted than their countrymen at home to be trusted in their dealings with the natives. But the fitness of individuals is not in question. As individuals the British settlers . . . are in no way inferior in integrity or in their sense of justice to the officials, and indeed would compare favourably with any body of men in the Empire. The difficulty lies in the fact that they constitute only one class in the community. . . . Their interests may come into conflict with those of the natives in regard to land. They are, as a class, employers dependent on the natives as a class for labour. They may have different interests in the incidence of taxation. They are not in a position to take the same detached view of questions in which their personal interests are involved.

'. . . In representative bodies the interests of the unrepresented are apt to receive scant attention. As the Natal Native Affairs Commission (1906–7) remarked, a white parliament by its origin and composition, "stands virtually in the relationship of an oligarchy to the natives, and naturally studies more the interest of the constituencies to which its members owe their position than the interests of those who had no voice in their election, more particularly when the interests of the represented conflict with those of the unrepresented".

'Experience has taught mankind that a man, however just and honourable, ought not to be made judge in his own cause. An unconscious bias tends to deflect his judgment. . . . That one part of the community should govern the whole, or that one class should make laws for another, was declared by Pericles more than two thousand years ago to be a form of tyranny. The foundation and only sure defence of freedom, a principle for which more than any other the British Empire stands, lie in a proper balance of interests and powers in the State.'

Theoretically, it is true, the Southern Rhodesian legislature did not represent an exclusively white electorate. When the Legislative Council was created in 1898, the vote was given to all men over twenty-one who were British subjects or made a declaration of allegiance, who were literate enough to complete an application form, and who had an annual income of at least

£50 or property worth at least £75, or a mining claim. For the time being, the financial qualifications excluded the Africans, but they were not high enough to do so indefinitely. But in 1912 they were doubled, and in 1917 the Treasurer, an official employed by the Company, assured the Legislative Council that they could be raised again in due course if the need arose. In 1951, the income qualification was raised to £240 and the alternative property qualification to £500: the Government explained this action on the ground that it merely compensated for the fall in the value of money, and all who had already been enrolled as voters were allowed to remain on the roll. By that time there were 52,761 European voters and 453 African;[1] in 1938 there had been 39 Africans in a total electorate numbering 24,626.

Such is the interpretation which has been given, in one matter of crucial importance, to Rhodes's principle of 'equality of rights for every civilised man south of the Zambesi'. What did Rhodes himself mean by it? He meant 'that any men, provided they can write their names, place of residence and occupation, and that they are workers or possessed of some property, quite irrespective of colour, would be entitled to these rights' (speech of 20th July 1899). It can scarcely be denied that between Rhodes and his interpreters there has been, to say the least, a marked difference of emphasis.

The history of the franchise illustrates how easy it is to contrive racial discrimination without explicitly mentioning race at all, and how very meagre is the value of constitutional 'safeguards' intended to prevent it.

Other and worse examples are to be found in the perversion of the criminal law. In 1903 the death penalty was imposed for attempted rape, though a lesser penalty might be inflicted at the discretion of the judge. The law did not state that the death penalty was intended exclusively for African men who were guilty, or even seriously suspected, of intending to rape European women; but that is what it meant. When, in 1910, the High Commissioner commuted a death sentence in such a case

---

[1] There were also 613 'coloured' voters (i.e. persons of mixed race), and 574 Indians.

to one of penal servitude for life, there were passionate protests from the settler community, and Coghlan was enthusiastically applauded at a public meeting when he threatened that the settlers would resort to lynching if they could not trust the lawful authorities to give adequate protection to their women. Yet white men could rape black women with impunity, and such instances were by no means rare. So it is clear that the settlers were not motivated by a fierce hatred of immorality, or of mis-cegenation, nor were they impelled by a chivalrous desire to protect women. And if they thought they were defending civil-ised standards of conduct against the savages who surrounded them, they tolerated a far lower standard of conduct from mem-bers of their own community than from the savages whom they despised. 'There will never be peace between the black man and the white man', said an old Matabele chief, 'until you give our women the protection you demand for your own.'

The introduction of trial by jury in 1899 greatly increased the danger of injustice in criminal cases involving both races, for the jurors, being drawn from the list of voters, were all white. In 1908 a jury acquitted four white men who had flogged to death two natives suspected of theft; in 1911, after the acquittal of a confessed murderer, the jury system was modified in cases where both Africans and Europeans were involved. In such cases the juries were in future to consist of five specially selected Euro-peans, instead of nine chosen haphazardly. It is important to recognise that this change had the widespread though reluctant approval of the settler community. Though their sense of justice might be distorted by collective self-interest, they could not approve of injustice in its more gross and flagrant forms; and they have become more sensitive in these matters as their community has grown more mature. In 1955 there was a wave of protest when a farmer who had killed an African employee was sentenced only to imprisonment for one year, with a sus-pended sentence of two years more.

The attitude and policy of the Southern Rhodesian settlers towards the African population may be said to fall into three successive phases, between which the transitions were gradual

M   177

and scarcely noticed, amounting merely to a quiet, general recognition of altered circumstances.

In the first phase there was a natural gulf between the races, but it was essentially a culture-bar, not a colour-bar. European and African had so little in common that they did not associate together at all, except as master and servant. After the rebellions of 1896, when fully one-tenth of the settlers were murdered, the survivors could not entirely forget the possibility of another insurrection, which, although it would undoubtedly be suppressed, would take its victims from among them; beneath the amused tolerance with which they treated a cook who poured a savoury sauce over a pudding or used his master's toothbrush to scrub out a saucepan there was a latent bitterness and distrust. But they were dependent on African labour, and could never get enough of it. The idleness of the native was a constant source of exasperation to men who were facing the enormous task of developing a land where nature had until then been almost untouched by human endeavour.

Today, it is true, it is considered ignorant and unenlightened to speak of the 'idleness' of the African male living under tribal conditions. He did some useful work from time to time, such as building huts or cutting trees. Perhaps he hunted, fished, or made a canoe; he might even smelt iron to make spear-heads and hoes. But although these activities were important and indispensable in the tribal economy, they left him plenty of time for doing nothing at all while his wife was engaged in constant toil. His apologists have therefore to admit that he had a great love of 'leisure'. But 'leisure' is not the right word. He was no Aristotelian, spending his days in intense intellectual activity; he was neither a thinker nor a mystic. His delight, apart from consuming all the beer and beef available, was endless, aimless talk—circuitous argument, moving round and round from irrelevancy to irrelevancy, and trivial gossip. 'The way in which the men pass the day, except something extraordinary occurs, is almost incredible: and one wonders that a creature with the form of a man and having an immortal soul can so exist'—so Bishop Knight-Bruce noted in his diary during his journey through Mashonaland, before the settlers came to disturb them.

The problem of drawing these people into the European economy was difficult, but it was not insoluble. What was needed was time—time for them to develop such a desire for the things which money could buy that they would be prepared to do enough regular work to earn the money to buy them; time for the first adventurers into the strange world of European employment to return home and tell their friends and relations how they had fared and whether or not they would advise anyone else to follow in their footsteps. As the years have passed the proportion of African men working for wages has steadily increased. It is reckoned to have risen from 23 per cent in 1921 to 48 per cent in 1946; these figures serve to illustrate a general trend over a much longer period. In addition, the supply of African labour from within Southern Rhodesia has, since before the turn of the century, been augmented by immigrants, mostly temporary, from neighbouring territories: in the inter-war period the non-indigenous African workers numbered between 55 and 60 per cent of the total, and the census figures for 1951 showed that the proportion was still rather more than 50 per cent.[1]

Unfortunately the settlers could not afford to wait until the Africans were ready to come to them for work. They needed labour at once, and without it they would soon be bankrupt. As their numbers increased, so did their labour requirements. In view of the high cost of transport to and from a country which was only moderately blessed with natural resources, the costs of production would have been prohibitive if Europeans had been employed as unskilled workers. A cheap labour force was indispensable, and—since the Government of India wisely refused to sanction the recruitment of Indians—this meant that African labour was indispensable; if its real cheapness was greatly diminished by its inefficiency, its inefficiency would be to some extent offset if it was available in sufficient numbers.

[1] In 1951 the countries of origin of male Africans employed in Southern Rhodesia were as follows: Southern Rhodesia, 241,683; Portuguese East Africa, 101,618; Nyasaland, 86,287; Northern Rhodesia, 48,514; other territories, 10,353: Total, 488,455. The number of African women in employment was only a few thousand.

European Progress and 'Native Policy'

Finding that the Africans whom they needed as workers preferred to spend the day sitting under a tree and talking, the early settlers turned to the Administration and asked it to use compulsion. But after the arrival of the Resident Commissioner the Administration had to be careful not to take any action which, when reported in England, would arouse the anger of the supporters of the anti-slavery movement. For Britain had not devoted herself to a century-long struggle against the slave trade merely to create conditions in which Africans could be compelled to work for private profit. And under the direction of Sir William Milton the Administration itself was anxious to keep its hands clean and avoid any act of oppression; its attitude in connection with the procuring of labour was, indeed, one of the major 'grievances' which the settlers cherished in their conflict with the Chartered Company. Native Commissioners—the administrative officials in charge of districts—were instructed to do their best to persuade Africans to go to work, but not to use compulsion. But, as was afterwards repeatedly pointed out during the controversy aroused in Britain when exactly similar instructions were in force in Kenya from 1919 to 1921, it was quite impossible for the native to distinguish between insistent exhortation and authoritative command when both came from the man in authority; indeed the exhortation derived its effectiveness almost entirely from the very fact that it *was* mistaken—as perhaps it was meant to be—for command. There was in effect a large measure of compulsion in the recruitment of African workers in the early years, though not nearly as much as most of the settlers, chronically short of labour, would have liked.

In 1903 the Legislative Council tried to increase the native tax levied on adult males from 10s. a head to £2, but to exempt those who had been in employment for four months of the previous year; average wages at that time were reckoned to be about 30s. a month, together with food and shelter. The proposed ordinance was primarily a device for compelling Africans to enter employment, not for raising revenue; it was, however, disallowed by the Secretary of State on the advice of the Resident Commissioner. As a compromise the tax was fixed at £1 in

1904, with a further 10s. for each wife after the first; the justification for the taxation of additional wives was that they were a sign of unusual wealth and therefore of more than average taxable capacity. The tax remained at this rate for more than half a century. It therefore became less and less burdensome, and an ever-diminishing element in the territory's budget, as earnings increased and the economy expanded.

In 1902 a Masters and Servants Ordinance was passed to regulate conditions of employment. Although its primary purpose was to oblige workers to remain at their jobs for a definite period—of not more than three years—specified in a written contract which could be enforced by a court of law, it also gave the worker some security against bad employers, who could be fined or imprisoned for withholding wages or failing to supply suitable food. Minimum standards of diet and housing were prescribed for mineworkers, and, probably in consequence, the death-rate from disease per thousand mineworkers fell steadily from 66·9 in 1906 to 16·7 in 1919: a powerful deterrent to accepting work in the mines was thus greatly reduced even if not eliminated. Mine work became much more popular than farm work, because it was more firmly regulated by law and because wages were higher. By about 1920, however, farmers as well as other employers could usually obtain enough labour if they had a reputation for treating their workers well, and it was only the notoriously bad employers who were still seriously short-handed.

Closely related to the question of labour was the question of land. But the problem of labour shortage gradually diminished in importance, and, indeed, became in the 1950s a valuable stimulus to the raising of wages, and consequently to the investment of capital to increase the productivity of a given amount of labour; the land question, on the other hand, became increasingly difficult and increasingly urgent.

The Chartered Company was lavish in its early grants of land, so lavish that by the time the Matabele Rebellion was over it regretted its offhand conduct in transferring enormous areas to so-called 'development companies' consisting of speculators who made no attempt at development, but held their properties in mortmain until the rise in value caused by the increase of settlement should enable them to sell at a handsome profit. The conquest of the Matabele in 1893 diverted the attention of settlers and speculators from Mashonaland, which was in any case more remote; consequently the extent to which the best areas of Mashonaland were alienated was much less than in Matabeleland, where almost the whole of the high veld and much of the middle veld was brought under European ownership. In Mashonaland the settlers picked out and appropriated the mineral-producing areas, and acquired ownership of the greater part of the most desirable uplands, but considerable areas were left unalienated. A notable exception was the country near the eastern border, around Umtali and south of it in the Melsetter district. A party of Boers had trekked into the Melsetter district in 1893, and taken possession of almost the whole of the high ground.

After the Matabele Rebellion it was obviously necessary to make provision for the needs of the tribe by supplementing the two big but unsuitable reserves which had been provided for them in 1895. For the Matabele had to be placated, and not all of them were prepared to live as tenants of European farmers. Native Commissioners were therefore instructed to allocate sufficient land for their requirements, but each Commissioner was left to use his own judgment as to what was sufficient, and there was nothing scientific about the method of allocation. It was understood that the land allocated as native reserves must be land which had not been alienated to Europeans: the vast, empty spaces in European ownership on the high veld were sacrosanct. It is not surprising that the settlement of 1902, which approved the Commissioners' recommendations, was ill-suited to be more than a temporary expedient. In Mashonaland, where reserves were demarcated at the same time and in the same way—they had not been thought necessary before the revolt of 1896–7—the result was more satisfactory, because, except on the eastern border, the areas in European ownership were more limited.

In 1914 a commission was appointed to report on the reserves, ascertaining whether any of them were insufficient for, or in excess of, native requirements. The commissioners were instructed to take account of the future as well as the existing needs of the native population, and to allocate enough land to meet African requirements for all future time. The purpose of these instructions was not to segregate the Africans from the European community by confining them within reserves, but to enable the European population—which had increased substantially following the Company's change of policy in 1907— to know definitely what lands were available for purchase; a final settlement of the reserves would also give a greater sense of security to the Africans living in them. The commission, however, proceeded on the assumption that large numbers of Africans would continue to live outside the reserves, either as tenants on European-owned farms or on the remaining unalienated Crown land. On any other assumption its estimate of native requirements would have been grossly inadequate, and it has, indeed, been accused of strong bias in favour of settler interests. But to make such an accusation is to ignore its own explicit statement about the limited and essentially temporary function of the reserves:

'The sudden immigration of a European community into a country previously inhabited only by African natives living in a state of tribal barbarism, and the rapid growth of that community, must have the immediate effect of dislocating the whole normal process of tribal development. . . . The native cannot at once be assimilated, and it is necessary to set apart areas in which those not ready for the new order can live under the old conditions' (quoted in Mason, *The Birth of a Dilemma*, O.U.P., 1958, p. 261).

The commission's recommendations were given the force of law by Order in Council in 1920. The net effect of the increases and diminutions which it recommended was to leave the reserves more than 1 million acres smaller than the 1902 settlement had done. About 23 per cent of the land in Southern Rhodesia now consisted of reserves, in communal, rent-free ownership; 32 per cent was owned by Europeans, and 45 per cent was Crown land, which could be sold to persons of any race.

Of course the Africans had little purchasing power, and there was no prospect that they would become owners of much of the Crown land for a long time to come. But already a few of them were beginning to show enterprise, and to become semi-permanently settled away from their kindred as wage-earners; the savings of some members of this developing 'black proletariat' might be sufficient to buy a piece of land at the prevailing low prices—land which would be their own property, unlike their share of a tribal reserve, where it was not worth any man's while, if indeed it was socially permissible, for him (or his family) to cultivate better than his neighbours. By 1925 Africans had purchased some 45,000 acres. It was a small enough beginning, compared with the 31,000,000 acres purchased by Europeans; but the Europeans began to wonder where it would end.

So, just as there had previously been a demand for a final delimitation of the native reserves, there was now a demand for a definite line of division to be drawn between areas of Crown land which only Europeans could buy and areas purchasable only by Africans. The assent of the United Kingdom Government was duly obtained, and a commission appointed in 1925 produced a report whose recommendations were, with minor modifications, embodied in the Land Apportionment Act, passed in 1930.

The total area of the territory is 96·2 million acres. Of this, 49·1 million were allocated to Europeans, including the 31 million already alienated to them. The native reserves amounted to 21·1 million acres, and remained unaltered, but 7·5 million acres of Crown land were declared a Native Purchase Area. Apart from comparatively small areas reserved as forest land and for other purposes, the remainder of the country was left unassigned, most of it being infested with tsetse fly or too arid to attract either race. Almost 3 million acres of this unassigned area were afterwards set aside as the Wankie game reserve.

At the time when the Act was passed more than a third of the total African population was living either on European farms or on the areas of Crown land which were now allocated for future purchase by Europeans. The startling innovation made by the Act was to require all these people to move into the reserves, unless they were under contract to provide labour in return for their right of occupation. Previously, in accordance with the Private Locations Ordinance of 1908, farmers had been at liberty to keep up to forty adult male Africans and their families on each 1,500 morgen of land in return for payment of rent, in addition to as many resident labourers as they cared to make contracts with. Rent-paying Africans had, indeed, no security of tenure, and many were evicted by farmers exasperated by their soil-wasting agricultural practices and their tendency to pilfer. The majority of farmers disapproved of the practice of permitting 'Kaffir farming' on European land, especially as it diminished the labour supply; at the same time many found the rent paid by these undesirable tenants a useful source of income. But the prevailing opinion among Europeans was that Africans ought not to be tolerated in the European area except as labourers, and this opinion was now given the force of law. The Africans for their part preferred to pay rent to the farm-owner rather than enter into a labour contract with him: if they paid rent they could earn it by selling their own produce or by choosing their own employer. But, since Africans had no votes, their opinions did not matter.

Thus the Land Apportionment Act established the principle of racial segregation. It is the most important enactment in the history of Southern Rhodesia.

The Act did not, of course, aim at a complete segregation of the races, because the African was still wanted in the European area as a labourer. Indeed one of its purposes was to stimulate the flow of labour by eliminating the rent-paying residents on European estates, for many of these people would accept labour contracts rather than be turned off the land which they and their fathers had occupied. 'I have not the slightest doubt myself,' said the Prime Minister when the Bill was being debated, 'and I can speak from personal experience, that that is going to be, at any rate in Matabeleland, to a certain extent the solution of the labour difficulty: getting the native himself, his wife and

family, to live on the farm as servants permanently of the farmer . . . the native will more and more tend to settle down with
his master and remain on with his master's son when he takes
over, and so on—permanent servants in the employ of the
estate.'[1] It is sad to reflect that the man who thus hopefully
looked forward to an extension of what was virtually a form of
serfdom was a son of J. S. Moffat.

The adoption of racial segregation as a matter of deliberate
policy during the early years of settler self-government marks
the beginning of the second phase of Southern Rhodesia's native
policy. The basic reason for the change was the emergence of
some Africans, at first only a few, as competitors with Europeans,
and as their potential equals. 'Kaffir farming' was merely an
incidental irritant. As the culture-bar which was inevitable in
the early days—and which, in the case of very large numbers of
Africans, is still inevitable even today—began to show signs of
breaking down, the European felt no desire to welcome his black
compatriot as a fellow member of a civilised community, worthy
of equal rights and equal respect. Instead, he felt himself
threatened, and made haste to erect a colour bar.

The underlying fear which motivated the settlers in the 1930s
was expressed candidly by the Prime Minister, Mr. (later Sir
Godfrey) Huggins, in a speech on 30th March 1938, quoted by
the Rhodesia-Nyasaland Royal Commission in its *Report* (Cmd.
5949, p. 170):

'Because of the presence of the white man the Bantu is, with
accelerating speed, lifting himself out of his primitive conditions.
His inter-tribal wars have been prohibited, and his once fre-
quently-recurring epidemics checked. His numbers are increasing. Tribes once separated by traditional animosities are developing the ideal of racial unity—an idea fostered by the development of Bantu newspapers and the publication of books in their
own dialects. The Bantu is resolved to learn, and within as yet
undetermined limits is capable of learning. To forbid him opportunities is contrary to natural justice, but are we to allow him

[1] I am indebted for this quotation to R. McGregor, *Native Segregation in
Southern Rhodesia* (unpublished Ph.D. thesis, London, 1940).

to develop and in the course of time, because his requirements are so small, gradually to oust the European? . . .

'While there is yet time and space, the country should be divided into separate areas for black and white. In the native areas the black man must be allowed to rise to any position to which he is capable of climbing. Every step of the industrial and social pyramid must be open to him, excepting only—and always—the very top. . . . The senior administrative officer must be white. The native may be his own lawyer, doctor, builder, journalist or priest, and he must be protected from white competition in his own area. In the European areas the black man will be welcomed, when, tempted by wages, he offers his services as a labourer; but it will be on the understanding that there he shall merely assist, and not compete with, the white man. If he wishes to stop in his own area, let him. The two races will develop side by side under white supervision, and help, not hinder, each other's progress. The interest of each race would be paramount in its own sphere.

'The policy I suggest enables the two races to live side by side to the benefit of both.'

It is in the light of this policy that the distribution of land effected by the Land Apportionment Act must be scrutinised.

More than half the total area was allocated to Europeans, although there were twenty Africans for every one of them. Still, they hoped to increase their numbers by immigration, and the land allocated to Africans was, by South African standards, generous in amount; moreover, it has subsequently been augmented by much of the area which was at first unassigned. It was not adequate to support a steadily growing African population, especially if African methods of agriculture remained static —but then there is no place on earth where population can grow indefinitely without increasing productivity, and the growing shortage of land in the native areas—including the native purchase areas, which have had to be used in part as supplementary reserves—has compelled the Government to devote considerable money and effort to conserving the soil and increasing the yield per acre.

But there are other and more important considerations. The European areas contained all the known minerals and a disproportionate amount of the best land—that is why the early settlers and speculators had chosen them—and the railways had been built to serve the European areas. The Royal Commission found that 'of 1,350 miles of railway approximately only 60 miles traverse native land, and the position as regards main road communication is little better' (*Report*, p. 171). Yet the European areas have been very inadequately used: as recently as 1957 a Select Committee reported that only 1·1 million acres were under crops—a figure which the Committee's report itself described as 'deplorably low'.

Again, the doctrine of 'parallel development' in European and African areas implied that there would be social change in the African areas, presumably on distinctively African lines. But there was no possibility of adapting primitive tribal society to twentieth-century conditions: either the African must preserve his tribal institutions and his economic inefficiency, or he must jettison both, as the Anglo-Saxon conquerors of Britain had themselves done by a more gradual process in a more unhurried age. If the African was to develop into a modern civilised man, what was the point of segregating him for all time in a separate area? But if he was to be preserved on his own lands as an interesting anthropological specimen, comparable to the wild life in the Wankie game reserve, what was the point of talking about 'parallel development' and the 'two pyramids'?

The Land Apportionment Act was frequently referred to by white Southern Rhodesians as their country's Magna Carta; it was still considered sacrosanct as late as the 1950s. Presumably they were confusing England's Great Charter of liberties with the granting of her soil by William the Conqueror to enfeoff his following of Norman adventurers.

The colour bar was introduced into industry by the Industrial Conciliation Act of 1934. The Act was concerned with the conciliation of European trade unionists, who were anxious to safeguard their standard of living by monopolising the skilled and semi-skilled jobs at artificially high rates of pay. In 1930 Professor (afterwards Sir) Henry Clay had prepared a most penetrating and authoritative *Report on Industrial Relations in Southern Rhodesia*; he had shown that average money wages in the building, engineering and printing industries and on the railways were two and a quarter times those paid in London, and although the cost of living was also higher, the real wage was at least one and a half times that of the Londoner. 'There can be no doubt', he declared, 'that the high level of wage rates was originally established by the necessity of attracting skilled workers to a new country'; it was now being maintained by strongly organised trade unions. But, he went on, the lowering of the cost of living could only be achieved by lowering the costs of production, and if this was to be done the Southern Rhodesian home market must be expanded. This could be done by European immigration, but there was an alternative or supplementary possibility, that of raising the consuming power of the Africans. 'If the natives all lived on a European standard the population of the country would no longer be 45,000 Europeans and 850,000 natives, . . . but 900,000 persons with a combined spending power perhaps ten times that of the present population. . . . If the Europeanisation of the native population must be slow, so far as it goes it is equivalent economically to the immigration of more Europeans.

'Such a development of native capacity is sometimes regarded with fear, and . . . in the Union has inspired colour bar legislation. . . . Such fears do less than justice to the economic quality and adaptability of the white worker, and imply that his present wage is based not on his skill and capacity as a worker, but on an artificial scarcity of skilled labour, maintained by excluding natives and the under-payment of the mass of natives employed [as unskilled workers]. They are, moreover, unfounded. The relation of advanced and backward labour is much more complementary than competitive. The increased employment of natives increases the number—and possible remuneration—of supervisory, responsible and specially skilled posts which white men must always fill. Even if in some occupations the native does displace the white man, now that he is able to earn more he can demand more, and so offers a market for an increased output of goods in general, in which additional white labour will find employment. Already the railway receipts from native passenger traffic exceed those from first-class passenger traffic. . . . There is no rigid limit to the work awaiting additional resources in labour and capital. There is no more social danger in cheap labour than in cheap capital, cheap power or cheap land. . . . There is every reason for confidence in the future. . . . The greatest flexibility, elasticity and freedom in the fitting of workers into jobs and the arrangement of the terms of employment is called for if the economic growth of the country is not to be retarded. . . . It is only depressed and underpaid labour that calls for Government intervention; in its absence the Government of a country which is engaged in building up its primary industries and absorbing new population may spare itself the trouble, and industry the rigidity and inconvenience, of the detailed regulation and determination of wage questions.'

As a guide to enlightened public policy, aiming at the greatest possible extension and diffusion of prosperity and at the avoidance of injustice, this was magnificent; but as a guide to the narrow class interest of European trade unionists it was distinctly dubious. For it assumed that a white worker with enough intelligence and skill, say, to drive a locomotive, would, when displaced from that job by an African capable of doing it equally well for a much lower wage, be competent to move into a more highly skilled job, demanding intelligence above the average. Such new vacancies would indeed be created, as Professor Clay made clear; but if fresh immigrants had to be recruited to fill them they would be no safeguard for the standard of living of the whites already in the country. And even if their own future could be secured by agreement with their employers, what would be the future of their children in a country where only those with outstanding ability and qualifications could hope to find jobs well enough paid to support what was commonly called 'a European standard of living'?

Moreover, by the time the Clay Report was in print the great depression was beginning to afflict Southern Rhodesia. In

Britain the depression made workers so afraid of 'working themselves out of a job' that they took refuge in restrictive practices,
and this defensive, restrictionist outlook became so deep-seated
during the 1930s that it has long outlived the circumstances
which gave rise to it, and to a considerable extent remains as a
drag on the British economy even to the present day. The
Southern Rhodesian counterpart of trade union restrictive practices in Britain has been the industrial colour bar.

The Industrial Conciliation Act of 1934, and likewise the
revised version of it enacted with the same name in 1945, authorised employers and employees to set up Industrial Councils
which, when approved and registered by the Government,
would have power not only to negotiate agreements between the
parties concerned but to ask the Minister of Labour to make
them legally binding, enforceable by the courts, upon the entire
industry; in effect the Councils and the Minister, acting together, were given powers of delegated legislation, which were
used to make apprenticeship and other regular training, to
which Africans were denied access, a condition of employment.
The term 'employee', it was explicitly stated, 'shall not include
a native'. Thus white trade unions were placed in a highly
favourable position to bargain for their own interests, while
African trade unions were denied any legal recognition whatever—though with the passing of time some were in fact
formed.

The white trade unions took their stand on the principle of
'equal pay for equal work', by which they meant equal pay for
holding the same category of job, regardless of competence to
do it. Provided that employers would pay Africans the full,
artificially high European wage rate, they would not object—
because they well knew that employers would not pay it, since,
at least initially, the African could not perform skilled work as
well as a European, and in any case there was a feeling of racial
solidarity between European employers and employees which
to some extent counterbalanced the obvious economic advantage to the former of reducing costs of production by employing
Africans at lower rates of pay. Even farmers, while grumbling

bitterly about high freight charges on the railways, seldom suggested the obvious way to reduce them, that of replacing overpaid white railwaymen by reasonably paid Africans.

The statistics published by the Federal Government showed that in 1954, the first year of federation, the wages and salaries of Africans in Southern Rhodesia averaged £60, while those of Europeans averaged £909. Whatever allowance may have to be made for the relative inefficiency of African labour, the gap which separates these figures is striking when compared with the 'differentials' in Britain, or in any other socially homogeneous country, between the wages of skilled and unskilled workers.

Although the white employee was exclusive in his attitude to his African subordinate and potential equal, he was not at all exclusive in relation to European immigrants. Like the rest of the settler community, he welcomed them, because they would help him to man the fortress of white privilege. But the more numerous the white community became, the larger was the number of people whose standard of living was excessively high when the nature of the work they were doing was considered in relation to the still under-developed condition of the Southern Rhodesian economy as a whole. 'I want Europeans to come in because Europeans will bring skill, capital and initiative,' said Sir Roy Welensky in 1955. If he had said that he wanted them *on condition* that they brought capital or supplied professional qualifications and specialised skills not yet available locally, no one could reasonably have objected. As it was, the economic progress of the African depended upon the rate of growth of the economy being faster than the rate of white immigration.

During the post-war years this situation in fact existed: the boom was so great that even the African workers were swept up by it, and the colour bar was weakened and in places breached because there was so much work crying out to be done that could not be done at all unless Africans were allowed to do it. Even by 1950 there were a few opportunities for exceptional Africans to earn £30 or even £37 10s. a month. Like the trade union restrictive practices which were its British counterpart, the industrial colour bar long outlasted the depressed conditions in which it was created, but its importance was diminishing. And in other respects too there was a slow, very incomplete, yet unmistakable thaw in the frozen rigidities of the segregationist policy based on the Land Apportionment Act. The economic factor made its contribution, but was not all-important—for in the neighbouring Union of South Africa similar conditions of prosperity did not prevent the hardening of segregation into doctrinaire *apartheid*. But the white Rhodesian is not a fanatic. He is not attracted by the authoritarian outlook of the Dutch Reformed Church, with its exaltation of *apartheid* to the status of an integral part of Christian doctrine.[1] There is indeed an intolerant Afrikaner minority in Southern Rhodesia, but it is comparatively small in numbers and even smaller in political influence. The victory of the South African Nationalists in the General Election of 1948 produced a revulsion of feeling in Southern Rhodesia; Dr. Malan, by bearing the standard of *apartheid* to triumph in the Union, made it easier for Sir Godfrey Huggins on his side of the Limpopo to raise the standard of 'partnership', and to carry the great majority of his electorate with him. He was the more ready to do so since it facilitated, and indeed made possible, the bringing of Northern Rhodesia and Nyasaland into the Southern Rhodesian orbit.

Thus in the post-war years the trend of Government policy—and, even more slowly and tentatively, of social attitudes—was away from the 'two-pyramid', segregationist policy of the 1930s, with its economic rigidities, social injustices, and political delusions. This period may therefore be regarded as a third distinct phase, in which 'native policy' matured into 'race relations' and even showed promise of developing into plain 'human relations'.

In Northern Rhodesia the control of native policy remained, in legal form if not altogether in fact, with the Governor, respon-

[1] See Leo Marquard, *The Peoples and Policies of South Africa* (O.U.P., 1952), pp. 210–15. But in his third edition (1962, pp. 246–8), Mr. Marquard shows that a serious challenge to this tenet has developed within the Church itself.

sible to the Colonial Office in London. In 1924, when Company rule ended, the elected representatives of the settlers were given only a minority position on the newly created Legislative Council. But in 1929 their numbers were increased from five to seven, while the number of officials in the Council remained unchanged at nine. It seemed to be only a matter of time until the expansion of the economy—made possible by the new-found wealth in copper—together with the consequent growth in the European population, would lead to the withdrawal of official control and the establishment of a settler oligarchy on the Southern Rhodesian model. As for the African population, the Legislative Council concerned itself scarcely at all with their affairs. Their proper management, it was held, could be and ought to be entrusted to individual European employers; this was indeed explicitly stated in 1927 by the most prominent of the elected members, Sir Leopold Moore, founder and editor of the *Livingstone Mail*: 'They are governed', he declared, 'by the people of this country; not governed in the sense that they are legislated for by the people, but they are governed by the people who employ them.' This is the sort of statement which has to be read several times to be properly relished. (It is quoted in J. W. Davidson, *The Northern Rhodesian Legislative Council*, Faber and Faber, 1948, p. 68.)

It was therefore with astonishment and passionate indignation that the settlers received the *Memorandum on Native Policy in East Africa*, published as a White Paper in 1930 by the Secretary of State for the Colonies, Lord Passfield (Sidney Webb), and commonly referred to as the Passfield Memorandum. The basic doctrine which was then laid down was, indeed, so far from being new that it was quoted verbatim from Lord Devonshire's White Paper, *Indians in Kenya*, published in 1923: 'His Majesty's Government think it necessary definitely to record their considered opinion that the interests of the African natives must be paramount, and that if, and when, those interests and the interests of the immigrant races should conflict, the former should prevail.' The passage quoted from the Kenya White Paper immediately went on to give the assurance that 'obviously, the interests of the other communities, European, Indian or Arab, must severally be safeguarded', and that there would be no drastic change of policy at their expense; nevertheless 'in the administration of Kenya His Majesty's Government regard themselves as exercising a trust on behalf of the African population, and they are unable to delegate or share this trust, the object of which may be defined as the protection and advancement of the native races'. Kenya was a long way from Northern Rhodesia, and the Northern Rhodesian settlers had scarcely noticed the declaration of 1923. But when it was reiterated and elaborated in 1930, its application was extended to the whole of East Africa, which at that time was regarded as including both the so-called 'central' African territories north of the Zambesi.

The heightened sense of Imperial responsibility for the welfare of Africans, as shown in the Passfield Memorandum, clearly implied that the Northern Rhodesian settlers would have to be denied the self-government which Southern Rhodesia had obtained, since 'self-government' involved government of the African population subject to safeguards which were scarcely more than formal. The statement that the British Government was 'unable to delegate or share' its trust meant that Northern Rhodesia must remain under British tutelage until the Africans were sufficiently developed to be capable of upholding their own interests.

The elected members of the Northern Rhodesian Legislative Council promptly drew up a protest and forwarded it by way of the local Government to the Secretary of State. 'British colonists', they declared, 'hold that the British Empire is primarily concerned with the furtherance of the interests of British subjects of British race, and only thereafter with other British subjects [e.g. the handful of Indian traders in the country], protected races [e.g. the African population], and the nationals of other countries, in that order.' Having thus asserted with startling candour the paramountcy of their own self-interest, in opposition to the official doctrine, they saw no inconsistency in continuing thus:

'The natural trustees of barbarous and less developed races are their more civilised neighbours. . . . The assumption of

European Progress and 'Native Policy'

Trusteeship by the Imperial Government is uncalled for and inadvisable, since that Government cannot know, as do the white settlers in the country, living among the natives, the needs, the opportunities, and the capabilities of races who are as unknown by as unknown to the Imperial Government. Interference, directed by uninformed or misinformed authorities, resident many thousands of miles away, in the relations and affairs of the white settlers and the African races can lead only to resentment and antagonism' (printed in *Correspondence with regard to Native Policy in Northern Rhodesia*, Cmd. 3731).

Although Lord Passfield himself treated the protest with contempt, it achieved its more immediate purpose. A Joint Select Committee of Parliament was set up soon afterwards to soothe ruffled feelings in East and Central Africa, and in furtherance of this task it explained away the offending doctrine of 'paramountcy'. According to its interpretation, published in October 1931, 'the doctrine of paramountcy means no more than that the interests of the overwhelming majority of the indigenous population should not be subordinated to those of a minority belonging to another race, however important in itself'. But if it meant no more it certainly meant no less; the change in emphasis from what it did mean to what it did not amounted in effect to beating a retreat.

The way was thus made clear for the rise of a new doctrine, or rather slogan, called 'partnership'. Whereas 'paramountcy' assumed that there was a conflict of interests between the races and that the Protectorate Government must therefore uphold the weaker though more numerous race against the powerful minority, 'partnership' presupposed that the interests of African and European were essentially in harmony; and it was indeed eminently reasonable that different races or social classes who had their homes in the same territory should try to co-operate for constructive purposes, instead of wasting their energies in a struggle for supremacy. African advancement required European enterprise as surely as European enterprise required African labour. But it did not follow that the terms of the partnership would be just if they were dictated by one community and imposed upon the other. The duty of the Government was to hold a just balance, and from 1931 onwards it was compromised.

But it was not abandoned. Until 1938 the officials who were members of the Northern Rhodesian Legislative Council were numerous enough to outvote the elected members; and since, in accordance with the normal practice in British dependencies, the officials were required to vote for the policy decided upon by the Governor with the advice of his Executive Council—which consisted wholly of senior officials—the Governor, and through him the Colonial Office, was firmly in control. Nevertheless the minority of elected members exercised great influence, since they were the chosen spokesmen of the most socially prominent and politically active of the governed. In 1938 their numbers were made equal with those of the officials, so that the Government had either to co-operate with them or fall back on the Governor's casting vote, a distasteful expedient to be used only in the last resort. And the stresses of war, followed by the post-war need for dollar-saving copper, so enhanced the value of their co-operation that they were able to strengthen their place in the constitution to the point of being almost, though not quite, the ruling element in the Protectorate.

The changes made in 1944–5, followed by others in 1948–9, gave them a majority of one over the officials in the Legislative Council. This in itself, however, was not of decisive importance, for by this time the council also included four spokesmen of African interests (two of them being Africans, the others nominated Europeans), whose votes, added to those of the officials, would suffice to enable the Governor to block any measure which he regarded as an inadmissible encroachment upon African rights. In addition, the Governor was given 'reserved powers' by which he could, in an emergency, override a hostile majority in the council.

More important in strengthening the political position of the settlers was the change in the Executive Council, where the seven officials were joined by four unofficials from the Legislative Council. One of these unofficials was a nominated spokesman of African interests, but the other three were elected members, chosen by the elected members of the Legislative Council; and in September 1949 a precedent was established that elected members of the Executive Council were responsible to their elected colleagues in the legislature, so that if they lost the confidence of a majority of those colleagues yet refused to resign, they would be dismissed by the Governor. Though these arrangements certainly did not amount to cabinet government, they unmistakably went a long way towards it—and this approximation to cabinet government had as its basis the European electorate, not the vast majority of the people of the territory. In 1953, at the beginning of the Federation, the number of officials in the Executive Council was reduced to five, and it was provided that in future each of the unofficials who were members of it should be in charge of a Government department.

But the process was still incomplete; the home authorities had never consciously abandoned their 'trust', and it is arguable that they had even succeeded in fulfilling it. At every stage the changes, accepted by the Colonial Office as the price of harmony with the ascendant local interests, had been carefully devised in a way that to some extent left the future open. It now seems clear, indeed, that the changes made in the Northern Rhodesian constitution in 1953 represented the high-water mark of settler power, and even, perhaps, the turning of the tide. For while the number of European elected members of the Legislative Council was increased by two (from ten to twelve), so was the number of African members—a more than proportionate gain.

In Northern Rhodesia the privileged position of white trade unionists was never protected against African competition by discriminatory legislation, as it was in Southern Rhodesia by the Industrial Conciliation Acts of 1934 and 1945. The white workers had to rely on their own efforts. But most of them were miners, organised in a single powerful trade union, which was well placed to protect its members in their monopoly of skilled work. According to a special correspondent of *The Times*, writing in 1953 (19th January), 'apprentices after four years are earning £1,000 a year, ordinary artisans £1,400, and occasional rock crushers £3,000. Their housing is of good quality and they are provided with magnificent clubs and recreational facilities. On a gala night at these clubs nearly everyone is in evening clothes, smoking Havana cigars.' But African miners' wages, though they had increased by several hundred per cent since before the war, averaged about £5 a month, and the highest monthly level attainable was £20 5s. The disparity between the remuneration of skilled and that of unskilled workers was quite as glaring in Northern as in Southern Rhodesia, and was due to the same cause, the colour bar.

So direct and obvious an affront to the principle of 'trusteeship' was looked upon with disfavour by the Colonial Office. Nevertheless the authorities made no assault on the citadel of European privilege, and contented themselves with a couple of cautious reconnaissances. The first was made in 1948, when a commission of enquiry published what is commonly referred to as the Dalgleish Report, after the name of the commission's chairman. But the European miners' union, having begun by refusing to co-operate with the commission in any way, went on to block all attempts to implement its recommendations for the gradual advancement of African miners to more skilled and responsible positions: their slogan was 'equal pay for equal work'. And in face of this intransigence the home authorities reconciled themselves to a confession of helplessness. Nothing could be done—the House of Commons was told on 29th October 1952—without 'the agreement of all parties concerned': that is, the consent of the Northern Rhodesia Mine Workers' Union.

But in 1953-4 the two great copper-mining companies, Rhodesian Selection Trust and Rhodesian Anglo-American, undertook direct negotiations with the union to try to persuade it to agree to the construction of a ladder of jobs of intermediate status, carrying intermediate remuneration. They offered to guarantee their existing European employees security in their jobs, and to limit for several years the number of Africans to be promoted; but it was in vain. The negotiations broke down in July 1954. Thereupon the Northern Rhodesian Government appointed another committee, this time presided over by Sir John Forster, Q.C.; the committee presented its report in the following October. This report, like the Dalgleish Report before it, was rejected by the union.

But now the Selection Trust lost patience[1] and terminated its agreement with the union. This prompted the union to change its mind; further negotiations conducted during 1955 led to an agreement by which twenty-four categories of jobs were opened to Africans, so that a definite though limited breach was made in the industrial colour bar. By 1957 an African could earn up to £53 3s. a month, more than two and a half times as much as in 1953.

This not inconsiderable victory was won by the mining companies, not the British and Northern Rhodesian Governments, which preserved a rather timorous though benevolent neutrality. The Colonial Office had, however, helped and encouraged the Africans to do battle on their own account. The formation of the African Mineworkers' Union, and of other though much less important African unions in other industries, was greatly assisted by the advice given by a British trade unionist sent to Northern Rhodesia shortly after the Second World War to stimulate and guide these developments. The African Mineworkers' Union has secured large increases in wages for its members; it has, however, been primarily interested in obtaining higher wages for the mass of unskilled workers, rather than in pressing for the advancement of the skilled minority, and in consequence a Mines' African Staff Association has been formed to promote the interests of the minority of African salary earners.

Just as Northern Rhodesia has had no Industrial Conciliation Act, so it has had no Land Apportionment Act. It has, however, had its land problems.

Since the Order in Council of 1900 stated that sufficient land must be assigned for occupation by the natives, each of the two companies with enormous estates in North-Eastern Rhodesia, the North Charterland (in the Fort Jameson area) and the

---

[1] Rhoanglo was less determined, partly, in all probability, because its parent organisation is in South Africa.

South Africa Company itself (in the Abercorn area), thought it well to set aside part of its domain as a native reserve, so that the remainder should be definitely available for leasing to settlers. The construction of the railway from Victoria Falls to the Congo border opened up what proved to be one of Northern Rhodesia's most fertile regions, and caused the belt of land which extends for about twenty miles on either side of the railway to become by far the most important area of European agriculture in the territory; here, too, white settlement had its accompaniment in the creation of native reserves.

The boundaries of the reserves were demarcated by three Orders in Council—one for each of the three areas concerned—in 1928–9. The reserves included, in all, rather more than $34\frac{1}{2}$ million acres, compared with 8·8 million acres alienated to Europeans. The areas affected by these arrangements, alienated land and reserves combined, amounted to a total of between a fifth and a quarter of the surface of the Protectorate. Barotseland, which had in effect been made a reserve by Lewanika's treaty with the Chartered Company, covered a further 37 million acres, more than all the other reserves combined.

After some $11\frac{1}{4}$ million acres had been classified as 'forest, archaeological and game reserves', there still remained $94\frac{1}{4}$ million acres, half the land in the Protectorate, neither alienated nor reserved. It might seem that the areas affected by white ownership were almost negligible in relation to the total size of the territory, and that a population whose average density was only six to the square mile would have nothing to lose by sharing these empty spaces with almost any number of immigrants. In fact, however, the widespread lack of water supplies, added to the poverty of most of the soil, resulted in a dense concentration of subsistence cultivators in those parts of the reserves where a living could be obtained. In one part of the North Charterland reserves, twenty-one miles in extent, the population reached a density of 240 to the square mile. Over-population necessitated over-cultivation, and was accompanied by over-grazing; the result—as in Southern Rhodesia—was a deplorable amount of soil erosion. In the railway belt the story of the reserves was much the same, and in the Abercorn area it received an added bitterness from the fact that millions of acres which Africans were required to vacate were not taken up by Europeans, and in the absence of human occupants were invaded by tsetse fly.

Between 1938 and 1947, however, Northern Rhodesia achieved land reforms of the utmost importance. In 1938 the South Africa Company handed over to the Government, for a nominal payment, 947,000 acres from its 'Tanganyika Estate'; subsequent purchases by the Government reduced that estate to the area, less than 100,000 acres in extent, actually alienated to settlers. Then, in 1941, the Government purchased 3,800,000 acres from the North Charterland Company. The lands thus recovered were restored to the local tribes. Finally, in 1947, the Northern Rhodesian Native Trust Land Order in Council was belatedly issued, after being under consideration for ten years: its effect was that only about $5\frac{1}{2}$ per cent of the land surface of the Protectorate still consisted of land either alienated or available for alienation, while all the rest was either native reserves or Native Trust land vested in the Secretary of State, under whose directions it was to be 'administered and controlled by the Governor for the use or common benefit, direct or indirect, of the natives of the Protectorate'. Some of this land might possibly be leased to Europeans, but only on condition that the lease would be, on balance, advantageous to the natives.

It seems reasonable to conclude that the vindication of the Africans' right to their land in Northern Rhodesia was due far less to any firmness of purpose shown by the Imperial authorities in discharging their 'trust' than to the absence of such extensive economic opportunities for white farmers as would have made large-scale immigration, followed by the expropriation and segregation of the African, worth while. Nevertheless, in Northern Rhodesia and also in Nyasaland, the fear that their land would be threatened by the cupidity of white settlers was the strongest, even if the least substantial, of the Africans' reasons for fearing and hating the establishment of a federal constitution by which their future was linked with that of Southern Rhodesia.

CHAPTER 8

The Nyasaland Protectorate

The history of Nyasaland in the first half of the twentieth century was comparatively uneventful, whether the comparison is made with what has occurred before and since in the same territory, or with the history of the Rhodesias or of the world as a whole during the same fifty years. Changes were indeed taking place, and cumulatively they were of great importance, but they were gradual and indeed for the most part depressingly slow.

The repercussions of the two World Wars were, it is true, felt even in the heart of tropical Africa: particularly those of the first, when Nyasaland had a common frontier both by land and lake with enemy-held territory. The largest vessel on Lake Nyasa was the German *Hermann von Wissmann*, and its presence was regarded as a dangerous threat to the whole British position in the Protectorate. But before it was ready for action it was attacked and disabled by H.M.S. *Gwendolen*, one of the small gunboats which, although originally under the direct control of the Admiralty, had since 1895 been part of the Protectorate's own armed forces. Thus from the beginning of the war Britain had command of the lake, and when the *Hermann von Wissmann* was refloated in March 1918, it was renamed the *King George*.

On the night of 8th September 1914 a German force attempting to penetrate southwards attacked Karonga, but on the following morning the place was relieved, and the enemy was defeated and driven back across the River Songwe, which formed the frontier. From then on the Germans were on the defensive, since they had to face an invasion from Kenya. In the latter part of 1915 reinforcements came up from the Union of South Africa, and in the following February General Northey arrived at Karonga to take command of the forces on the Nyasaland and Northern Rhodesian front. On 25th May 1916 a British advance began along the whole front from Lake Nyasa to Lake Tanganyika.

The success of this advance, which contributed greatly to the conquest of German East Africa, was due in very large measure to the service rendered by African carriers in bringing up supplies to the troops. The farther the advance continued the more difficult this task became. The carriers themselves had to be kept supplied with food; each man ate the equivalent in weight of his own entire load in three weeks, and he could not be expected to march fully laden for more than fifteen miles a day.

The native population had to be mobilised to meet the emergency. Men were recruited for a period of twelve months in 1916–17, and again in 1917–18. Some 58,000 were recruited as carriers in the first of these years, and 67,000 in the second; in addition, 14,500 were employed on road-making and related tasks in 1916–17, and in 1917–18 some 57,000 were recruited for particular jobs, chiefly transporting foodstuffs locally, in addition to those recruited for the whole year. At that time the total fit adult male population of Nyasaland was only about 200,000, and of these 19,000 were already serving in the King's African Rifles, at least 20,000 were absent from the country as migrant labourers in Southern Rhodesia and on the Rand, a further 20,000 were constantly required as carriers to meet the normal transport needs of the territory, and yet another 30,000 were required for about four months a year as labourers on European estates, of which the produce was more than ever necessary in time of war. 'It is apparent', wrote Sir George Smith,[1] who was Governor of Nyasaland during these years, 'that the Protectorate was practically exhausted in meeting the military demands.' And he added:

'All this was done in a cause in which they took little interest

[1] In *The Empire at War*, ed. Sir Charles Lucas (O.U.P., 1924), vol. iv, pp. 272–3.

and which they understood less, but the Government they respected required the service from them and it was readily and loyally given at much personal risk to themselves and not a little inconvenience to their families. A great debt of gratitude is also due to the native chiefs for the assistance most readily rendered by them at all times in meeting the recurrent demands for more and more of their men. It speaks well for the Nyasaland population generally that this great disturbance of their ordinary lives and pursuits, extending over so long a period, led to no serious resistance at any time.'

Similar efforts and sacrifices were required, and were made, in the neighbouring north-eastern part of Northern Rhodesia. It was actually on Northern Rhodesian soil that the campaign came to an end, for the gallant and resourceful German commander, General von Lettow-Vorbeck, did not allow himself and his small army to be rounded up and imprisoned by the British. He slipped out of the net, thrust his way through Portuguese East Africa, and invaded Northern Rhodesia. He was advancing upon Kasama in the Bemba country, and Broken Hill and the railway lay undefended before him, when the news of the armistice caused him to terminate his operations.

In the Second World War Nyasaland's part was neither so dramatic nor so exhausting, for the enemy no longer held any territory in Africa south of the Equator, and transport was now by motor-lorry instead of on the heads of porters. Nevertheless, at a time when considerable efforts had to be made to increase agricultural production, nearly 30,000 men served in the armed forces.

The psychological effects of the wars upon the African population cannot, of course, be measured, but they must have been profound and lasting, not only in Nyasaland but throughout the continent. The war of 1914 showed that although the white man had long since outgrown the tribal stage of social development, and was capable of preserving peace and the rule of law over vast tracts of country for long periods of time, he had not as yet progressed beyond the stage of nationalism, and the framework of public order which he upheld was not proof against the outbreak of a conflict which in its scale and destructiveness far exceeded anything that the Bantu tribesman had ever known or dreamed of. Great as were the white man's achievements and power, there were evidently limits to both.

In the Second World War the soldiers from Nyasaland saw much service overseas, and their experiences broadened their horizons and quickened their minds, already stimulated by visits as migrant labourers to the more developed parts of southern Africa. In the first annual report on the territory published after the war, the Government itself recognized that 'the individual African soldier, impressed by what he had seen during his service, was writing to his family from Madagascar or India descanting upon the value of education and enclosing sketches of the neat brick cottage he proposed to build on his return home, and this changed attitude had to be taken into account by the Development Committee in formulating its plans'. It might with advantage have been taken into account again, a few years later, by the makers of the federal constitution.

But apart from their lasting psychological impact the wars had no great effect upon the general course of the Protectorate's history. The main factors influencing that course have been geographical. The country was too remote to attract much capital unless it had minerals which were considered to offer great promise, and it had none. True, no less than forty-six different minerals have been found, and in the 1950s the Government considered it worth while to undertake the systematic geological mapping of the Southern Province, the country south of the lake. There has also been a good deal of private prospecting. But these investigations have not yet opened up any prospect for the development of a mining industry on a significant scale. A small amount of mineral working has, indeed, been undertaken in the past—for instance, a few thousand pounds' worth of mica were mined and exported during and shortly after the First World War—but it has never been important, and it has died out. Not all of the known mineral deposits have yet been prospected sufficiently to establish their value, but those which have been closely examined have been found to be uneconomic, when the costs of production and transport were considered in relation to world prices.

To pay her way in the world, in so far as she managed to do it at all, Nyasaland was therefore dependent on her agriculture. She had not only to grow enough food for her own comparatively large and rapidly increasing population but also to produce crops for export. Coffee was the first to be tried, with great initial success and apparently even greater promise; early in the twentieth century, however, disease attacked the bushes, and coffee production almost ceased. Then cotton was tried; it is still an export of some importance. Soon afterwards it was far surpassed in value by tobacco; a few years later tea began to run a close second to tobacco, and has more than maintained its position for over twenty years. Exports of tobacco were worth £2,733,000 in 1951, and those of tea were worth £2,029,000, out of a total (including re-exports) of £5,899,000. For 1960 the comparable total was £9,472,000.

In the 1950s the production of groundnuts increased from small beginnings until it became of major importance, and in 1962 it was two and a half times that of 1959. Another recently developed crop is tung, less important than groundnuts but far from negligible.

At first the production of export crops was undertaken only on land alienated to white settlers, but during the inter-war period it passed to a large extent into the hands of Africans. To the African cultivator a bad season or low prices merely meant absence of gain, without which he would still be self-sufficing, whereas for a European estate-owner such a set-back might threaten bankruptcy. By 1930 cotton had become almost entirely a native crop, and tobacco, which was then worth three times as much as all other exports put together, was mainly in native hands. Groundnuts, too, are an African crop. But the European planter was not eliminated. He continued to produce moderate quantities of good quality flue-cured tobacco, while the African produced only the cheaper fire-cured variety. More important, the European estate-owner found his economic salvation in the development of tea plantations. Tea is a crop which is not easily cultivated by peasant farmers, and its production has come to be by far the most important contribution made by the settlers to the economy of the Protectorate.

The role of the white settlers in Nyasaland's agriculture has thus been limited, though unquestionably of great importance. Between 1931 and 1945 the planters and farmers declined in number from 290 to 171, and when Sir Sidney Abrahams made his enquiry into the Protectorate's land problems in 1946 he remarked that he 'was struck by the modesty and sincerity of European representations in respect to land acquisition'; they asked only that the door should be kept open for another forty or fifty settlers on the land.

This moderation was the fruit of experience. When the country was taken under British protection in 1889 its prospects had been looked upon with far more optimism, and by the time Johnston arrived in 1891 to establish his Administration very extensive tracts of land had already been ostensibly acquired by purchase from chiefs. Johnston at once issued a circular declaring that no further purchases or leases of land from Africans would be recognised unless made with his sanction, and demanding that full particulars of those already made be sent to him for investigation. In his subsequent enquiries he undoubtedly did his utmost to be strictly just, and aroused the bitter resentment of a number of impecunious adventurers who had been trying to set themselves up as landed magnates, and who now had their claims rejected or drastically reduced in extent. His main objects, as he himself stated them, were, 'firstly, to protect the rights of the natives, to see that their villages and plantations [i.e. cultivated patches] are not disturbed, and that sufficient space is left for their expansion; secondly, to discourage land speculation; and thirdly, to secure the rights of the Crown [i.e. in effect the Protectorate's own Administration] in such a way that the Crown shall profit by the development of this country'. But he had no wish to hamper or discourage genuine enterprise, and he believed that there was plenty of land to meet fully the needs of the Africans and those of white immigrants as well. At that time much of the Shiré Highlands had been completely depopulated by the slave trade.

Provided, then, that certain conditions were fulfilled, Johnston issued 'certificates of claim' which, when duly approved by the home Government, became freehold titles. The conditions were that the chief who sold the land was the real ruler of the country in which it was situated, that he understood what he was doing when he made the bargain, and that he received fair payment. The purchase price on which Johnson usually insisted was 3d. an acre, equivalent in value, perhaps, to a shilling in the currency of seventy years later, and not at all a trifling sum in relation to the prevailing conditions.

The objection has, indeed, been raised that the chief had no power under native legal custom to alienate land in perpetuity; he could merely allocate it for temporary use. But if the chief could not sell it, who could? Even the tribe as a whole had no definite ownership, but moved about from place to place at intervals of a few years as the land became exhausted and the villages became insanitary beyond endurance. The only alternatives to paying the chiefs for vacant land were either to let the land remain vacant or to occupy it without paying anything to anyone.

The certificates of claim issued by Johnston determined the main features of the land problem almost to the present day. According to the Land Commission of 1920 they applied to 3·7 million acres, more than one-seventh of the land surface of the Protectorate. Of this total, however, some 2·7 million acres were accounted for by the 'North Nyasa Estate' which covered the entire area extending northwards from the River Rukuru as far as the territorial boundary; this was acquired by the African Lakes Company and was transferred to the South Africa Company as part of the agreement made between them in 1893. But the North Nyasa Estate did not attract settlers, and the South Africa Company's ownership appears to have made no practical difference whatever to the life of the African population. Eventually, in 1936, the Company renounced its title to the ownership of the surface, but received confirmation of its mineral rights in the area.

The Nyasaland Protectorate

It was the remaining million acres which mattered. They were situated in the Shiré Highlands, and it was there that most of the white settlers, including all the early ones, became established. By 1920 a further 140,000 acres had been alienated in freehold and 118,500 had been granted under lease. Some of these later grants were in what is now the Central Province, the region between Fort Jameson and Lake Nyasa; but it was only to a very limited extent that European farming was attempted outside the Shiré Highlands.

Unlike the Rhodesias, Nyasaland has had no native reserves. There was at no time enough white settlement to make it seem necessary to allocate any. And by the early 1930s it had become apparent that not only was there little European demand for additional land, but there was little additional land that could still be spared for alienation to Europeans. So, in 1936 the Native Trust Land Order in Council was issued, eleven years earlier than its Northern Rhodesian counterpart, to safeguard the interests of the natives.

By 1946, when Sir Sidney Abrahams investigated the situation, Native Trust Land comprised about 20·5 million acres, or 87·25 per cent of the total land in the Protectorate. The area alienated in freehold was 1·2 million acres, or 5·1 per cent of the total; the remaining 1·8 million acres included forest reserves, townships, and leasehold Crown land.

But although the European area was relatively small, it was much larger than the handful of farmers and planters could cultivate. And even when Johnston issued the certificates of claim there were some estates—it is not clear how many or how extensive—on which considerable numbers of Africans were already settled; in Johnston's own words, such land had 'so to speak, been bought "over the heads" of the people by a bargain between the Chief and the purchaser'. Here, he explained, 'I have (usually) insisted that the native occupants should remain in undisturbed possession of their land and villages, and have only allowed the purchaser to make use of waste land.' When the estate-owner's right to use the land was limited in this way, Johnston regarded a penny an acre as a fair purchase price: that is, one-third of the usual amount.

Nevertheless, the position of the occupants was merely that of legally protected squatters on private estates. And, of course, their right to reside rent-free and without fear of eviction applied only to themselves and their descendants, not to Africans subsequently permitted by the landlord to settle alongside them. Such persons were mere tenants at will, and were liable for payment of rent. But in the early twentieth century, and particularly during the 1920s, there was a large-scale movement of immigration to the Shiré Highlands from Portuguese East Africa. These people are commonly called Anguru, but are said to dislike this repellent-sounding name and to prefer the alternative of Alomwe—a preference in which they deserve to be followed by the authors of books in English. By 1945 they were estimated to number 373,000, while the total population of the whole Southern Province was 916,000. In the Mlanje and Cholo districts, where most of them were concentrated, they numbered 230,000 out of a total of 329,000. This immigration, added to the rapid natural increase of the previous inhabitants, had brought the density of the population in the Zomba district up to 152 to the square mile, and in the Cholo district it was even higher, 192 to the square mile. But in these two districts at least two-thirds of the land was owned by Europeans; it inevitably followed that a large proportion of the Alomwe became tenants on European estates.

There they proceeded to intermarry with the descendants of the original occupants, as did other Africans from villages outside the estate. The 1945 census itself pointed out that in the Shiré Highlands members of four or five tribes might be living together in a single village, so that in some cases classification according to tribe had become meaningless. On the European estates it had become almost impossible to distinguish between those who were entitled to reside undisturbed and rent-free and those who were liable for payment of rent and who might be evicted.

The distinction was, in fact, completely ignored by an Ordinance passed in 1928, which rendered all natives residing on private estates, except labourers and domestic servants, liable to pay rent at a figure amounting annually to between two and three months' wages at the average rate earned by agricultural workers in the district. The landowner could evict not only those who failed to pay rent, but also, once in every five years, up to a tenth of the total number on his estate, provided that he gave them six months' notice.

Thus the man who lived on a private estate was subjected to a heavy burden of rent, and to the threat of eviction, while his neighbour on Native Trust Land lived rent-free and enjoyed security of tenure. And the one had to pay as much tax to the Government as did the other. Nor were these the only grievances; and although it is impossible to say how many landlords behaved harshly towards their tenants, the mere fact that they were in a position to do so was itself undesirable. Sir Sidney Abrahams quoted an experienced administrative officer as having said that the tenants were 'constantly being chivvied by estate owners', and that they had 'very little security regarding either their houses or garden lands'. But the point of view of the owner, who saw his land being devastated and eroded by ever-multiplying numbers of incompetent and thriftless cultivators, is understandable too.

It was not until 1946 that the obvious and only adequate method of reform was set out boldly and in detail. Sir Sidney Abrahams, in his Land Report, pointed out that this was a matter which required a clear-cut remedy, not a compromise. Alienated land which was occupied by Africans or was lying unused should be bought back by the Government for conversion into Native Trust Land. The status of 'resident native' should be abolished, and those Africans who had held that status, and whose holdings were so situated that they could not be excised from the estate, should be given the option of remaining and entering into a written contract with the landlord, or of withdrawing to Native Trust Land and being compensated for the loss of their former huts and gardens.

In accordance with these recommendations, the Nyasaland Government proceeded to buy some 300,000 acres—a third of the total alienated land in the Southern Province, and a quarter of the total in the whole Protectorate—at a cost of about £190,000. When the estates were originally acquired in Johnston's time at a penny an acre, the cost of this land was £1,250.

Subsequent purchases have reduced the area of alienated land by a further 260,000 acres, so that the European freehold estates in the whole of Nyasaland now comprise only 623,000 acres, about 2·7 per cent of the total area. The area held in leasehold amounts to 174,000 acres. In 1946 the number of families living on private estates had been 49,600; by the end of 1961 it had been reduced to 14,800. But this was still more than a quarter of the number at the time of the Abrahams Report. Nor had anything been done to improve the position of Africans living on private estates in the Central Province: in 1946 about 10,000 families. These people are even more insecure than tenants in the south: they make an annual contract with their landlord, who provides them with seed and other forms of assistance to enable them to grow tobacco, which he sells on their behalf, taking an agreed share of the proceeds; they have to leave the estate at the end of the year if he is not prepared to enter into a new contract with them. Nyasaland's agrarian problem has been greatly eased, but it has not yet been solved.

In Nyasaland, as in the Rhodesias, there is a striking similarity between the extent of white settlement and the degree of economic development. The Southern Province has from the beginning had most of the settlers, the Central Province has had a few, and the Northern Province has had scarcely any. The Northern Province, which extends over the country north of the Kota-Kota district, was gloomily referred to in the inter-war period as 'the dead north'. But if the absence of economic development was partly due to the absence of European enterprise, this in turn was due to the absence of sufficient economic opportunity to attract it. The north is a land of steep mountain-slopes and high, wind-swept plateaux; it is also the remotest and least accessible part of the Protectorate.

'Poor little Nyasaland, she has nothing to sell but scenery and labour'—so, Professor Debenham relates, a senior official remarked to him a few years ago. This is more nearly true of northern Nyasaland than of other parts. The Angoni and the Tonga are foremost among the tribes whose young men travel hundreds of miles from home, to Southern Rhodesia and even to the Rand, in search of employment. In recent years there has been a rapid development of groundnut production in the Mzimba district, west of the Vipya range of mountains. Some cotton has been grown on the lake shore near Karonga, and the cultivation of rice for the market has extended northwards from Kota-Kota to the area around Nkata Bay. There are now thousands of growers of coffee in the Northern Province. Nevertheless it remains true that the agricultural possibilities of the north are small, and unless industrial development can be brought to the region it is never likely to be able to support even its present population, still less the steady annual increase in numbers, at a decent standard of living.

The most notable attempt to bring employment and a measure of prosperity to the north has been the planting of some thousands of acres of tung on the Vipya Plateau: the nuts which grow on the tung trees yield an oil which is used in the making of varnish. The project was initiated in the immediate post-war years, and was taken over in 1949 by the Colonial Development Corporation. By the end of 1958 the Corporation had spent nearly a million pounds on its Vipya estates, including over £200,000 which were written off in 1955. Even so, the enterprise had only a marginal effect in providing employment. In 1957 it employed 600 Africans, under the direction of five Europeans. But in 1958 the price fetched by tung oil after being transported to Beira fell from £115 to £68 a ton: the minimum economic price was considered to be £100 a ton. This fall in price was due to world-wide over-production, and there seemed little prospect of improvement, because of the increasing use of synthetic substitutes. In the event, however, prices more than recovered, and in 1961 were the highest for ten years. The area planted has remained unchanged since 1959 at about 16,000 acres, slightly less than before.

Northern Nyasaland suffers from a further handicap. The

lake, which is its natural means of communication with the south and with the outer world, rises and falls by as much as twenty-five feet over a period of years. It is consequently impossible to construct harbours or even jetties for the lake steamers, so that goods have to be transhipped by barge or canoe in open roadsteads. This lack of harbours is dangerous as well as inconvenient, for the storms which sweep down the rift valley are sudden and violent, and many a boat has foundered when caught in one of them. The worst of these disasters occurred in 1946, when the steamer *Vipya*, a new vessel making only its third voyage, capsized in a storm and sank in a minute and a half, with the loss of 140 Africans and 10 Europeans.

The variations in the level of the lake are due, at least in part, to the choking of the slow-flowing upper Shiré by the silt which is deposited in it by a number of minor tributaries, and by the mass of vegetation which springs up in this silt and assists in the collection of more. As the river becomes choked the lake rises behind it, until eventually it overflows in sufficient volume to start wearing down the bed of silt which has been built up during the preceding years; this erosion continues until, when the lake has fallen, the river becomes sluggish again, and the cycle begins to be repeated.

It follows that the level of the Shiré itself depends upon whether the lake is rising or falling. In the 1870s and 1880s there was enough water in the river to enable the missionaries and the African Lakes Company to use it as their line of communications; had the river not been navigable at that time they could scarcely have established themselves, and Nyasaland would have been left to the Portuguese and the Germans. But by the turn of the century navigation was becoming increasingly difficult, and in 1907–8 a railway was built from Blantyre to the southern extremity of the Protectorate at Port Herald. The line was extended to the Zambesi in 1913–15, and shortly after the First World War a railway was built from the Zambesi to the port of Beira. From 1922 to 1935 the two lines were connected by a ferry. But this proved inconvenient and expensive, and it was found worth while to construct the Lower Zambesi Bridge, whose 12,064 feet make it the longest railway bridge in the world. About the same time the line was continued northwards from Blantyre to a point about ten miles from the lake: the lake was rising at the time, and no one knew how much farther it would rise, so the railway-planners decided to keep well away from it.

Thus Nyasaland was made completely independent of both the Shiré and the lower Zambesi as a means of communication, but at the cost of being burdened with a crushing load of debt, until, in 1945, the British Government relieved her of it.

The Nyasaland railway was operated mainly by Africans, together with some Indians, whereas in both the Rhodesias work on the railway long remained a European preserve, jealously guarded by a single powerful trade union. Nyasaland has always been a land of equal opportunity for all races, because its opportunities have been too limited to draw any significant number of white artisans into the country. The entire white population was still not quite 2,000 in 1945. By 1950 it had, indeed, more than doubled, and a few years later it had more than quadrupled—it was estimated at 8,800 in 1961—but this marked increase was due at least as much to the expansion of the activities of the Government as to the beginnings of industrial development, chiefly at Blantyre. Moreover there has never been any scope for Europeans to engage in small-scale trade, for this function was secured by a frugal, industrious and fast-multiplying community of immigrants from India, who increased in numbers from 1,600 in 1931 to 10,700 in 1961. The Indians have played a most valuable part in economic development, but they have not been quite numerous enough to become a major element in politics.

Nyasaland had, in fact, very little politics, except at the tribal level, until the issue of federation arose in 1950. The white settlers were obviously too few to become dominant, and the country was quietly administered by a small band of hardworking and devoted civil servants, of whom the most important in practice were, perhaps, those who were most junior in

The Nyasaland Protectorate

status—the district commissioners who represented the authority of Government in direct contact with the chiefs and people. Constitutional development at the centre of administration, Zomba, proceeded at the same slow tempo as economic and social change. At first the Commissioner and Consul-General (the two offices were complementary and were entrusted to one man) exercised authority entirely at his own discretion, within the limits of the Orders in Council laid down by the home Government, and subject to the supervision and control of the Foreign Office. In 1904 control was transferred from the Foreign to the Colonial Office—a suitably belated recognition of the fact that Nyasaland (like Uganda, which was transferred at the same time) had ceased to be anything less than a full-scale colonial responsibility, in spite of its Protectorate status. The Commissioner and Consul-General now became the Governor. And in 1907 the Protectorate was given a constitution by Order in Council. From then on it had an Executive Council, consisting of the Governor and three senior officials, and a Legislative Council, in which three prominent unofficials, nominated by the Governor, deliberated with the members of the Executive Council. One of the first group of unofficials to be nominated by Sir Alfred Sharpe in 1907 was Alexander Hetherwick, who had by this time mellowed into a respected ecclesiastical statesman, well fitted to act as a spokesman for African interests; while his two unofficial colleagues represented the interests of the European settlers. When Hetherwick's five-year term as a member of the legislature came to an end, Dr. Laws reluctantly consented to take his place.

With the passing of time the number of unofficial members of the Legislative Council was gradually increased, and the number of officials was increased correspondingly, so that the Governor remained in control without the use of reserved powers. At the end of 1948 the Council consisted of the Governor, six officials, and six unofficials. Up to that time the representation of African interests had been entrusted to a missionary, but in 1949 two Africans, and also an Indian, were nominated in addition, and three more officials were nominated to preserve the official majority. A third African and a tenth official were included in 1953.

In 1955 an Order in Council was issued, modifying that of 1907 by introducing the principle of election in place of nomination. Separate Indian representation was abolished: there were in future to be five elected Africans and six non-Africans, the latter being in fact Europeans; the Governor's phalanx of officials now numbered eleven. This was still the constitutional position at the time of the disturbances of 1959.

The only change made in the Executive Council between 1907 and 1939 was the inclusion of one more official. During the war two unofficials were brought in, and subsequently the number of officials was increased by a further two, bringing their total number to six, in addition to the Governor, while the number of unofficials remained at two.

The broad conclusion to which these facts point is that the settlers in Nyasaland were indeed influential, as they might reasonably expect to be in view of the contribution they made and still make to the country's economy, but that the growing representation of the Africans in the legislature was likely to have much greater long-term significance. The country was being held by the Imperial authorities in trust for its own native inhabitants, to whom it would be gradually transferred as they became ready to assume the responsibility. The genuineness of this trusteeship was not seriously in doubt, until the British Government thought fit to yoke the territory in a federation with the Rhodesias.

CHAPTER 9

The Africans' Response

Before the narrative is carried to its climax in the making of the federal constitution, it will be well to consider how the Africans have adjusted their outlook and way of life under the influence of those European initiatives and activities which have been of most direct concern to them.

The pacification of the country may be considered first, for in a sense it is the most important thing the British have achieved: the spiritual influence of Christian teaching and the social influence of modern industry and commerce would have been exceedingly slow to take effect if they had not been given a framework of public order in which to operate. The ending of tribal warfare and of the export of slaves has to a large extent been the pre-condition of every other form of change initiated by the white man. It has also been exceedingly important for its own sake. The gradual depopulation of the country not only ceased but was followed by a dramatic increase in African numbers. The statistics are only approximate, being based on tax returns, but the general trend is clear enough: the combined population of the three territories has more than trebled in the past fifty years, and has probably quadrupled since British rule began. Here are the estimates in more detail:

Year	Southern Rhodesia	Northern Rhodesia	Nyasa-land
1911	752,000	820,000	969,000
1931	1,081,000	1,330,000	1,600,000
1951	1,970,000	1,890,000	2,330,000
1961	3,520,000	2,400,000	2,870,000

The Africans' Response

The exceptionally high birth rate, which in the past enabled the Africans as a race to survive all the afflictions that befell them, has thus caused a 'demographic explosion' which would have been catastrophic if the numbers had not initially been so low in relation to the areas of land which they occupied.

To the predatory tribes the imposition of peace was not immediately recognisable as a blessing. It involved the conquest and humiliation of the Matabele, with the confiscation of all their best land and the loss of many of the cattle in which they reckoned their wealth. It compelled the Bemba to live by their own labour instead of exploiting their neighbours. As for Mpeseni's Angoni, Professor J. A. Barnes concludes his study of their affairs by observing that 'the Ngoni sovereign State has become more and more like a rural district council in a backward area, . . . and the great warrior chief has become in effect the only member of the Administration who never goes home to Britain on leave'.[1]

With their blood-lust curbed by the Government and their other lusts frowned upon by the missionaries, vigorous young men of the warrior tribes found that village life had grown exasperatingly dull. They craved new opportunities for adventure, for proving that they were real men. That is one reason, though perhaps not the most important, why they began to migrate to and from the mines and farms of the white men in search of work.

Migration of labour, on which the economy of all southern Africa heavily depends, should not be confused with *mobility* of labour, as we understand it in a country such as Britain. Wherever there is economic development it is necessary that workers should be to some extent mobile—willing and able to move from jobs and areas where they are no longer required to others where the expansion is taking place. But if a man moves from his place of work to one which is several hundred miles distant,

[1] 'But', he adds, 'in the eyes of his people, the Paramount Chief still belongs to the Ngoni, and not to the Administration.' (*Politics in a Changing Society*, p. 172.) That was in the late 1940s; one wonders if it is still true, and, if so, how much longer it can continue.

we should normally assume that he would move his home as well, taking his wife and family with him; whereas the distinguishing feature of *migrant* labour is that a man's home remains in the village where he was born, and in his place of work he is merely a temporary visitor.

So far as the Rhodesias and Nyasaland are concerned, the migration of labour began as an internal movement in Nyasaland itself. As early as January 1893 Johnston reported that Angoni from Chikusi's country supplied 'nearly all' the labourers on European estates in the Shiré Highlands. An even longer journey in search of work was made by Tonga from the vicinity of Bandawe. Although formerly harried and terrorised by Mombera's Angoni, these remarkable people have shown enterprise and ambition unsurpassed by any other tribe in the whole region, and have been foremost in engaging in migrant labour.

The demand for labour was far greater in Southern Rhodesia than in the Shiré Highlands, and by the turn of the century the southward migration both from Nyasaland and from Barotseland was well under way. Some men, attracted by higher wages, journeyed as far as the Rand. Others went to the copper mines in Katanga. Political boundaries meant little to the African; in choosing his destination he was influenced only by what he had heard about the hardships of the journey and about the rates of pay. Thirty years ago the foremost authority on the subject, Major (later Sir Granville) Orde-Browne, remarked that 'it is easy to hear a camp-fire conversation in the Congo during which conditions in the Union, [Southern] Rhodesia, Tanganyika and Angola are all discussed and commented upon; brothers from Nyasaland may go one to the north and the other to the south, and may be trusted to compare their experiences on their return home' (*The African Labourer*, pp. 120–1).

The rapid development of the Northern Rhodesian copper mines in the years immediately before the depression created an urgent demand for African labour. Recruiting agencies, properly controlled by the Government to prevent malpractices, were employed by the mining companies to seek workers in their own villages and provide them with free transport for their journey to the mines, and for the return journey after their contracts had expired—that is, after a period which was limited by law to two years. By 1931 the number of Africans employed in the mines had risen to 25,000.

A year later, owing to the depression, it had fallen to 7,000. The recruiting agencies collapsed, and have never again been required. Although wages fell sharply and remained low until the war, the habit of looking to the copperbelt for employment had been formed, and the supply of labour more than kept up with the increasing demand. In 1957 the number of Africans employed in copper-mining was 37,600. Men were prepared to walk hundreds of miles through the bush, accepting the risk of being seized by beasts of prey on their journey, to present themselves, exhausted and emaciated, at the copper mines in the hope of obtaining employment. In the 1940s a number of rest-houses were set up by the Government at convenient points on the most-frequented routes, to mitigate the hardships of the journey. Those who could afford it travelled by lorry; more recently it has become usual to make the journey by bus, if necessary borrowing the fare.[1]

Even before setting out from his native village on the long journey to work the tribesman was likely to be suffering from malnutrition and disease. His diet was monotonous and was usually unbalanced and deficient in vitamins. For weeks and even months before the harvest there was often an acute shortage of grain, due partly to low agricultural productivity, partly to the improvidence of a people too much given to converting their grain into beer, and partly to the depredations of rats and other vermin. From the beginning the mining companies understood that a man cannot do good work unless he is well fed and in good health; as Major Orde-Browne reported in 1938, they 'fully appreciate the value of a healthy and contented labour

---

[1] 'The journey by bus is a significant change from the past. A man no longer expects to go ragged and on foot to the Copperbelt and return clothed and by bus. Now he both goes and returns by bus, properly dressed. If he cannot find the money for both suitable clothes and the bus fare of £2 10s. [from Abercorn], his relatives must stake him.' (W. Watson, *Tribal Cohesion in a Money Economy* (1958), p. 51.)

6. The Copperbelt.

Surface plant, African & European Housing, Sports field and Headgear at Nkana Mine, Kitwe, May 1961

7. The Kariba Dam, photographed in May 1963

force, and go to considerable lengths to secure this. Frequently the requirements of the law will be found to be far exceeded. . . . Generally in this country [Northern Rhodesia] the rations will be found to be sufficient and well-balanced . . .; sanitation, bathing provision and water supply are good; and some attempt at amenities is made by the provision of playing-fields, bands, reading-rooms, and amusement grounds. Conditions may be said to be appreciably higher than those of the home village; in particular, the ration is both ampler and better balanced, the seasonal shortage characteristic of native life being, of course, entirely absent. Again, the employee enjoys, for the first time in his life, an efficient medical service; latent disease, such as malaria or hookworm, will be cleared up, while any trouble contracted during employment will be speedily detected and treated. Routine monthly recording of weights will detect insidious diseases such as tuberculosis, and the discharged worker is probably freer from ailments than he has ever been before.'

Professor Frankel, visiting the copperbelt in 1936, formed the impression 'that in many respects those responsible for this development are succeeding in creating a model industrial system for tropical areas'. This achievement owed little or nothing to pressure either from the Government of Northern Rhodesia or from the African workers. Until the mines themselves began to yield a large and growing revenue in the form of income tax, the Government was never able to avoid an annual deficit, incurred under the vigilant and disapproving eye of the British Treasury. The services of Government were therefore kept to the barest minimum, and the mining companies were of necessity left to manage their labour relations by the light of whatever wisdom they themselves possessed. It was not until after the thorough investigation carried out by Major Orde-Browne in 1938 that a Labour Department was set up in Northern Rhodesia, with a Labour Commissioner to collect and classify the relevant information, and Labour Officers residing in the copperbelt and elsewhere with the special duty of promoting good relations between British employers and African employed.

The Africans themselves, illiterate or barely literate tribesmen bewildered by the machinery and organisation of modern industry, speaking a babel of different languages and dialects and with no tradition of inter-tribal solidarity, were at first incapable of collective bargaining. They were not, indeed, wholly at the mercy of their employers, for, in addition to the safeguards provided by law, they had the alternatives of returning to subsistence agriculture and of going outside the territory in search of work. But neither the Government nor even the mine managements had any satisfactory means of knowing what grievances were being felt and what misunderstandings were fermenting unexpressed among this heterogeneous mass of workers. As early as 1931 'Tribal Elders' were instituted by the management at one of the mines, Roan Antelope, to try to meet this need. The Elders were elected by their fellow tribesmen among the workers, and might be expected to enjoy their confidence. For a time the experiment was popular with the workers and helpful to the management. It was afterwards extended to the other mines. But tribal groupings were irrelevant to the organisation of work and labour in the industry, and even to the selection of football teams and to the social life which centred in the Beer Hall—the main social centre on the compound. The Tribal Elders, chosen because they were closely related to the chiefs of the tribes which they represented, were usually dignified, conservative, and illiterate, ill-suited to control a crowd when it became excited, and receiving little respect from young men of better education though of humbler birth. The 'Elder system' broke down completely, though only temporarily, during the violent disturbances which took place in 1935 and again in 1940; on both occasions a number of people were killed and many others were injured. It was significant that during the disturbances in 1940 a strike committee was formed at one of the mines, Mufulira, and this committee kept the situation there under control, avoiding violence, and negotiating with the management. Elsewhere the strikers themselves hardly knew what they were demanding, and there was no group of leaders with whom the management could negotiate. The establishment of the African Mine Workers' Trade Union in 1949 remedied this situation; it also led, shortly afterwards (in 1953), to the abolition of the system of Tribal Representatives, as the Tribal Elders had come to be called.

The 'Elder system' had been introduced on the assumption that the African was only a temporary visitor to the mines; that he would soon return home and be replaced by another villager as raw as he had been when he first arrived; that he was essentially a villager and not a townsman, a tribesman and not a potential trade unionist. But the mining authorities failed to realise how great would be the strains which the new conditions would place upon traditional loyalties. Although men seldom remained for long periods at a single mine, they did not always return to their native village when they left their employment. Growing tired of one job or one compound, they moved to another job and another compound; and some of them tried their luck in neighbouring territories. From time to time, it is true, most of them went back to their home village, but their visits tended to become little more than holidays. Often they took wives or concubines from tribes other than their own. The obligation to share their earnings with a wide circle of relations sometimes became so irksome that they preferred and adopted the alternative—that of making themselves permanent outcasts from the community in which they had been born and reared.

Thus there was a strong and growing tendency for Africans who entered modern industry to lose, or deliberately to cast off, their ties with their kindred in the countryside. This tendency was as strong at Broken Hill as in the copperbelt, and in Southern as in Northern Rhodesia. From a segregationist point of view it was deplorable: the African's roots ought to be in his own area, and he must not be encouraged to transplant himself and settle down in the European area, with nowhere else to go. From the point of view of the mining companies, too, it was unwelcome, because it implied an extension of their own already great responsibilities for African welfare; the depression had been a warning to them, and they hesitated to burden themselves with the obligation to provide for all their workers in the event of any future collapse of the market. Migrant workers, if they became unemployed, could and would return home and fall back upon their traditional subsistence agriculture, whereas workers who cut themselves off from home and kindred by becoming permanently urbanised would need unemployment relief to save them from starvation. Besides, it was manifestly undesirable that swarms of children should grow up in the mine compounds, without either tribal discipline or modern education. If they were to be educated, who was to pay the heavy cost? It was much less troublesome to take the view that the proper place for African family life was the African village, not the European town.

During the 1930s, however, it became clear that the migration of labour was causing widespread hardship and demoralisation among the tribes from which the workers came. A Committee of Enquiry presented an alarming report on the situation in Nyasaland in 1935, and in 1937 a second enquiry collected statistics which showed that in that year (1937) 18·3 per cent of the total fit adult male population was employed outside the Protectorate, and a quarter of these men had not been heard of since 1930. These were the *machona*, the 'lost ones', mostly married men who had forsaken their wives. The proportion of emigrants from Northern Nyasaland was much larger than from the Southern Province, and among the Tonga it reached 60 per cent. Yet among the Tonga the proportion of *machona* was exceptionally small. The effects of migrant labour, indeed, varied greatly from tribe to tribe. Whether or not a man would be likely to desert his wife under the stress of the temptations of urban life depended to a large extent on the kind of upbringing that his tribe had given him.

Again, the effect of his absence—whether temporary or permanent—on agriculture depend partly on the type of agriculture practised by his people and partly on whether or not he is able and careful to arrange that someone else will give his wife whatever help she needs during his absence. For example, the Bemba, who have poor soil, grow their crops in beds of ashes made by lopping branches from trees, piling them in a central clearing, and burning them. This tree-lopping is arduous work which has to be done by young men, and so is the erection of fences to protect the crops from wild pigs. When the young men are away from the village, this work is not done, and although the actual cultivation of crops is women's work the village suffers much more from hunger than it would if the migrants were at home. About half the younger Bemba men are away at work at any one time But this does not mean that half of those belonging to any particular village can be relied upon to remain behind; if it did it might not be serious. Instead, most of them are absent together, while in another village most may be at home. Among the neighbouring Mambwe, by contrast, an equally large proportion of total emigration does not result in any loss of agricultural production, partly because they organise their departures with a sensible measure of co-operation, and partly because they occupy grasslands where the arduous—and destructive—work of tree-lopping is not among their tasks.

The Nyasaland Committee of Enquiry in 1935 found that the tax collected in the five northern districts (Kota-Kota and the present Northern Province) in 1934 amounted to £18,379; the total wages earned locally were about £12,000, and there were few opportunities of earning money by the sale of produce. If the inhabitants of these northern districts were even to meet the demands of the tax-gatherer, quite apart from having anything to spend, they must emigrate. At that time the rate of tax was only 6s. a year[1] for a single man or a man with one wife: the inability of the people to find such a trifling sum without going to work hundreds of miles away gives some indication of the undeveloped condition of Nyasaland's 'dead north' in the inter-war period.

But although the Committee gave first place to the native tax among the causes of labour migration, it did so only 'from the point of view of immediate necessity', and did not 'wish to stress it unduly as an omnipresent and overwhelmingly important cause of the exodus', except perhaps in the case of the Chewa, 'an

---

[1] By 1958 it had risen to 30s. Of this 30s. tax, 5s. was paid to the Native Treasuries, belonging to and managed by the (essentially tribal) local authorities.

unambitious and almost pathetic people'. Twenty years later, when studying labour migration as it affected the Mambwe in the remotest northern corner of Northern Rhodesia, Dr. W. Watson found that Mambwe youths were so far from being driven to work by the demands of the tax-collector that many of them pestered the district commissioner to register them as taxpayers before they reached the age of eighteen at which they became liable for payment, because on becoming taxpayers they would receive an identification certificate, which they required when seeking work. They wanted work because they wanted money for their own purposes: the purchase of clothes, household goods, bicycles, and even wireless sets—these are now possessed by large numbers of Africans, and broadcasts in the more important vernacular languages were sent out to the whole Federation from Lusaka, the capital of Northern Rhodesia. The most important single private purpose for which money is wanted is still, as it was in 1935, the payment of *lobola* to one's prospective father-in-law. Formerly paid in cattle and in scarce goods, it is now paid wholly or partly in cash, and the usual practice appears to be to screw as much as possible out of young men eager to marry. Often they borrow the money from their kindred so that they can marry before going away to work; thus one effect of *lobola*, and perhaps nowadays its main effect, is to impose upon the young couple a heavy burden of debt. The desire to marry stimulates the desire for money in other ways, too. 'Even to be considered as a potential husband', Dr. Watson writes, 'a Mambwe youth must be smartly dressed, able to give presents, socially accomplished, adept in the Sava-Sava (a popular African ballroom dance based on the foxtrot), and generally he must have the sophisticated air and fashions of the urban worker' (*Tribal Cohesion in a Money Economy*, p. 43). Indeed, the practice of going away for a time to paid employment is now so nearly universal that a young man would be considered odd if he did not go, and this expectation on the part of his kindred and acquaintances is not the least of the pressures which urge him on.

Migrant labour is notoriously inefficient. By the time that a man has become semi-competent at his work he has earned enough to pay his taxes and other debts and to buy what he wants, and he leaves his job and goes home. If he afterwards enters employment again, it will probably be in a different type of job, where he will have to learn almost everything afresh. This inefficiency is one reason for the lowness of the wages paid to unskilled workers—much lower until recently, in real as well as cash terms, than they are now. Even if higher wages could be afforded, the effect of paying them might be to make the worker an even quicker bird of passage, by enabling him to earn the amount required in a shorter time.

In all three territories of the Federation farmers and estate-owners have found it comparatively difficult to prosper, and farm wages have consequently been lower, and conditions less attractive, than in the towns. That is probably why farmers have usually been bitterly dissatisfied with the quality of the work done by their employees, whereas urban employers, if they have provided capable and sympathetic management, have found that in many cases Africans work as well as Europeans. According to an authoritative survey published by the U.S. Department of Commerce in 1956, such employers 'claim that good training, constant supervision, and exemplary managerial behaviour contribute as much to higher productivity as do good wages, regular health check-ups, and exemplary living conditions; and that African workers generally are more encouraged by promotion to the types of jobs traditionally reserved for Europeans than by monetary rewards. . . . Higher productivity may be attained if the worker lives with his wife and children in sanitary, reasonably spacious, and secluded surroundings. . . . If they can buy their house and the land around it, so much the better. . . . Most Africans are interested in getting a better home of their own, and will work harder to own one than for any other thing. The present inability of an urbanised African to obtain freehold title of land in or near his place of work [in Southern Rhodesia] is considered by many employers as the main reason for the large labour turnover that is still characteristic of most industries.' In other words, it was economically desirable to encourage instead of discouraging the tendency of migrant workers to settle down in the towns.

For social as well as economic reasons, the Governments concerned have all adopted the view that migrant labour should be gradually replaced by 'stabilised' labour. In 1960 Southern Rhodesia amended the Land Apportionment Act to enable Africans to obtain freehold ownership of their houses, with the security of occupation and the sense of permanence which that alone could bring. It had previously been unattainable because the African locations, as appendages to the European towns, lay within the European area; they were now set apart with the special status of 'Native Townships Area'.

The ending of migrant labour is still a distant dream: the exodus from Nyasaland actually increased during the 1950s, when a fall in the demand from Southern Rhodesia was more than offset by increased migration to South Africa. And in 1961 some 45 per cent of Southern Rhodesia's African workers still consisted of immigrants, including 117,000 from Nyasaland and 45,000 from Northern Rhodesia. It is probable, however, that these figures include a considerable number who will settle down permanently as town-dwellers. It seems that the permanent African town-dweller seldom deliberately chooses to become so: he drifts into it, his desire to return to his village gradually diminishing the longer he prolongs his stay. Of course he is much more likely to remain if he has his wife and children with him; there is, moreover, a world of difference, morally and socially, between the prolonged absence of married men who have left their wives behind and have picked up concubines in the towns, and that of men who are able to live a normal family life at their place of work.

The Nyasaland Government has long been aware that it must try to regulate an exodus which it has been in no position to forbid. Its early attempts, however, proved almost futile, because it was at the point of arrival and not at the point of departure that controls were needed, and Southern Rhodesia with its insatiable thirst for labour was slow to co-operate. But in 1936 the 'Salisbury Agreement' was made between the

The Africans' Response

Governments of the two Rhodesias and that of Nyasaland, and in 1947 it was replaced by a much more stringent and valuable agreement. This provided for the compulsory repatriation, free of charge, of all workers who had been absent for two years, unless their wives had accompanied them or had subsequently joined them: united families might remain absent as long as they liked. It also provided for deductions to be made from wages of a worker whose family remained behind; part of this money was to be remitted to his dependants, and the remainder paid to him after his return home, so that it would be spent in his own territory. A further control was the exclusion from the copperbelt, by law, of African women other than wives accompanying or joining their husbands.

On the copperbelt, too, a system of pensions for long-service African workers was introduced by the mining companies, and the problem of educating the large numbers of African children, instead of letting them grow up without any kind of training or discipline to become hooligans, was faced seriously if not altogether successfully both by the missions and by the Government.

At least as important as the establishment of a settled population of urban industrial workers is the development of African agriculture. The most urgent need has been to stop the spoliation of the land by practices which lead to soil erosion; the further need has been to improve the yield per acre from the miserable $1\frac{1}{2}$ or 2 bags of maize (a bag contains 203 lb.) to the 8 bags or more which can be produced by competent farming.

Owing to the overcrowding of the reserves caused in part by the Land Apportionment Act, it is in Southern Rhodesia that the need has been greatest, and it is there that the boldest policy has been followed and the greatest financial outlay incurred. At first, until after the Second World War, the Government relied mainly on education by instruction and example. By 1937 there were 64 trained African agricultural demonstrators supervising 3,533 demonstration plots; by 1944 the staff of the Native Agricultural Department consisted of 30 Europeans and 219 Africans. Yet in 1947 the Director of Native Agriculture admitted in his report that 'to date we have only started to cope with the problem, and more intensive efforts must be made to avoid disaster', because the population was increasing more rapidly than its deeply-rooted conservatism concerning the use of the land was being overcome.

In 1950 Professor Sir Frank Engledow of Cambridge prepared an official report on Southern Rhodesian agriculture; in it he called attention to 'the extravagance of land and of effort occasioned by the miserable level of soil fertility' in the reserves, and to the scrawny condition of African-owned cattle, whose meat was 'small in amount and wretched in quality', and was being 'raised with no less extravagance of area and injury to condition of land than the food crops'. He concluded that 'the disorderly way in which the land is distributed to and worked by individuals seems likely so to handicap reform as to hold it perpetually in arrear of increase of population and therefore of despoliation'. Moreover, about 70 per cent of able-bodied males were believed to spend at least part of the year in paid employment outside the reserves, so that agriculture within the reserves was scarcely more than a part-time occupation for industrial workers and housewives. There could be little hope of improvement until it became men's full-time work. The industrial workers and their families must become permanently urbanised, and the reserves and other native areas must cease to be regarded as the real home of the whole African population. The numbers permitted to remain in the reserves should be limited, and rules of good husbandry should not only be taught but enforced.

Partly as a result of these recommendations, the Native Land Husbandry Act was passed in 1951 to enforce good husbandry, control the number of livestock, and, most important of all, to effect the gradual replacement of communal land-tenure by individual ownership, and to put a stop to the fragmentation of holdings into uneconomic units. Thus, four years before the publication of the famous report of the East Africa Royal Commission, Southern Rhodesia embarked on a policy broadly in accord with that which the Royal Commission recommended for Kenya and its immediate neighbours. And in 1955 the

The Africans' Response

Government speeded up the implementing of the Act under a five-year plan involving an expenditure of £6,600,000.

These changes amount to an economic and social revolution, the introduction of twentieth-century conditions into the whole of rural as well as urban production. When this process has been completed, tribal habits of thought and conduct will survive for a long time, but will be little more than the lingering shadow of a way of life whose substance has been buried in the past. More immediately significant, however, has been the creation of a multitude of grievances on the part of the new landless proletariat, and of peasants whose holdings were inadequate for more than subsistence—though, as Dr. J. W. Rowland has recently shown at the Henderson Research Station, those same holdings might become highly productive if groups of smallholders combined and co-operated to make them so.

In Nyasaland and Northern Rhodesia little or no attempt has been made to interfere with traditional customs of land tenure, in spite of the density of population in the Shiré Highlands and in some parts of the Northern Rhodesian reserves. The Protectorate Governments have concentrated their attention on the use of land, as distinct from its tenure. In 1949 the Nyasaland legislature passed the Natural Resources Ordinance, which authorised compulsion to reinforce persuasion for such purposes as the control of cultivation on hill slopes, to prevent soil erosion. The rules involved extra work and some sacrifice of immediate advantage, and their enforcement was greatly resented. The Devlin Commission in 1959 found them to be 'a very happy hunting ground' for agitators wishing to make political capital out of any Government action, necessary or unnecessary, which was not immediately palatable.

Viewed as a whole, the social effects of participating in the cash economy of the Europeans have obviously been greater in the main areas of white settlement—Southern Rhodesia and the copperbelt—than in the outlying parts of Northern Rhodesia and in Nyasaland, especially northern Nyasaland; they have been greater in the case of those Africans who have settled down to permanent family life in the towns than in the case of those who have continued to look upon wage-labour as merely an occasional supplement to subsistence agriculture, practised to a great though diminishing extent with tradition-hallowed inefficiency. The permanently urbanised African has broken with his tribal organisation, even though he still thinks of himself as belonging to his tribe in much the same way as a Scot in England or an Englishman in Australia retains a lifelong attachment to the country in which he was born, and to its people. The rural African, however, retains his place in his tribal structure, though for many years the younger members of the Angoni and perhaps of some other tribes have been finding the authority of the tribal elders obscurantist and irksome, and in Southern Rhodesia tribal institutions must be greatly and increasingly weakened as a result of the implementing of the Native Land Husbandry Act.

It is sometimes said that in one respect the influence of European civilisation has made no change whatever—that belief in witchcraft continues to be universal among Africans. It has even been suggested that the pressure of social change and the emotional disturbance and loss of self-confidence attending it have actually intensified superstitious beliefs, which provide a convenient ready-made explanation for every mishap. Of course the introduction of European rule was quickly followed by the suppression of the poison ordeal, and the smelling-out of suspected witches was made a criminal offence. In the eyes of the Africans, however, it was the witches who were the enemies of society, not the witch-doctors who smelt them out; since witches could now go unpunished and even unidentified, the feeling of insecurity to which they gave rise was increased. The persistence of witchcraft beliefs is sometimes regarded as proof that the African remains and will always remain at heart a primitive savage, however superficially civilised some individuals may contrive to appear. This is to overlook the fact that in European society in the seventeenth century belief in witchcraft was equally strong, not least among the highly educated; and in our own times otherwise intelligent and sensible white people avoid the number 13 and sometimes even take a serious interest in what the stars are alleged to foretell.

The fear of witches is inseparable from belief in the existence of evil spirits, since it is by co-operating with them that the witches work evil; this belief cannot be disproved, and in our own society it is considered irrational merely because it is out of fashion. The missionaries for their part have made little or no attempt to attack it, not only because such an attempt would be hopeless, but primarily because they have seen no need to contend against a belief which was held by the New Testament writers themselves. They have been content to insist that spiritual protection against all evil must be sought through Christian prayer and not through pagan hocus-pocus. They have made many sincere converts, who have tried hard to follow their teaching; but the temptation to lapse has been strong.

It is impossible to assess with any precision the importance of the missions as a factor in the general history of the territories after the establishment of European rule. The initiative in shaping the course of events and in influencing the African had passed to other white men, the administrators and the settlers. In Africa, as elsewhere, example seems to be more important than instruction; if the Africans assumed, as in most cases they probably did, that the conduct of white men represented Christianity in action, the presence of settlers served to dilute the influence of missionary teaching. What were they to think if, after being admitted to membership of the Christian community—'where there is neither Jew nor Greek, circumcision nor uncircumcision, Barbarian, Scythian, bond nor free; but Christ is all, and in all'—they found themselves excluded as far as possible both from social intercourse and from economic competition with their European fellow Christians, as a result of the deliberate erection of a colour bar based on selfishness and pride? 'It seems to follow', wrote W. M. Eiselen in 1934, 'that contact with a population of white Christians has raised the quantity and has lowered the quality of Bantu Christians. . . . Native Christians are now following the white man's example in being good Christians when convenient only' (quoted in C. P. Groves, *The Planting of Christianity in Africa*, Vol. IV, p. 157).

The Africans' Response

On the other hand the conquest of the Matabele greatly facilitated the work of conversion among them by shattering their complacent arrogance and removing the almost insuperable institutional obstacles to the spread of the Gospel. In 1899, after forty years' work, the L.M.S. had made only three converts among them; by 1905 the number was already over 400. Another effect of the conquest was to encourage other missionary bodies to enter the country: before the end of the century eight new missions had entered Southern Rhodesia, where until 1890 there had been only the L.M.S. (since 1859) and the Jesuits (since 1880). A similar inrush of new missions took place in the northern territories after the establishment of British rule. When the U.M.C.A. completed its long movement of westward expansion by entering Northern Rhodesia in 1910 and founding a separate diocese there, it was the fourteenth mission to undertake work in that territory (though the first Anglican mission to do so).

On the whole the missions have worked amicably together, each keeping within boundaries agreed with its neighbours—though there have been one or two sharp disagreements as to where a particular boundary should run. In the copperbelt, where workers belonging to several Christian denominations were working side by side with one another and with pagans, the Free Church missions drew together in 1936 to form a Union Church of the Copperbelt, which has worked in close co-operation with the Anglicans, though the Roman Catholics, who were about as numerous as the others combined, have held aloof. In Nyasaland the young churches brought into being by the Livingstonia and Blantyre Missions, each organised in a presbytery, united in 1924 to form the Church of Central Africa (Presbyterian). The united church was soon joined by a third presbytery, formed by the Dutch Reformed Church, which for many years had been at work in western Nyasaland in close co-operation with Livingstonia. Some years later the Presbyterians in Northern Rhodesia united with the converts of the L.M.S.—which has a decentralised, Congregationalist organisation—to form a single presbytery.

The Africans' Response

All the missions have aimed at fostering the growth of a church rooted in African soil, drawing its ministry increasingly from its own African members, and relying less and less on instruction, advice and financial help from outside. Some indication of the extent to which this aim has already been achieved is given by the consecration of an African, in 1957, as Roman Catholic bishop in Nyasaland, and by the transfer in 1959 of all the Church of Scotland's authority and property in Nyasaland to the Church of Central Africa (Presbyterian).

These changes were timely, for the rise of nationalism among Africans has led to an increasingly critical attitude to the missionaries. They have been accused of being 'in the pocket' of the white settler communities, and of being far too complaisant towards the policy of European-controlled Governments. No doubt the Church of Scotland has to some extent escaped this censure, because of its militant support for Nyasaland's cause against the Federation. But in the Rhodesias the word 'missionary' has sometimes actually become a term of abuse, and during the disturbances in 1958 and again in 1961 several churches were burnt down. Even the Reverend Colin Morris, that robust and fearless opponent of racial discrimination, has been driven to ask: 'Is the price to be paid in retaining the friendship of the African people one hundred per cent uncritical acceptance of all that they say or do? . . . Within the churches themselves a silent and secret struggle is going on to eradicate all missionary influence and evolve a policy line which would make the Church the spiritual wing of black nationalism' (Morris and Kaunda, *Black Government?*, pp. 96, 104).

The work of the missionaries has increasingly consisted in the training of teachers and clergy rather than in continuing personally to teach letters to the illiterate and to preach to people wholly ignorant of Christianity. As early as 1894 Dr. Laws moved from his mission-station at Bandawe on the lake shore te a carefully chosen site on high ground overlooking Florence Bay—the little plateau of Kondowe, which projects towards the lake from the great mass of the Nyika Plateau. Here, with his rare vision and capacity for organisation, he founded the Livingstonia Institute, and he spent the remainder of his career in Africa in building it up as a combined teachers' training college, theological college, and technical college. It was largely because of the work of teachers and craftsmen trained at this institute that men from Nyasaland gained the reputation for being better educated than any other workers in the Rhodesias, indigenous or migrant. And while the achievement of Livingstonia was particularly outstanding, the other missions too were vigorously active in educational work.

For many years after the establishment of British administration the missions continued to represent the only, or almost the only, attempt on the part of the white man to communicate his knowledge to the African. When the Administrations did take a hand in the work, it was by paying them a small grant in aid. In 1901 Southern Rhodesia made its first such grant—£133. When Nyasaland passed under the control of the Colonial Office, Sir Alfred Sharpe managed to obtain an annual grant of £1,000 for the same purpose. During the inter-war period the contributions gradually increased, but it is only in the post-war years that they have become really substantial; at the same time the Governments have been building some schools of their own. The total expenditure of the Southern Rhodesian Government on African education increased more than twenty-fold between 1946 and 1961, from £208,441 to £4,794,000. In Nyasaland the total Government expenditure on education in 1946 was only £88,759, and this included about £9,000 spent on the education of Europeans and Indians; in 1961 the expenditure incurred for Africans alone was £1,154,000. (In 1961 the amount spent by voluntary agencies on African education in Nyasaland was £404,000—most of this came from the missions, but some from European estates, from commercial enterprises, and from the Moslem community. A further £60,000 was spent on primary schools by African local authorities.) This increased expenditure has, of course, been made possible by post-war economic development; in the case of Nyasaland it also reflects the financial advantages of federation. In each of the three territories the amount spent by the Government on African education alone now equals or exceeds the entire amount collected from the Africans in direct taxation.

Even today, however, there are still some children who redeive no school instruction at all: in Southern Rhodesia it is claimed that these are now less than 5 per cent of the total, but in each of the Protectorates the percentage is at least twice as large. Of those who go to school at all, only a tiny proportion obtain a thorough education. In Southern Rhodesia in 1961 there were 465,000 attending 'lower primary' classes, 61,000 in 'upper primary' classes (Standards IV to VI), and only 5,000 in secondary schools. For Northern Rhodesia the corresponding figures were 244,000, 61,000, and 3,800; for Nyasaland they were even more pathetic: 261,000, 26,000, and 1,700. Yet in all three territories the numbers receiving secondary education had roughly trebled during the previous five years.

By 1962 the number of Africans attending the new University College of Rhodesia and Nyasaland was 74, together with 241 Europeans and 15 Asians and Coloureds. Much larger numbers of Africans, however, were attending universities abroad, especially in the United States and Britain.

In the earliest days of missionary effort the Africans were not easily induced to attend school or to send their children, and those who did attend usually did so too irregularly and for too short a time to learn anything at all. With the coming of European administration and European enterprise the situation was transformed. As soon as he grasped the fact that literacy would make it easier for him to fend for himself in the strange world of township and mine, and that a few years of schooling might bring him a clerkship, the African developed an insatiable thirst for knowledge.

'Education is an obsession with the African nowadays,' wrote Mr. Kenneth Bradley in his *Diary of a District Officer*, just before the Second World War; Mr. Bradley was recording his experience in a remote district in the region of Fort Jameson. 'It is the road to a clerical post, and therefore to liberal support for fathers and mothers and uncles and aunts and cousins of the nth degree. For these reasons severally it is eagerly demanded by both young and old. . . . The first thing the Ngoni did with their money when they achieved a Native Treasury was to start a school. The Ngoni father may be reactionary and tiresome about windows in his hut, rubbish-pits, latrines, or selling his cattle, but he differs not a whit from his Chewa cousin in his enthusiasm about education. . . . What I like about the school is its spirit. We never say when we are coming, and we have yet to find a single person idling—which, in Africa, is in itself remarkable. . . . In Africa the schoolboy is so athirst for knowledge that his punishment is to be kept *out*, not *in*. . . . "Impots" are rewards and "half-hols" punishments!' A generation previously Sheane had remarked that 'boys reading by the camp-fire and by moonlight are a common sight'.

The missionaries were well aware that it was the desire for secular rather than for spiritual knowledge that brought most of the pupils to their schools. They had no pious illusions about the significance to be attached to an expression of eagerness to learn, or even of desire to be baptised. Coillard referred to 'spontaneous professions, some of which have moved our hearts; but I do not encourage them. . . . To speak candidly I am not without apprehensions. I fear lest this movement, which seems so widespread, may yet be without depth.' The attitude of the other missions was on the whole equally reserved; at Livingstonia, for instance, no one was baptised without at least two years' preparation, and teaching in special classes was insisted upon after baptism. The missionaries certainly did not assume that all who attended their schools would ever be converted to Christianity. When a pupil was guilty of persistent misconduct, they dismissed him. But he then went in search of employment, and made the most of the fact that he had attended a mission school; his employer's subsequent disillusionment tended to give the schools a bad name, and to foster the idea that the white man's education, while good for the white man, 'spoiled the native'. So did the arrogant conduct frequently shown by native clerks and teachers, half-educated men with all the presumption of a self-conscious intellectual *élite*. Nevertheless Dr. Laws, although sometimes grieved to the brink of despair by the lapses of men in whom he had put confidence, remained convinced that the remedy was to be found in more education, more widely spread, and accompanied by more practical experience and responsibility in the ways of civilised life—not in trying to stifle ambition and to protect the African in the enjoyment of his traditional ways undisturbed by intellectual and spiritual training.

There was however one mission distinguished from the others both by the perversity of its teaching and by the harmfulness of its influence—though even it seems to have done some good. This was the Watch Tower movement, which originated in the United States about the beginning of the twentieth century. It proclaimed the imminence of the end of the world, denounced all secular Governments and the whole of the existing social order as accursed, and declared that all the Christian churches were ranged on the side of the Devil, not of God. The movement was particularly active in Northern Rhodesia in the inter-war period, and took such an extravagant form that an American who was sent by the parent organisation to inspect it was horrified by what he found. The excitement which it stirred up culminated in several murders, and the Commission of Enquiry into the copperbelt disturbances of 1935 found that it was 'an important predisposing cause' of the murderous violence which then occurred.

The influence of the Watch Tower movement entered Nyasaland a few years before the First World War, and there it acted as a stimulus to what is called 'Ethiopianism'—the state of mind which leads to the founding of separatist African sects, independent of missionary influence, rejecting the moral discipline of the Christian life but emphasising the importance of baptism. This combination of religious emotion, pagan ethics, and the cry of 'Africa for the Africans' had—and continues to have—an obvious attraction. It has been aptly compared with Anabaptism in sixteenth-century Europe; like Anabaptism it is religious in form but is political and social in content. Political nationalism as such did not find organised expression in Nyasaland until 1944, when the African National Congress was formed; thirty

years earlier, however, the syncretistic sects were already preparing the soil for it. In the Shiré Highlands the problem of
tenants on European estates was already causing discontent,
which was being made worse by the boorish discourtesy which
some at least of the estate-owners and managers showed towards Africans. An African was expected to raise his hat when he
met a white man, yet, according to Hetherwick, 'many Europeans absolutely ignore a boy's [i.e. an African's] salutation'.
Hetherwick—who was giving evidence before a commission of
enquiry—continued: 'The smallest drummer boy in the British
Army, if he salutes Lord Kitchener, receives a salute in return.
There will be no difficulty if the European makes acknowledgement: it indicates that two gentlemen have met and not only
one.'

That was in 1915, and the occasion for the enquiry was a
petty revolt headed by a comparatively well-educated separatist
clergyman name John Chilembwe. The rebels had burgled the
house of an unpopular estate-manager and murdered him and
another white man; they had then attacked the store of the
African Lakes Corporation at Blantyre to secure arms and ammunition, killing the night watchman, but running away in
disorder when the Corporation's employees approached. Within
a few days they had been hunted down and either killed when
trying to escape or captured and summarily tried and shot. But
although three women and five children had been captured at
the house of the murdered estate-manager, Chilembwe and his
followers had taken care of them and had seen that they suffered no injury. The whole incident was even more foolish than
criminal. The great majority of the African population took
care not to be caught up in the disturbance. Yet after his death
Chilembwe became something of a nationalist martyr, on whom
the Nyasaland nationalists of today look back as on a kind of
patron saint, since they lack any better alternative.

CHAPTER 10

Federation

The idea of uniting Northern and Southern Rhodesia was put forward as early as 1915, by the Directors of the South Africa Company. Their aim was the same as it had been a few years previously when they had united North-Eastern and North-Western Rhodesia: to reduce administrative costs. They tried to make the scheme attractive to the settlers in Southern Rhodesia by depicting the country north of the Zambesi as a land of rich natural resources—though the wealth of the copper-belt was as yet unknown—and by the argument that Rhodesia as a whole would gain enhanced importance through amalgamation and through the extension of elective representation in the legislature to settlers in the north. If Sir Drummond Chaplin had been more tactful in his advocacy of the proposal, it might possibly have gained the support of a majority of the elected members in the Southern Rhodesian legislature. In the event, however, it was rejected, because its acceptance would have been likely to retard the attainment of responsible government, the settlers' chief political objective, by doubling the number of Africans whom they would have had to manage without bringing any comparable increase in their own numbers or financial resources. And without the approval of the settlers the Company could not obtain that of the Imperial Government.

After the ending of Company rule in 1923-4, it seemed for a time as if the new Protectorate north of the Zambesi had more in common with the older Protectorate on its eastern border and with the three dependent territories farther north on the East African mainland—Tanganyika, Kenya and Uganda—than with the self-governing colony in the south. In 1924 a Parliamentary Commission visited all five territories, and for the next few years, when the question of 'closer union' in East Africa was being discussed, it was discussed with reference to them all.

In November 1927 Mr. L. S. Amery, as Secretary of State for the Colonies, appointed a commission, with Sir Hilton Young as Chairman, to enquire into the desirability of federation or some other form of closer union between all five territories. The commission reported in January 1929. It recommended the establishment of a Central Authority for Kenya, Uganda and Tanganyika, but found that this group did not have adequate communications with Northern Rhodesia or even with Nyasaland, nor did it have sufficient community of interests with them, to justify their inclusion within the jurisdiction of the proposed Central Authority. The commission then turned its attention to the possibility of forming a second group of territories, by linking Northern Rhodesia and Nyasaland to Southern Rhodesia.

It found that since the referendum in 1923 the large minority in Southern Rhodesia which had then voted in favour of joining the Union of South Africa had greatly diminished, and that the policy which was now generally acceptable was one of cautious advance towards a 'Greater Rhodesia', possibly including Nyasaland. One reason for this change of attitude was the defeat of the Smuts Government by General Hertzog's Nationalists; another reason (not mentioned in the report) was the recent discovery of the wealth of the copperbelt.

In Northern Rhodesia and Nyasaland the opinion of the settlers was divided. In the railway belt it was, on the whole, favourable to amalgamation, though some doubted whether Northern Rhodesia could hope for enough representation in a joint legislature to safeguard her special interests. In the Fort Jameson area, where the tobacco-planters relied on the Nyasaland Railway, it was opposed to any union with Southern Rhodesia unless Nyasaland were included. In Nyasaland the trading interests and the larger planters were uneasy about Southern Rhodesia's native policy; the smaller farmers, however, favoured it, and expressed dislike of what they called the 'pro-native' policies pursued in Tanganyika and Uganda.

The commissioners themselves were unable to agree in their recommendations. Sir Hilton Young submitted a minority report in favour of uniting the central part of Northern Rhodesia —the railway belt and all north-western Rhodesia except the Barotse Province—with Southern Rhodesia; Barotseland should be administered by the Rhodesian Government as an inalienable reserve; north-eastern Rhodesia should be united with Nyasaland, and this enlarged Nyasaland should be loosely linked to the new Rhodesian state through the Governor—not the Government—of Southern Rhodesia.

The other three commissioners, of whom Dr. J. H. Oldham was the most notable, rejected any proposal 'to place any further tracts with a large native population under the Government of Southern Rhodesia until that Government has demonstrated its ability to cope with the extensive native problems that already confront it'.[1] For various reasons they thought it 'premature' to partition Northern Rhodesia so as to include only the railway belt in the enlarged Southern Rhodesia. For the present, therefore, they thought the best course was 'to maintain the independent status' of the two Protectorates. The question clearly was one of race relations as well as of economics. Sir Hilton Young was preoccupied with the economic interdependence of the three territories, whereas Dr. Oldham and his colleagues were primarily concerned with the Imperial responsibility to promote social justice in the East African dependencies. That is why the three Commissioners could not support the recommendations made by their Chairman.

In the following year, 1930, Lord Passfield issued his uncompromising *Memorandum on Native Policy in East Africa*. It was the shock that they received from this pronouncement that drove the settlers of Northern Rhodesia to cast aside all doubts and hesitations about the desirability of amalgamation with Southern Rhodesia. If the British Government was going to insist on 'the paramountcy of native interests', and was there-

[1] Cf. the passage from the report quoted above, pp. 174–5.

fore going to deny them the steady advance to self-government on which they had previously counted, then, as they said in their protest, 'they may seek, and find, sympathy and aid (interested thought it may be) from neighbouring colonies enjoying freer institutions and more equitable opportunities'; that is, Southern Rhodesia and possibly even the Union of South Africa.

Such an attempt to circumvent the British Government's position was so obvious that it could not succeed at once. Yet in 1931 the Government was bent on conciliating the settlers, and in addition it did not wish to offend the Southern Rhodesians. It therefore temporised instead of being categorical. In a statement of 2nd July 1931 it admitted that it did not wish to reject the idea of amalgamation 'in principle', for all time; it said that it 'fully realise[d] the prejudicial effect upon progress in both countries if such a rejection were regarded as a permanent bar to their future evolution'. This was virtually an invitation to renew the pressure after a decent interval.

Accordingly, in January 1936, a conference was held at Victoria Falls, attended by all the elected members of the Northern Rhodesian Legislative Council and by representatives of all three political parties in Southern Rhodesia, and it resolved that: 'This Convention is of the opinion that the early amalgamation of Northern and Southern Rhodesia under a Constitution conferring the right of complete self-government is in the interests of all the inhabitants of both Colonies.'

As a result of discussions which followed the passing of this resolution, a royal commission was appointed in March 1938, with Viscount Bledisloe as Chairman, to enquire 'whether any, and if so what, form of closer co-operation or association between Southern Rhodesia, Northern Rhodesia and Nyasaland is desirable and feasible, with due regard to the interests of all the inhabitants, irrespective of race, of the Territories concerned and to the special responsibility of Our Government in the United Kingdom of Great Britain and Northern Ireland for the interests of the Native inhabitants.'

The royal commission was not a body of comparable calibre with the commission which had reported ten years previously.

For the sake of producing an agreed report it carefully blurred issues of principle, not realising that where principles are undefined policies will drift, and the direction in which they will drift will be that in which they are pushed by interested parties. Yet what authority the agreed report would otherwise have possessed was undermined by the action of its members in adding concluding notes in which each explained how far he agreed or disagreed with the main document to which he had put his signature.

The commission presented its report on 1st March 1939. It expressed the view that the problems confronting the three territories were 'fundamentally similar', and that Southern Rhodesia 'stands to benefit if her future is planned as part of a "bloc" of British territory stretching from the Limpopo to the southern boundary of Tanganyika'. Northern Rhodesia and Nyasaland, it added, with no great air of conviction, 'should also derive some advantage', since their own resources were unlikely to attract the European enterprise necessary for development. Why a closer political union with Southern Rhodesia should serve as a substitute for natural resources in attracting privately owned capital to such regions as the Bemba, Chewa or Tonga country is a question which the commission did not attempt to answer.

It believed that the three territories would 'become more and more interdependent in all their activities, and that identity of interests [would] lead them sooner or later to political unity'. Nevertheless it recognised that the native policy of Southern Rhodesia was 'in some respects restrictive', and, 'if persisted in, [would] limit the opportunities open to Africans, as they gradually emerge from their present backward condition'; it therefore thought that amalgamation should not be put into effect until there was 'a greater degree of certainty' than there was at that time that the policy of 'parallel development', with whatever modifications might be adopted, was in the best interests of the Africans.

The commissioners also called attention to 'the striking unanimity' of African opinion in Northern Rhodesia and

Federation

Nyasaland in opposing the withdrawal of the Crown's protection consequent upon the merging of these territories with Southern Rhodesia, and they were 'agreed in doubting the practical wisdom' of amalgamation as long as African fears and suspicions remained alive and threatened to 'prejudice the prospect of co-operation in ordered development' in the united territory.

They proposed, therefore, that in the immediate future unity should be promoted solely by co-operation between the three Governments; there should be neither unification nor even federation. Nevertheless they assumed, for no explicit reason, that the obstacles would before long disappear, and that the United Kingdom Government would be justified in proceeding at once to announce its acceptance of the policy of amalgamation in principle, while postponing indefinitely the adoption of that policy in practice.

Had the British Government made such a statement, it can hardly be doubted that the Protectorates would in due course have been absorbed in a Dominion of Rhodesia. But, just when the Prime Minister of Southern Rhodesia was in London for discussions, Hitler invaded Poland, and further consideration of the matter had to be postponed. It was not until 18th October 1944 that Colonel Stanley, as Secretary of State for the Colonies, announced in the House of Commons that the British Government had 'after careful consideration, come to the conclusion that the amalgamation of the Territories under existing circumstances cannot be regarded as practicable'. In reply to questions he made it clear that by 'existing circumstances' he was referring not merely to the fact that the World War was still continuing, but to disagreement on the subject of native policy.

Colonel Stanley also stated, however, that the Government recognised the desirability of 'the closest possible co-ordination of the policy and action of the Governments of the three Territories' in such matters as communications, economic relations, industrial development, research, labour, education, agriculture and health; with this end in view a permanent Central African Council, assisted by a permanent secretariat, was to be set up. The creation of this Council had been suggested by the royal commission as a practical step which could be taken at once, to improve the methods and strengthen the habit of co-operation between the three territories, and thereby to help to smooth the way to eventual amalgamation. In certain matters the habit of co-operation was already well developed. Arrangements had been made for European children from Northern Rhodesia and Nyasaland to receive their secondary education in Southern Rhodesia, since no provision for it existed in the Protectorates themselves; in 1937 there were 209 children from Northern Rhodesia and 70 from Nyasaland at school in the Colony. Again, the 'Salisbury agreement' on migrant labour had been concluded in 1936. In addition, there was a good deal of exchange of scientific information concerning agricultural, medical and veterinary problems, there was consultation about the development of communications in the common interest, the same banknotes circulated in the three territories, and coin minted in Southern Rhodesia was legal tender in the Protectorates, along with United Kingdom coins. The task of the Central African Council was to stimulate and guide this tendency toward inter-governmental co-operation. But the Council was not an executive body, still less a legislative one. It was merely an agency for consultation and co-operation, and the three territorial Governments did not give up any of their powers to it. The Governor of Southern Rhodesia was its Chairman, and its most important members were the Prime Minister of Southern Rhodesia and the Governors of Northern Rhodesia and Nyasaland.

Sir Godfrey Huggins, the Prime Minister of Southern Rhodesia, said afterwards (on 3rd December 1949) that it was 'nothing more than a sop', and that his cabinet had agreed to it only because they thought it would bring them a stage nearer to amalgamation.

But on 5th February 1947 Mr. Creech Jones told the House of Commons that the British Government still adhered to the view expressed by Colonel Stanley in 1944, that amalgamation was not practicable in 'existing circumstances'. In the following year, when the dominant unofficial member of the Northern

Federation

Rhodesian Legislative Council, Mr. Welensky, was in London trying to obtain fully responsible government for his own territory, he discussed the question of amalgamation both with Mr. Creech Jones, the Secretary of State for the Colonies, and with Colonel Stanley, who was now in Opposition; he found both of them determined never to accept amalgamation.

Colonel Stanley, however, suggested that he take up a policy of federation as a compromise. The idea was not new, but although it had been considered by both the Commission on Closer Union (1927–9) and the Rhodesia-Nyasaland Royal Commission, they had both rejected it on the ground that any scheme of federation between a self-governing colony and two dependent territories could only lead to endless friction between the federal Government and the Colonial Office. But by 1948 Northern Rhodesia—though not Nyasaland—had reached the very threshold of responsible government. The United Kingdom authorities had no intention of effacing themselves completely, but on the other hand they could scarcely pretend that they were still in full control. If such an unpromising constitutional arrangement could be made to work tolerably well in one territory, might it not work equally well in a federation of the three? The Colonial Office could then continue to act as trustee for African interests in the two Protectorates, while giving the settlers' elected representatives a free hand in the economic development of the whole region.

Mr. Welensky returned to Africa convinced that the cause of amalgamation was hopeless, but that a policy of federation had a reasonable prospect of success. With some difficulty he persuaded Sir Godfrey Huggins to join him in pursuing the more modest aim.

Accordingly, in February 1949 a conference of delegates from the three territories met for two days at Victoria Falls; its Chairman was Sir Miles Thomas, who was in Southern Rhodesia to advise the Government in drawing up an ambitious programme of economic development. Sir Godfrey Huggins and Mr. Welensky both took part in the proceedings, and under their influence a resolution in favour of federation was passed unanimously. It was agreed that the Australian system should be taken as a model. When the conference was over Sir Miles Thomas told the press that not only had the foundations been laid but the house had been built, and all that remained was to move in the furniture and fittings.

But if the house had been built it had been without the approval of the planning authority in London, and without any attempt to ascertain the views of most of the people who were to live in it—the Africans. According to *The Times*, however, 'there appeared to be general agreement that Africans would not oppose federation as they had opposed amalgamation, and that thus the Colonial Office's consent to federation might be expected'—especially as Sir Godfrey had said that he would not oppose the nomination of some Africans to the Upper House of the federal legislature.

Two months later Mr. Creech Jones visited the three territories, and was assailed with complaints of the complete insufficiency of the Central African Council, which, he was told, was altogether unacceptable as a substitute for federation. He replied that, if the need was so great and the Council so unsatisfactory, it was odd that the matter had never been laid before him in a single official dispatch. In the absence of any cogently argued case in favour of federal institutions rather than functional co-operation, he could only conclude that the actual practical necessities were being met perfectly adequately by the existing machinery, and that the settlers were simply aspiring to an increase in political power for its own sake. In a farewell broadcast from Lusaka he did promise that the British Government would 'study' any proposals on federation submitted to it, 'but', he added, 'it cannot transfer its trust and neglect its solemnly pledged duties'.

By the end of the year the high hopes entertained in February had sunk very low. 'Since the war,' Sir Godfrey Huggins complained in a bitter speech on 3rd December, 'I have had several talks with Ministers of the present British [Labour] Government, and it became apparent to me that amalgamation was looked upon by them with even greater disfavour than by their predecessors in office [the wartime coalition]. I say this with deep regret, but it is perfectly plain to me that we in this country are not considered fit and proper persons to whom the future destinies of native Central African people should be entrusted.' When the idea of federation was taken up in place of amalgamation, the problem, he said, was to determine what part the Africans should be allowed to play in federal politics. 'I gather that the United Kingdom Government would require representation of Africans by Africans from the start. I am quite sure that the time has not arrived for that, and further that there are as yet not enough civilised natives to justify one constituency; so, while the ultimate participation of Africans in the central Government was accepted, the fact that they are not yet ready seems to provide a complete deadlock.'

From this languishing condition the cause of federation was rescued by the British General Election of February 1950. The huge Labour majority in the previous Parliament was almost wiped out, and among the casualties was the Secretary of State for the Colonies, who consequently lost his office. Mr. Creech Jones is a man whose lifelong passion has been the study of colonial problems and the endeavour to redress injustices and promote advancement among the dependent peoples of the British Empire; he was thoroughly familiar with the background to the demand for federation, and profoundly distrusted the motives of its Rhodesian advocates. His successor, Mr. James Griffiths, had had little if any previous acquaintance with African affairs, and, like most Ministers in comparable circumstances, was amenable to the guidance of his professional advisers. One has only to refer to the names of the civil servants who took part in the London Conference in March 1951, and who then produced the first rough draft of the federal constitution, to realise that the idea of federation had powerful advocates in the Colonial Office itself and in both the Protectorates. Indeed the Governor of Northern Rhodesia, Sir Gilbert Rennie, was so much in accord with the Rhodesian politicians that he was appointed to be the Federation's first High Commissioner in London.

Federation

So, before the year 1950 was out, Mr. Griffiths announced that the British Government had formed the conclusion that there should be a fresh examination of the question of closer union between the Rhodesias and Nyasaland, and had accepted a suggestion by Sir Godfrey Huggins that a conference of officials from the Colonial Office, the Commonwealth Relations Office and the three territories concerned should be held in London for this purpose. His statement, it is true, contained important reservations: first, the work of the conference was to be 'purely exploratory', so that none of the participating governments would be committed to adopting any proposals it might make; secondly, African opinion in Northern Rhodesia and Nyasaland would be consulted, and full account would be taken both of it and of the British Government's special responsibilities in the two Protectorates. Nevertheless the conference could hardly have been expected to do otherwise than try to chart a navigable passage between settler ambitions on the one hand and, on the other, Britain's responsibilities as trustee for the native populations. It could therefore be expected to recommend federation, though on terms rather more favourable to the Africans than those agreed upon at Victoria Falls in 1949. This it did in a report published in June 1951.

It expressed the view that there was 'a compelling case' for establishing an effective form of closer union between the territories, and it repeatedly emphasised that the need was urgent. In support of this conclusion it dwelt upon the economic interdependence of the three territories, and upon the increased prosperity and improved welfare services which closer association would bring. This economic argument for federation came to be almost universally accepted in Britain, without detailed examination, and was not subjected to close scrutiny until the federation had already existed for several years. *The Economist* did indeed look at it with academic detachment, in an article in the issue of 23rd June 1951, and dismissed it as totally unconvincing. But *The Economist* did not press the point, because it was itself at that time favourably disposed towards federation on political grounds.

Federation

In 1951 it was Afrikaner, not African, nationalism which was regarded as the threat to partnership between the races in the Rhodesias, and the recent formation of an Afrikaner party (the 'Democratic Party'), in Southern Rhodesia, had made the threat seem more serious than it really was. Moreover, the Afrikaners actually formed a proportionally larger minority of the white population in Northern than in Southern Rhodesia, so that if South African influence extended northward to the Zambesi it would reach still farther north, and cause trouble among the white miners in the copperbelt. The conference of officials expressed anxiety about 'the course of native policy south of the Limpopo', and believed that the three territories would be better able to preserve and develop a distinctive way of life—a partnership of races as opposed to segregation and domination—if they combined to form a single bloc.

Mr. Griffiths and his advisers were sincerely convinced that federation was in the interests of the Africans as well as of the white Rhodesians. But Mr. Griffiths attached the greatest importance to convincing the Africans that this was so, and persuading them to be willing participants in the new enterprise. In a letter to *The Times* on 23rd September 1959, he discussed the immediate sequel to the officials' report in an attempt to justify his own conduct:

'We as a Labour Government regarded a decision on this matter, which inevitably affected the whole future destiny of these peoples, as one which they themselves should take. Neither we nor officials in the colonial service had any right to take this highly important decision for them. As democratic Socialists we believe in the right of all individuals to determine their own future.

'I spent some weeks in the two protectorates and had full consultations with representatives of the African people and the other communities. I was convinced then, and have seen no reasons since to depart from my view, that in an important matter of this kind the Secretary of State should himself consult the people concerned and not leave it to the officials. My colleague, Mr. Patrick Gordon-Walker, who was then Secretary of

Federation

State for Commonwealth Relations, undertook similar consultations in Southern Rhodesia.

'Following these talks a conference which both of us attended was held at Victoria Falls at which all the communities were represented. No final decision was taken at the conference—it was understood that further consideration would be given to the proposals. We were left in no doubt, however, that African opinion was overwhelmingly hostile to the federal scheme.'

In short: the decision must rest with the Africans; the Africans were overwhelmingly hostile to the scheme; no decision was taken, and the proposals were to receive further consideration.

No one is likely to question Mr. Griffiths' integrity or goodwill. But after his discussions at Victoria Falls he was torn between his conviction that federation was in the best interests of everyone concerned, including the Africans, and his doctrine that the Africans must choose for themselves. He was sorely perplexed, and he drifted, until, a month later, he was relieved of his responsibilities as a result of the change of Government (October 1951).

The next Secretary of State, Mr. Oliver Lyttelton, showed no such indecision. Once he had made up his mind that federation would have solid advantages and that the safeguards for African interests were perfectly adequate, he pressed ahead with all the vigour and singleness of purpose of a highly successful business man. A succession of further conferences and discussions was necessary before the federal scheme assumed its final shape, but early in 1953 the last details were settled, and, at a referendum held in Southern Rhodesia on 9th April, the proposed constitution was approved by a majority of nearly 2 to 1. The opposition to it in Southern Rhodesia came from the more uncompromising supporters of white supremacy and racial segregation, who distrusted the new orthodoxy of inter-racial partnership on which the advocates of federation took their stand. The fact that the constitution was attacked by white champions of European interests in Southern Rhodesia as well as by black champions of African interests in the Protectorates enabled its sponsors in Britain to represent it as a wise, statesmanlike middle course between the ruinous follies of opposing extremists. On 1st August 1953 the Federation of Rhodesia and Nyasaland (Constitution) Order in Council was issued, giving the constitution the force of law, and on 3rd September the Federation came into being.

In imposing the constitutional link with Southern Rhodesia upon the Protectorates the Conservative Government minimised the extent and importance of African opposition, attributing it to the self-interested misrepresentation of a small number of nationalist politicians. Its spokesmen rightly scorned the argument, freely used by these politicians, that federation would be followed by a northward rush of white settlers to occupy Native Trust Land in the Protectorates: the Orders in Council safeguarding Native Trust Land lost none of their effectiveness through the establishment of the federal authority. But Mr. Lyttelton and his colleagues wrongly went on to assert that as soon as the mass of the African people found that federation left them wholly unaffected, except for improved social services made possible by greater financial resources, the opposition would wither away and the nationalist demagogues would come to be despised as charlatans. They under-rated the depth of the fear and abhorrence with which ordinary Africans looked upon the transfer to Southern Rhodesia of any part of the authority previously exercised by the Colonial Office. Large numbers of men in both Nyasaland and Northern Rhodesia had first-hand knowledge of conditions in Southern Rhodesia, having worked there as migrant labourers; and although they were attracted by the wages which could be earned in Salisbury or Bulawayo, they were conscious when there of belonging to what was generally looked upon as a subject people, whereas in their own country they felt free. Southern Rhodesia, they said, was a good place in which to work, but a bad place in which to live.

Technically, of course, it was quite incorrect to regard federation as a transfer of power in whole or in part from the Colonial Office to the Colony. On the contrary, Southern Rhodesia was on the same footing as Northern Rhodesia and Nyasaland in giving up certain of its own powers to the new federal Govern-

ment and legislature; and in the legislature—the single-chamber
Federal Assembly—she was to be represented by only 17 of the
35 members. But the technicalities of constitutional law were not
the same as the political realities. The point of view of the elected
white representatives of Northern Rhodesia and even of Nyasaland differed little if at all from that of the Southern Rhodesian
contingent, and between them they had 26 of the 35 seats. It
could certainly be said with truth that the Federation was
created by the partial transfer of power to the white community.

It was, indeed, also true that the powers which were transferred did not include the control of African affairs. But the last
clause of the constitution itself provided that the constitution
was to be reviewed not less than seven nor more than nine years
from its coming into force, by a conference consisting of delega-
tions from the Governments of the United Kingdom, the
Federation, and the three territorial Governments—and who
could tell what would happen then? Did not the preamble express the hope that the Federation would 'go forward with confidence towards the attainment of full membership of the
Commonwealth'? This was, indeed, to be the culmination of
the achievement of partnership between the races, and was to
take place when the inhabitants of the Federation so desired.
But who could say when partnership had been achieved? And
would 'inhabitants' be interpreted to mean anything more than
'voters', the great majority of whom would be white? Was it
not, indeed, reasonable to interpret the preamble and the provision for constitutional review, taken in conjunction, to mean
that the Federal Government could have full independence
within the Commonwealth for the asking, subject perhaps to a
referendum, not later than 1962? And full independence, even
within the Commonwealth, would imply the complete elimina-
tion of the Colonial Office and the United Kingdom Parliament
from the control and protection of Northern Rhodesia and
Nyasaland.

These developments were not inevitable, but they were sufficiently probable to justify anxiety on the part of anyone who
thought it Britain's duty to retain her authority in the two Pro-

tectorates until the Africans were ready to take at least as large a part as the Europeans in governing them. And although a half-educated or wholly illiterate African could not explain his fears in logical terms, and made them appear groundless if he referred to the land issue, it is probable that very large numbers of humble folk sensed something of the kind.

When the cause of federation was tentatively taken up by Mr. Griffiths in 1951, the immediate reaction of most Africans seems to have been one of bewilderment and anxiety. They knew that they wanted to stay out of the Southern Rhodesian sphere of influence, and they relied on the Secretary of State for the Colonies to keep them out of it. Could it really be that he had found a long enough spoon to sup in safety with the vigorously self-assertive settler Government beyond the Zambesi? They went to their district commissioners, trusted friends and counsellors in all things, and asked for advice. But the district commissioners had been silenced, because Mr. Griffiths was too universalist a democrat to allow officials of another race to influence the African people. They could only say: 'This is your affair; make up your own minds.' Yet how could the Africans be considered competent to reach a wise decision on a matter of such weight and complexity if they were not yet competent to exercise the full franchise of citizens in an independent democratic state? Neither Mr. Griffiths nor any other sensible man in Britain thought that the Africans in Nyasaland and Northern Rhodesia were within a long distance of being ready for a democratic constitution, either territorial or federal. That was why Britain must continue to exercise her trust on their behalf. Yet in this one matter of federation these political minors were expected to carry the entire responsibility of adults.

This preliminary period of drift transformed an attitude of suspicion and uncertainty into one of confirmed opposition. The Africans could only suppose that the district commissioners had something sinister to hide, and when, after the change of Government in Britain, the officials were instructed to 'explain' the federal scheme and its advantages, the people had become too distrustful to listen.

Federation

Now that the Federation has come and gone, it is obvious to everyone that a state created mainly to suit the wishes and promote the interests of one-twentieth of its total population had no prospect whatever of long-term survival and development, unless, indeed, it could somehow conciliate its African opponents and enlist their support. But in the early 1950s it was quite impossible to foresee how rapidly African nationalism would grow in militancy, in strength of organisation, and in popular appeal. Those in Britain whose sympathies were with the Africans possessed no more gift of prophecy than did the advocates of federation. They did not argue that it was folly to provoke an awakening of the latent power of the multitude; their sole concern was to protect the weak from the strong, the helpless native population from the confidently thrusting settlers.

During the first half of the Federation's existence, the African nationalist agitation against it appeared to 'practical men' to be a matter of no consequence whatever. Even in Nyasaland, where the agitation was strongest, the violent disturbances of August 1953 in the Cholo district—involving the death of 11 Africans and injury to 72—were caused by agrarian discontent[1] and not by the issue of federation, although the latter did serve to heighten the existing unrest. Apart from this incident there was no serious disturbance or commotion for the next five years. Investors had full confidence in the future, capital flowed in, and the post-war boom continued unchecked. Having gained an overwhelming victory in the first Federal election, on 15th December 1953, Sir Godfrey Huggins ruled almost unchallenged; in 1955 he was raised to the peerage as Lord Malvern, and in the following year, when visiting London to attend the Conference of Commonwealth Prime Ministers, he took the opportunity to ask the British Government to concede what he called 'technical independence' to the Federation.

The purpose of his request, he said, was to enhance the Federation's status in relation to the rest of the world: 'This

---

[1] The reasons for this have been shown above, pp. 210–12. The immediate cause of the commotion in Cholo was a rumour that two Africans had been murdered by Europeans.

would enable us to talk to other countries as a separate state, and not as someone else's child.' The internal structure of the Federation would be in no way affected by the change, which was not intended to lead to 'amalgamation by the back door'; the very suggestion that it would do so was 'poisonous'. The Protectorate status of Northern Rhodesia and Nyasaland could, he said, be safeguarded by treaty between Britain and the newly independent state. But acceptance of this change would have put Britain in the extraordinary legal position of exercising authority within the boundaries of a state as sovereign as herself, and her Government rejected the proposal. As Mr. Wellington Chirwa said in the Federal Assembly: 'There is no such thing as technical independence. . . . If a Dominion is independent it is independent.' The main effect of the incident was to sharpen African suspicions. On the other hand the *Rhodesia Herald*, one of the two leading daily papers in the Federation, denounced the British Government as a 'gutless crew': it was referring, of course, to the Conservatives of the pre-Macleod era, the habitual apologists of the white Rhodesians, and not to the Labour Party, their habitual critics. The *Herald* concluded that, almost to a man, the electorate of the whole Federation desired that all ties with the Colonial Office should be cut.

A few months later Lord Malvern retired from office, and was succeeded as Prime Minister by Sir Roy Welensky. Sir Roy had already acquired a considerable reputation as a formidable public figure in the territorial politics of Northern Rhodesia, and he had worked in Salisbury since the Federation was established as Lord Malvern's foremost Cabinet colleague. Nevertheless he did not at once command the same affectionate loyalty from the electorate of Southern Rhodesia as his veteran predecessor had enjoyed. And by this time a serious challenge to the ruling Federal Party was developing on its right flank. In February 1956 the Dominion Party had been formed, and the Government felt obliged to take the challenge seriously. White Rhodesians were not content to wait indefinitely for independence while it was being granted to the Gold Coast (Ghana) and the Sudan, with Nigeria following at no great distance behind; their patience might not last even until 1960, the earliest date for the promised review of the constitution. It was because of this feeling of impatience among the electorate, and because of the danger that the Dominion party might be able to exploit it sufficiently to win the next Federal election, that Lord Malvern had made his unsuccessful bid for 'technical independence'. Sir Roy could not afford to let the matter rest. He therefore went to London in April 1957 to resume negotiations.

The British Government was ready to do all it could to help him to consolidate his political position in the eyes of his electorate, for it had no wish to see the federal experiment endangered by the victory of a right-wing party devoted to the maintenance of racial segregation. It agreed to entrust responsibility for external affairs to the Federal Government 'to the fullest extent possible, consistent with the responsibility which Her Majesty's Government must continue to have in international law so long as the Federation is not a separate international entity'. It also recognised 'the existence of a convention applicable to the present stage of the constitutional evolution of the Federation, whereby the United Kingdom Government in practice does not initiate any legislation to amend or to repeal any Federal Act or to deal with any matter included within the competence of the Federal Legislature, except at the request of the Federal Government'. This, said Sir Roy at a press conference, ruled out the possibility that the British Labour Party, if in power, 'would endeavour to inflict some of their half-baked ideas on us by legislative act'.

The British Government also agreed that all Civil Services in the Federation, territorial as well as Federal, 'would eventually be locally based, and look for their future to the Federal area'. The conference to review the constitution would be held in the earliest of the three possible years, 1960: it would 'consider a programme for the attainment of such a status as would enable the Federation to become eligible for full membership of the Commonwealth'. And both Governments reaffirmed that 'they are opposed to any proposal either for the amalgamation into a

Federation

unitary state of the Territories now composing the Federation or for the secession of any of those Territories from the Federation'.

'I do not want you to assume that we are not determined to attain independent status within the Commonwealth,' said Sir Roy to the press in London. 'We are—but I believe the time to settle that is in 1960.'

Nor was that all. The Federal Government was already making plans to enlarge the Federal Legislature and to introduce a new franchise, and there were indications that these plans received British approval at the London conference.

The Constitution Amendment Act, 1957, was passed by the Federal Assembly on 31st July. The number of members was increased from 35 to 59, of whom the two Protectorates still had a majority of one over Southern Rhodesia. In appearance the ratio of African to European representation was not worsened, and was even marginally improved: there were to be four Africans from each territory instead of two, the previous number, and in addition there would continue to be, as there had been before, one European member from each territory charged with representing African interests. But this appearance was belied by the method of choosing the additional Africans from all three territories. All six of them were to be elected by the same almost wholly European electorate as chose the 44 ordinary elected members, voting together with an additional electorate consisting of persons registered on a new 'special' roll, who would have lower qualifications than the electors on the 'general' roll, and most of whom would be Africans. But even the Federal Government, when making out its own case, admitted that 'Africans will not preponderate in special elections [i.e. the election of African representatives] in all Territories at the outset' (Cmnd. 298, paragraph 27); only in Nyasaland was there any likelihood that the Africans on the special roll would outnumber the Europeans on the ordinary roll.

In the event, it was a predominantly European electorate which chose the two additional African members in every one of the three territories. And in the case of Southern Rhodesia it

262

was the predominantly European electorate which had from the beginning chosen the two original African representatives, and also the European representative of African interests. Thus, of the twelve Africans in the enlarged Assembly, only four—two from each of the Protectorates—would be in any genuine sense representative of their own people. If the Europeans, nominated by the Governors of the Protectorates to represent African interests, are included in the reckoning (as they ought to be), the Africans would have six genuine spokesmen in an Assembly of 59, exactly the same number as in the previous Assembly of 35. Their other nominal spokesmen would merely be additional lobby-fodder for Sir Roy Welensky's Government.

The Constitution Amendment Bill was referred to the British Government by the African Affairs Board, a standing committee of the Federal Assembly charged with the duty of watching over African interests, and armed with the constitutional right to ask the Governor-General to reserve any Bill which it deemed to be a 'differentiating measure' for consideration and possible disallowance at Westminster. The Electoral Bill, passed at the beginning of 1958 to give effect to the new franchise arrangements, was likewise a subject of complaint by the Board. But in each case the British Government advised the Queen to issue an Order in Council overriding the Board's objections, and both Bills became law without alteration. The inevitable result was loss of confidence in the practical value of the Board, which had been given great publicity when the federal constitution was being devised and inaugurated, as being a uniquely powerful safeguard for African interests. And, as a result of the constitutional changes and the ensuing elections, the Board itself came to be composed mainly of members of the United Federal Party, who could not protest against any future Bill without defying the authority of their own party and so destroying their own prospects of re-election.

When the Federal election was fought at the end of 1958, Sir Roy Welensky met the strong challenge of Mr. Winston Field's right-wing Dominion Party by refraining from advocating a more liberal racial policy than that of his opponents, and by concentrating on demonstrating to the electorate the inexperience and incompetence of the Dominion Party's leaders, in contrast with the proven ability and successful record of his own Cabinet. The electorate was satisfied: it gave him forty-six seats, while Mr. Field's Opposition gained only eight.

But Sir Roy and the electorate which he had come to personify had overreached themselves. By their impatient desire for more power and their indifference to African resentment they had already initiated their own overthrow.

CHAPTER 11

Malawi, Zambia, Zimbabwe

In the modern world no state can long survive unless its unity and its institutions are upheld by a national consciousness shared by all, or almost all, its people. Only the sense of community, of having more interests in common than in conflict, can generate the loyalty without which even the most imposing governmental authority is brittle and insecure.

The Federation of Rhodesia and Nyasaland rested upon the support of its dominant white minority; its initial success was made possible by the apathy or sullen acquiescence of most of the Africans, since those few prosperous and contented Africans who gave it their active loyalty were quite unrepresentative of the great majority of their own race. Its most vital need was to broaden the basis of its support by inspiring in its non-white population a pride in being Rhodesians, fellow citizens of the white people and fellow workers in building the future as a united nation.

In retrospect this may appear to have been impossible. Why, it may be asked, should Africans have agreed to share the future with a European minority, when by uncompromising hostility they could hope to win the entire future for themselves? No doubt some of their politicians would, in any event, have insisted on 'one man one vote' at the earliest possible opportunity, so that they could ride to absolute power on the support of the ignorant masses. No doubt, too, the eventual attainment of universal suffrage was almost inevitable, and was in principle greatly to be desired—but only when the masses had sufficiently emerged from their primeval poverty and ignorance to be capable of exercising the authority of an electorate in such a way as to make responsible democratic government a reality and not an ideological illusion.[1] But in the early 1950s it was not yet too late for the white community to try to make common cause with the emerging African middle class, including a fair proportion of its better educated members, in support of the 'civilised and responsible' standards which Sir Roy Welensky and other ministers repeatedly claimed to be upholding. The greater its success in winning over these people to its own side, the more time it would have for the great tasks of economic development and mass education.

No one realised this more clearly than Sir John Moffat, the grandson of J. S. Moffat and a prominent member of the Northern Rhodesian Legislative Council. On 29th July 1954 he introduced in the Council the famous 'Moffat Resolutions', which were adopted by acclamation with only one dissentient voice. They were aimed at the removal of all racial discrimination and all fear of racial domination; they were, he said, merely the highest common factor on which agreement might at that time be hoped for; 'this policy of partnership can mean a great deal more, but it cannot, to my mind, possibly mean anything less. . . . The core of the problem is how to find a system of government which will permit each race in Northern Rhodesia to make its full contribution towards the common good, and which will permit every individual in this territory to feel that he is a free man living in a free society of which he is proud to be a member. A solution is of tremendous importance to every African, but it is of absolutely vital importance to Europeans. . . . To me, Sir, the big question mark in Central Africa—if a permanent solution to the race problem is not found—is not African progress, but European survival as a political force or even as a civilising influence.'

[1] Of course it is true, as has often been remarked, that illiteracy may be combined with great practical shrewdness, and that, conversely, the highly educated man may be (and, in my experience, often is) a fool. But the illiterate's shrewdness can hardly extend beyond those local matters of which he has direct personal knowledge.

Malawi, Zambia, Zimbabwe

These were prescient words. But the acceptance of the Moffat Resolutions did not alter the law, nor did Sir John's grave eloquence prevail against the established customs of white society in Northern Rhodesia. The artisans of the copperbelt continued to combine proletarian uncouthness with the insolence of the *nouveau riche*. When a British Member of Parliament, Mr. Stonehouse, was deported by the Federal Government for telling Africans to stand up for their rights, he was jeered at by a crowd in Ndola with shouts of 'White Kaffir', 'Live in the compound next time,' and 'Go back to your black mammy.' Africans still had to put up with being called 'Kaffir', 'boy', and 'munt'. The long rearguard action against African advancement in the mines continued after the compromise of 1955, and was not finally ended until November 1960. And it was not until that same year that the Race Relations Ordinance was passed by the Legislative Council, making racial discrimination in such places as hotels, restaurants and cinemas a punishable offence. This legislation was deemed necessary after an eminent Nigerian, Sir Francis Ibiam, was refused a cup of tea at a café in Chingola; insults to distinguished foreigners were much more embarrassing to the authorities than similar insults to the people of the territory itself—even though some of the latter might be potential cabinet ministers. Such was Mr. Sikota Wina, who went to the restaurant car of a Rhodesia Railways train, politely asked for something to eat, and was told 'to get back with the Kaffirs where he belonged'. And this, he commented, occurred on a transport system under the direct control of the Federal Government, 'the great apostles of partnership'.

'I am regarded in my own country as a second-class citizen,' said Mr. Kenneth Kaunda in 1960. He went on to relate how, in April 1957, he had gone into a café in Kitwe, asked for sandwiches, and been told, 'boys are not served here'; he was then thrown outside by European customers. 'If this discrimination was on the grounds of education,' he went on, 'many Africans in spite of handicaps could remedy this situation by taking to night studies, as many of them are doing today. If this was an economic bar we could overcome it, as some of our people are fast doing. One could even change one's religion. But God has made me black, there is nothing I can do about it. This does not mean that I am not proud of my colour.'

At the Federal level, Sir Roy Welensky said that he deplored the 'pinpricks' of the social colour bar, but that they could not be removed by legislation, because changes in social conventions could not be forced. This meant that the wounded feelings of the progressive African—the increasingly important middle class who had most occasion to visit such places as hotels and offices—were less important than the prejudices of the average European. And, from the point of view of short-term political expediency, he was probably right—for the Europeans had votes, and the Africans did not have enough of them to matter. When Sir Edgar Whitehead was asked what, in his opinion, was the chief reason why he lost the Southern Rhodesian election of 1962, he replied without a moment's hesitation, 'Because we proposed to legislate against racial discrimination in public places.'

As for Sir John Moffat, he became increasingly disillusioned; he turned against the federal experiment after the British Government overrode the African Affairs Board in 1957, and attempted to build a genuinely non-racial party in opposition to the United Federal Party: first the Central Africa Party, in which he joined forces with a like-minded group in Southern Rhodesia led by Mr. Garfield Todd, then the Liberal Party, which was confined to Northern Rhodesia. But he was too liberal for more than a handful of Europeans, and too conciliatory for more than a handful of Africans. At last, when his party had been ruined by defeat in the election of 1962, he decided that the only way in which he could still promote the cause in which he believed was to throw in his lot completely with African nationalism, and to join the United National Independence Party led by Mr. Kaunda.

Magni esse mereamur—let us deserve to be great—was the motto of the Federation. White Rhodesians interpreted this in terms of enterprise and hard work, leading to economic development; they looked at the mighty Kariba dam, the Federation's enduring monument, and congratulated themselves on having fulfilled their aspirations. Now, it is altogether foolish to blame or deride them for emphasising the importance of economic development, without which the prospects before a rapidly expanding population would have been miserable indeed. And yet the greatness by which states stand and prosper is, in the last resort, greatness of spirit, not the greatness of the gross national product. White Rhodesians were assuredly no more lacking in this respect than any other community, white or non-white, in Africa, Europe or elsewhere. It was not, after all, in Salisbury that non-white students required the protection of armed police in order to avail themselves of their lawful right to enter the university. And yet, in the supremely important matter of race relations, the Federation allowed its motto to turn to irony, to become its indictment.

It is true that there were great improvements. They had begun before 1953, and they continued at least until the change of Government in Southern Rhodesia in December 1962. But the most active period of reform was the early 1960s, and by that time the Africans had been so aroused that they no longer cared about the removal of 'pinpricks', and would be satisfied with nothing less than power: not a small share of power, giving them the status of junior partner with the white Rhodesians; not even a preponderance of power; but power absolute and unfettered, based on universal suffrage—'one man one vote'.

Nationalism in Africa both resembles and differs from nationalism in Europe. The resemblance lies in the demand for a government based upon one's own people, instead of alien rule. And, in Africa as in Europe (or in Asia), this demand acquires such an intensity that its fulfilment comes to be regarded as the one thing which is all-important, to which everything else, including the basic moral obligations of human beings, is subordinated; it is deemed to be the one Absolute Good. For this reason it has often been called a religion; it vies with Marxism for the dedicated devotion of twentieth-century idolaters.[1]

---

[1] I do not, of course, wish to imply that nationalism is intrinsically evil,

Malawi, Zambia, Zimbabwe

In Europe, however, nationalism was the assertion of the historic identity and collective personality of limited though large groups of people: of Poles or Greeks, Germans, Italians, Hungarians, Irishmen or Finns. In Africa the only possible comparable development would have been a reversion to tribalism. But Africans had no wish to revert to tribalism, much as they might long to be able to take pride in their pre-colonial past. The presence of the white man had awakened a consciousness of being African, a consciousness which could never have developed in his absence. Members of tribes which had formerly hated and harried each other came to realise that they had blackness in common, and that they were equally subject to the power and arrogance of people who, by contrast, were not black. Hence, in Africa, nationalism and Pan-Africanism are inseparable, and are almost alternative names for the same phenomenon.

When this general characteristic of African nationalism has been pointed out, it must nevertheless be added that in Nyasaland, the part of the Federation where nationalism developed most early and most strongly, there was a real sense of a distinctive 'Nyasa' identity already in existence before any widespread nationalist agitation developed. This was not because of any cherished memories of the pre-colonial Maravi (or Malawi) kingdom; the dominant Yao and Angoni had not had any share in that. It was because the Nyasas were in the habit of going to Southern Rhodesia, or to the Rand, as migrant labourers, and there they learnt to congratulate themselves on the freedom which they enjoyed in their own country, as protected persons, in contrast with the subjection of the conquered peoples to the south. The Nyasa's attitude to his docile fellow-Africans in Southern Rhodesia had something of the proud disdain which the free Athenian of antiquity felt towards the 'barbarians' who bowed under the yoke of the King of Persia.

or that every nationalist is an unscrupulous fanatic. It is indeed possible to be both a good nationalist and a good man; this is as true in Africa as in Europe or in India. But although it is possible, it is not, to say the least, altogether usual.

Malawi, Zambia, Zimbabwe

The national consciousness of the Nyasa people did not, then, develop in protest against subjection to alien rule; on the contrary, it was fostered by an awareness of being relatively privileged. The educated African, who throughout the continent has been the leader of the nationalist movement (in face of the apathy, scepticism or outright hostility of the traditional rulers —the chiefs and village headmen), was content to form groups called 'Native Associations' to promote educational and other welfare services. The first of these Native Associations was formed as early as 1912, and the movement spread all over the Protectorate during the inter-war years, most of its members being clerks. When the Bledisloe Commission made its investigation in 1938, the Native Associations were at one with the chiefs in an impressively unanimous and impassioned opposition to the proposed amalgamation of their country with the Rhodesias.

The upheaval of the Second World War, following immediately after the apprehensions aroused by the royal commission, brought about a decisive change, although its full significance was not apparent until much later.[1] A new climate of opinion, largely formed, no doubt, by the militancy of India's demand for independence, led to the formation in 1944 of the African National Congress, an organisation whose leadership and local organisation were provided by the Native Associations, and whose aim was the winning of political power for Africans, through an agitation aimed at gaining representation in the Legislative Council. The Congress soon made itself heartily disliked by the governing officials by its attitude of disrespect towards their benevolent paternalism, and by an impatience for power which the officials considered recklessly foolish in view of the country's economic and social backwardness. Government policy for African advancement was to build up 'native authorities' based as far as possible on traditional institutions, and to give these native authorities representation in Provincial Councils, with a council representing the whole Protectorate at the apex of the pyramid. The Protectorate

[1] Cf. above, p. 206.

Council was purely advisory; all power was in the hands of the Legislative and Executive Councils, under the Governor and ultimately the United Kingdom Government. But for a number of years it was officially regarded as a promising experiment; it was considered to represent the thoughts and feelings of the great majority of the people, in contrast with Congress, which was believed to be merely the voice of a few clamorous malcontents. Yet the Protectorate Council represented the past, with its traditional courtesy and its willing acceptance of the British administrators as protectors, guides and friends; the Congress represented the future, with its brash assertion of the black man's right and determination to take his destiny into his own hands and make or mar it as he himself thought fit.

In Northern Rhodesia a Federation of Welfare Societies was formed in 1946, and in 1948 it reconstituted itself as the Northern Rhodesia Congress; in 1951, under the stimulus of the officials' report recommending federation, it added the words 'African National' to its title. In Southern Rhodesia, where European control was complete enough to discourage opposition, the first attempt at forming a Congress was unsuccessful, and it was not until 1957 that an organisation inspired by those in the two Protectorates and in South Africa, and bearing the same name, came into being.

In both Protectorates the federal scheme was strenuously opposed by Congress, and the failure of this opposition to prevent the introduction of the new constitution led to disillusionment and a temporary loss of influence. But the Congress in Nyasaland recovered its prestige and self-confidence in 1956. In March of that year the African members of the Legislative Council were for the first time elected instead of being nominated; their election was by an indirect method, with the Provincial Councils acting as electoral colleges. (This was in consequence of the constitutional changes introduced in 1955; see above, pp. 217–18.) In these elections the only candidate who was prepared to work within the framework of the Federation received only a single vote. The results were a triumph for Congress, which won all five seats, and the two members with the largest majorities were Mr. H. B. Chipembere and Mr. M. W. K. Chiume, the most militant of the five successful candidates. By showing that even the Provincial Councils were now deeply under the influence of Congress, these results went far to disprove the belief of officials in Zomba and of Government spokesmen in London that Congress was merely a movement of smart young men with enough education to make them conceited but not enough to make them wise, and that it had little influence among simple, decent, respectful country folk.

'No doubt', wrote the Devlin Commission (reporting on the disturbances of three years later), 'it was hoped (by the Government) that the five Africans in the Legislative Council would treat the four years of the legislature's life as a sort of probationary period during which they would put the African viewpoint with moderation and make a thoughtful contribution to the formulation of policy which remained the exclusive responsibility of the Government; this was their chance to learn how to run the estate which would some day be theirs. Instead of that they behaved as if they were the opposition in a fully fledged democracy whose duty it was to harass and criticise the Government. Their speeches are largely designed as propaganda to be printed in Hansard at government expense; Hansard has become a best seller among educated Africans.' Mr. Chipembere stated his own position clearly on 4th July 1958, when commenting on the Government's refusal to reinstate Gomani, the former Chief of the southern Angoni, who had been deposed in 1953 for supporting the Congress campaign of non-co-operation with the Government at the time of federation. 'Anything like moderation will never get us anywhere. The only language which British imperialism can understand is the language of extreme conflict.'

But the real enemy was not 'British imperialism', but federation. The Devlin Commission found that, in 1959, 'even amongst the chiefs, many of whom are loyal to the Government and dislike Congress methods, we have not heard of a single one who is in favour of Federation. Witness after witness appeared before us for the sole purpose of stating that the cause of all the troubles we were investigating was Federation. . . . Very little was said against imperialism. One critic of the Government was so little anti-imperialist in his sentiments that he wound up a denunciation by saying that the Governor was a disgrace to the British Empire. Always Federation was the cause of all the trouble.'

As Messrs. Chipembere and Chiume gradually gained a dominant position in Congress it became apparent to the Europeans in Nyasaland that the previous leaders had been comparatively moderate men. Foremost among these was Mr. Wellington Chirwa, who, with another member of Congress, had been elected as Nyasaland's African representatives in the Federal Assembly. To Mr. Chipembere it appeared that even to take one's seat in such a place implied a measure of acceptance of it, and an intolerable degree of compromise. He insisted that they must resign their seats, and when they refused he caused them to be expelled from Congress. Mr. Chirwa's new-found respectability in European eyes came too late: he was now a man bereft of political influence among his own people. When Congress decided in January 1959 to draw up a black list of 'stooges and quislings', Mr. Chirwa's name was placed at the head of it.

If Congress was to achieve its aim of secession from the Federation, it must first become more than a vehemently but ineffectively protesting minority in Nyasaland's own legislature. The matter became urgent after Sir Roy Welensky's successful visit to London in April, 1957. Two of the concessions gained by Sir Roy caused particular concern in Nyasaland: the conference to review the Federal constitution was to be held in 1960, and was then to prepare the way for the Federation to become a full member of the Commonwealth—that is, a sovereign state independent of Britain. It seemed to Congress, therefore, that it had only three years in which to win control of the territorial Government in time to be able to frustrate Sir Roy's purpose of eliminating Britain's remaining control over the two Protectorates. Yet in the existing legislature they had only five seats, while the combined strength of the officials and the white unofficials was eighteen. They now proposed, in September 1957, that they should have forty seats and that the total number of non-African members should be only eight. And the Executive Council should be elected by the Legislative; they would concede that it should include two officials. Although the Government was willing to consider some further modest increase in African representation, it was totally unprepared to accept proposals so revolutionary as these. In June 1958 the Secretary of State for the Colonies, Mr. Lennox-Boyd, gave a conciliatory but quite inconclusive answer to a delegation which had gone to London to present the proposals to him in person. The leader of the delegation was Dr. Hastings Kamuzu Banda, who had recently agreed to become President of Congress. Early in July he returned to Nyasaland, where he had not set foot since early boyhood.

For some months Dr. Banda had been receiving urgent appeals from Mr. Chipembere and his associates to return to his native land. They themselves were young men in their middle twenties, and they recognised that he, at nearly twice their age, could become the object of popular veneration, of a quasi-religious cult, as none of them could hope to do. He was to be the 'Messiah', returning from afar to deliver his own people from bondage. The thoughts and feelings implanted in the people of Nyasaland by eighty years of Christian missionary effort were to be adapted and exploited for the achievement of a secular objective. Even in the Legislative Council Mr. Chipembere referred to the new President of Congress as 'our Mahatma', 'our Messiah', 'our Saviour'—terms of blasphemous hyperbole which it ill became an elder of the Presbyterian Church to allow anyone to use about himself. But Dr. Banda not only tolerated it, he found it exceedingly gratifying, and it has continued ever since. No politician since the death of Stalin, with the exception of President Nkrumah of Ghana and the late General Trujillo of Dominica, has been the recipient of such unconscionable adulation.

Dr. Banda's record of genuine achievement was, indeed, impressive. A man of humble origins, educated at a mission school in Nyasaland and afterwards in South Africa and the United States, he had graduated in medicine at the University of Edinburgh and then, in 1937, had settled down to medical practice in England, residing in London from 1945 to 1953. But he never lost interest in the affairs of Nyasaland, and in 1949 he joined with Mr. Nkumbula of Northern Rhodesia in preparing a memorandum expressing opposition to federation on the ground that the Africans of Southern Rhodesia were downtrodden and that the inhabitants of the Protectorates ought not to be made to share their fate. This was issued as a booklet in 1951. When, in spite of his efforts, the Federation was set up, he shook the dust of England off his feet and went to settle in Ghana, or the Gold Coast as it was still called, where he formed an enthusiastic admiration for the demagogue-rule of Dr. Nkrumah and the Convention People's Party. It was in Ghana that he received Mr. Chipembere's appeals to return to Nyasaland. He withheld his agreement until March 1958, when he was offered the Presidency of Congress, which had just been rendered vacant by the action of the militants in ousting his namesake, Mr. T. D. T. Banda, from that office.

In Dr. Banda the nationalists found a leader who could talk to any white man on a footing of complete personal equality. But his importance was chiefly as a symbol. By the time he reached Nyasaland on 6th July, an atmosphere of tense and fervent expectation had already been created by Congress propaganda: the Messiah was at hand, coming to deliver his people! He himself, although he had forgotten his own language and could speak only English, was capable of rousing an audience to wild excitement by his emotional rhetoric. As he himself boasted, he set Nyasaland 'on fire' on his triumphal progresses, and although he did not favour or encourage violence he did far too little to discourage it. The small European community and the numerically inadequate police force became thoroughly alarmed. Tension became so great that the Government was capable of believing as sober fact a highly coloured report by a single paid informer that a plot had been hatched to murder all the whites in the country, from the

Malawi, Zambia, Zimbabwe

Governor to the missionaries, and African 'quislings' too. The plot was imaginary, but there was sufficient inflammatory talk of sabotage and violence, including beatings and even killings, to justify the Government in declaring a state of emergency and rounding up the Congress leaders on 3rd March 1959. These arrests precipitated the worst phase of the disturbances in the course of which a total of 51 rioters were killed.

The scale of the disturbances and the extent of the bloodshed compelled the British cabinet to appoint a commission of inquiry, of which the Chairman was Sir Patrick Devlin. Its report, presented in July, contained such a candid and lucid exposition of the situation in Nyasaland that the cabinet was deeply embarrassed. It chose to evade the issue, and rejected the report. In the ensuing controversy in Britain there were some who argued that since it is Governments and not commissions which are responsible, through Parliament, to the electorate, they are perfectly entitled to reject a report which they do not like. But this is to confuse the issue; it is to employ truth to make falsehood plausible. A Government is indeed responsible for policy, and cannot delegate that responsibility to any commission; it has therefore the duty as well as the right to form its own judgement on whatever recommendations are submitted to it. But the Devlin commission was not appointed to formulate policy, but to ascertain facts. It was presided over by one of the most able and respected judges in the realm. To reject its report was, in effect, to declare that facts should be deemed to be un-facts if politicians in office found them inconvenient. Nothing in the record of the Macmillan Government was more discreditable than its bland repudiation of the unpalatable truths contained in this masterly report.

Shortly afterwards the Government won a general election with an increased majority; the British people were too contented with their own prosperity to punish political dishonesty and colonial misrule. Yet the Prime Minister himself was far less complacent than he appeared. As early as 22nd July 1959 he stated in Parliament that the authority of the British Government in Northern Rhodesia and Nyasaland would be preserved until they became fully-self-governing; only then would the Federation go forward to full independent membership of the Commonwealth. In other words, there would be no transfer of Imperial responsibilities in the Protectorates to the Federal authorities, either in 1960 or at any later date. Six months later, speaking in Nigeria on 13th January 1960, he made it explicitly clear that by 'real self-government' he meant that the people must be able to express their will through their own elected representatives; and on the 19th, he repeated this pledge in Salisbury itself, to the consternation of his white hearers and the delight of Africans. One of these, from Northern Rhodesia, is said to have humorously adapted to his own purposes the Americanism with which Mr. Macmillan had won the recent general election campaign: 'We have never heard it so good.'

The most notable of this series of statements was delivered on 3rd February, in Cape Town, in an address to the Parliament of South Africa. There could have been no more dramatic occasion for the affirmation that henceforth it was Britian's policy to seek an accommodation with African nationalism. From this long, urbane, and carefully prepared speech a single phrase lived in the public memory: 'the wind of change'. Having referred to the rise of nationalism, first in Europe, then in Asia, Mr. Macmillan continued: 'Today, the same thing is happening in Africa. The most striking of all the impressions I have formed since I left London a month ago is of the strength of this African national consciousness. . . . The wind of change is blowing throughout the continent. . . . Our national policies must take account of it.'

It is true that he went on to qualify these remarks by declaring, in the orthodox language of the era of 'partnership', that Britain's aim in its dependencies was 'to create a society which respects the rights of individuals; . . . a society in which individual merit, and individual merit alone, is the criterion for man's advancement, whether political or economic'. However sincere this genuflexion to orthodoxy may have been, it was of no practical consequence. For it was not the merit of the individual but the power of the mass which was rousing the wind of change, before which, it was now announced, British policy would in future spread its sails. This is not to say that there was any better policy available; there was none. But the Prime Minister deceived himself and others by pretending that his new policy was better than it was.

While he was making these speeches in Africa, his newly appointed Secretary of State for the Colonies, Mr. Iain Macleod, was presiding over the historic Lancaster House conference at which the balance of power in Kenya was decisively and irrevocably transferred from the side of the white settlers—who were approximately equal in numbers to those in Northern Rhodesia—to that of the Africans. Then, in March, he turned his attention to Nyasaland.

By that time the state of emergency had lasted a full year. Although several hundred of those detained had been released, about two hundred were still in prison, including Dr. Banda himself, who had been removed for greater security to Gwelo in Southern Rhodesia. The Government was in physical control of the country, having quickly regained its grip after a few anxious days when large areas, including virtually the whole of the north, were in the hands of Congress. Individual district commissioners might still be respected and liked. Nevertheless there could be no return to the old contented confidence in the white man's rule; the banned Congress movement had retained the loyalty of the mass of the people, and now a successor to it had been formed by Nyasaland's first African barrister, Mr. Orton Chirwa, so that there would be an organisation already in being for Dr. Banda to lead when he was eventually released. It was called the Malawi Congress Party. Clearly the only alternative to perpetual repression—an impossible policy for any British Government to pursue, since it would involve chronic and increasing political embarrassment at home—was to release Dr. Banda and anxiously hope that concessions would elicit from him the necessary minimum of co-operation. So, on 1st April, he was unconditionally released.

He had not failed to notice Mr. Macleod's handling of the

constitutional problem in Kenya, and he realised that the interests of his own nationalist movement could best be secured by giving the Secretary of State all possible help in bringing about a similar transformation in Nyasaland. He therefore appealed to his supporters for peace and calm. 'Do not spoil my work,' he said. 'If you listen to me you will have your own Government. I want everybody to keep quiet while I go to London.' And, after a visit to London (and also to the United States), he returned in May in high good humour. To the thousands of enthusiasts who acclaimed him at the airport, he said, 'I want to help Mr. Macleod. He is a good man. Many settlers are against him; even some of the Conservatives are against him; but he is the settlers' best friend. He is ensuring their future. He is the settlers' insurance broker.' And he added, 'Do not hate the white man. It is not the white man I am against, but the system.'

It was now possible to end the emergency, to release almost all the remaining detainees, and to convene a conference in London to devise the constitutional arrangements for handing over the government of the Protectorate to the Malawi Congress Party.

Already, during the emergency, the number of African members of the Legislative Council had been increased from five to seven; two more nominated officials had also been added, to retain the official majority. This concession had been received with contempt by the Africans, especially as the two additional African seats—and likewise the two rendered vacant by the arrest of Messrs. Chipembere and Chiume—were filled by nomination, not by election. Nevertheless the change was not wholly without significance, because for the first time the number of Africans now exceeded the number of non-African unofficials, which remained at six. Hence, in the eyes of the United Federal Party (which controlled both the Federal and Southern Rhodesian Governments, and was supported by most Europeans in both the Protectorates), even this modest change had appeared ominous in its implications for the future.

But the new constitution which was agreed upon at the Lancaster House conference at the beginning of August 1960 was incomparably more important than the changes made in the previous year. It might well be described as a revolution achieved with the consent of all parties. The number of officials in the Legislative Council was reduced to five, all of whom owed their seats to the fact that they were also members of the Executive Council. But the number of elected unofficials was increased to twenty-eight. Among these, Africans and non-Africans as such were no longer to be separately represented, but a division on the basis of class served substantially the same purpose. There were to be two electoral rolls: one for the relatively wealthy few, who would have eight representatives; and one with qualifications low enough to enfranchise many thousands of Africans, who would have twenty representatives. Thus the members elected on the lower roll would have a comfortable majority over the upper roll members and the officials combined—if they ever did combine. It was obvious that the Malawi Congress Party would win all twenty of the lower roll seats; it was almost equally obvious that the officials would do their utmost to maintain harmony with the dominant group. The only uncertainty concerned the upper roll members. Since there had never before been direct elections by a mass electorate in Nyasaland, it took a whole year to make the necessary preparations. But when the time came, in August 1961, the United Federal Party gained only five of the eight upper roll seats, and the Malawi Congress Party won the other three. This was largely because the great majority of the Asian community had decided that it could best secure its future by throwing in its lot with African nationalism.

The new constitution provided that the Executive Council should consist of five officials and five unofficials, presided over by the Governor. Of the unofficials, three were to be members of the Legislative Council elected on the lower roll, and the other two were to be members elected on the upper roll. In the event, it was possible for all five to be adherents of the Malawi Congress Party—four Africans and one Scot. With the complete co-operation of the Governor and the officials, Dr. Banda and his supporters were now in full control of the territorial Government.

The constitutional conference had ended in an atmosphere of cordial good will, with Mr. Macleod and Dr. Banda praising each other enthusiastically and Mr. A. C. W. Dixon, the leader of the United Federal Party delegation, accepting with a good grace an arrangement which he realised it would be futile and harmful to oppose.

In the Rhodesias, the United Federal Party accepted the decision on Nyasaland with resignation. But there could be no such acquiescence in any similar decision concerning the constitutional future of Mr. Macleod's other Protectorate within the Federation. Both in its economic resources and in the number of its settled white population, Northern Rhodesia was many times more important than Nyasaland. Besides, if Africans controlled the Governments of two of the three territories, they might be intelligent enough to abandon their demand for secession and instead to demand that they should be given control of the Federal Government. Rather than submit to such a demand, the Southern Rhodesian electorate would insist that Southern Rhodesia should itself secede; its Prime Minister, Sir Edgar Whitehead, had given an explicit warning to that effect on 29th January 1960, a few days after Mr. Macmillan's visit.

In the early years of federation the largest and most influential group in the Northern Rhodesian Legislative Council had continued to be the group of elected members, of whom there were twelve, representing an electorate which was non-racial in principle but was in practice almost wholly European. There were four African members chosen by the African Representative Council, which corresponded to the Protectorate Council in Nyasaland; there were also two Europeans nominated by the Governor to represent African interests. The officials in the Council numbered only eight, sufficient to hold a balance between the two other groups. For a number of years, however, even before federation was introduced, the territory had been on the verge of responsible government, and in 1954 it moved another inch towards that goal when the principle of collective responsibility—as distinct from the individual responsibility of particular members already established in 1949—was recognised.[1]

A new constitution was devised in 1958, with the aim of moving away from separate representation for each race, while ensuring that Africans would still be represented but also that Europeans would remain preponderant. Africans had hitherto been kept off the electoral roll not only by their lack of education and wealth but also by the requirement that a voter must be a British subject. It is true that they could obtain this qualification without much difficulty. But even if they were aware of this, they had no wish to become British subjects, since it was precisely their existing status as 'British protected persons' which differentiated them from their fellow Africans in Southern Rhodesia, who were British subjects in view of the fact that Southern Rhodesia was a colony. The new constitution provided that British protected persons had the same right as British subjects to be registered as voters, and to be eligible as candidates. There was to be a 'special' electoral roll in addition to the ordinary (and much more exclusive) roll, and the qualifications were such that large numbers of Africans would be able to register.

There were to be twenty-two elected members in the new Legislative Council, in addition to six officials and two nominated members. Eighteen of the twenty-two were of unspecified race, two must be Europeans and two must be Africans. Voters on both rolls would vote for all twenty-two seats, but the demarcation of constituencies and the other electoral arrangements were designed to ensure that Europeans would win twelve of the eighteen 'non-racial' seats, and Africans the other six. The other two Africans would represent their race only in name and in appearance, since most of their electors would be white, and it was probable that the successful candidates would be members of the United Federal Party. That party could therefore hope,

[1] See above, pp. 197–8.

at best, to win sixteen seats; the other six would go to Africans who would oppose it. With sixteen seats it would possess an overall majority in a council with a total membership of thirty. It would thus be entitled to demand that all the seats allocated to elected unofficials in the Executive Council should be given to persons nominated by Mr. John Roberts, its leader. There were now to be six such seats, while only four members of the Executive Council would be officials. It is true that two of the six had to be Africans, but if the United Federal Party could provide two Africans from its own ranks this provision would be no obstacle in its path. With an overall majority in both councils it would virtually have attained its goal of responsible government under European control. Sir Roy Welensky, himself a Northern Rhodesian, said cheerfully that if there were sixteen men of his party in the legislature 'it would be a very brave Governor who tried to rule them'.

The ensuing election, held in March 1959, was therefore of vital importance in determining the fate of Northern Rhodesia, which, as the future was to show, carried with it the fate of the Federation itself. But the African National Congress was so disgusted with the new constitution that it was unwilling to take part in the election at all. Like its counterpart in Nyasaland, it feared that European control over the whole Federation would be made complete in 1960 unless the Africans could in the meantime gain a strong enough position to exercise an effective veto. It had therefore demanded, as an immediate step, that the number of elected Africans in the Legislative Council should be as large as that of the elected Europeans and the officials combined. Mr. Kenneth Kaunda, who was then its Secretary-General, relates in his autobiography that he accompanied Mr. Harry Nkumbula, its President, on a visit to the Governor, Sir Arthur Benson, and that the following exchange took place. 'Mr. Kaunda,' said the Governor, 'don't you think Europeans would paralyse Government if we accepted your proposals?' He replied, 'Are you implying, Your Excellency, that for our demands to be met we have got to be in a position to paralyse Government?' His question, he adds, was never answered

Malawi, Zambia, Zimbabwe

(*Zambia Shall Be Free* (Heinemann, 1962), p. 87).[1]

When the Government's constitutional proposals were published, Mr. Nkumbula publicly burnt the White Paper. But the Government stood firm, and he decided to take part in the election rather than to boycott it. As a result, nearly 7,000 Africans registered as electors, and 85·7 per cent of these electors cast their votes. Mr. Nkumbula's aim was at all costs to deprive the United Federal Party of the overall majority which it sought, even if this could only be done by supporting a Dominion Party candidate. The participation of the Congress voters determined the result: the United Federal Party gained only thirteen seats in the legislature, and consequently it had to be content with only five seats in the executive.

Nevertheless the decision to contest the elections had precipitated a revolt against Mr. Nkumbula's leadership, which had already been under criticism for some time on the ground that it was both erratic and dictatorial. Since his grip on the Congress organisation was too strong to be broken, his opponents seceded and formed a new movement called the Zambia African National Congress—the name Zambia being invented, in the absence of a suitable historical alternative, as an 'African' substitute for the name 'Northern Rhodesia'. Mr. Kaunda became its leader. Like the parent Congress it professed to be nonviolent, and Mr. Kaunda's personal sincerity in this matter is, on the whole, convincing, although it would carry more complete conviction if he had shown more awareness of the very considerable extent to which violence was in fact being committed by his adherents. For the Zambia Congress, being the more militant and uncompromising part of the nationalist movement, attracted to itself the greater part of the brutal hooligan element in Northern Rhodesian society—men who had cast off the restraints of traditional tribal discipline without

[1] Sir Arthur was in fact, pro-African; that is why he was anxious that Africans should use their voting strength to the full and not play into the hands of the United Federal Party and of the Federal Government (which he strongly disliked—see his letter in *The Times*, 20 Feb. 1961) by boycotting the election.

paying any heed to the Christian gospel or even picking up the merest shred of Western humanism: men who found arson and even murder an exhilarating diversion. Now, it was the policy of the Zambia Congress to boycott the elections, and a boycott would be ineffective unless it was enforced. Mr. Kaunda himself told a public meeting at Fort Jameson on 26th February 1959, that they must not let *any other* African organisation go to the polls. If he supposed that such a boycott could be enforced in an African situation without violence and terrorism, he was too naïve to be a political leader; if he recognised the necessary consequences of his policy, his Gandhian asceticism and mild-spoken high-mindedness can hardly be altogether without the taint of hypocritical humbug.[1] There can be no doubt that he genuinely disliked violence, and used his influence to minimise its extent; he never planned any kind of violent outbreak. On the other hand, he was not prepared to be deflected from his chosen line of policy by the realisation that it would inevitably involve incidental atrocities. Nevertheless he was by far the best of the militant Congressmen, and if he had not taken the lead someone of coarser grain would have taken it instead.

Left to itself, the Zambia Congress would have made sure that scarcely a single African dared to cast a vote. So, on 11th March, the movement was outlawed, and its leaders restricted or imprisoned. There is no need to suppose that the authorities were unaware of the service that they were doing to their most dangerous opponents by presenting them with the politically invaluable 'prison graduate's cap'. Mr. Kaunda himself relates that a Federal minister visited the prison in which he was being detained, and, when the senior superintendent jocularly remarked, 'This man is here, sir, because he conspired to blow up the British Empire,' the minister replied, 'That should stand

---

[1] In his autobiography (p. 155) he refers to a statement which he issued on 9th February 1961, warning that if his party's demands were not conceded there might be a mass rising in Northern Rhodesia which would make Mau Mau seem a picnic. He explains that he was referring to the massacre of Africans which would occur when such a revolt was suppressed. This seems a singularly disingenuous excuse for a warning which was addressed to the British and Federal Governments, not to his own people.

him in good stead for his future responsibilities.' But, whatever the long-term consequences of the Government's action might be, the immediate need to maintain public order and protect law-abiding people had to be considered paramount. The crisis was far less serious than that in Nyasaland, and by about the beginning of 1960 the men who had been detained had all been set at liberty.

They now reorganised themselves as the United National Independence Party,[1] with Mr. Kaunda as President. The new party quickly established itself as the main nationalist movement in Northern Rhodesia, though the African National Congress remained fairly strong. The rise of the Independence Party was accompanied by a crescendo of violence in the areas where it was strongest, culminating in the notorious incident in May 1960, when a car was stoned and forced to a halt and the driver, Mrs. Burton, was covered with petrol, set on fire, and so hideously burned that she died in hospital a few days later. Already two African women and one African man had been murdered in petrol attacks, but these incidents had attracted less attention. The Governor, Sir Evelyn Hone, now banned all branches of the party in the Copperbelt. 'There is no doubt whatever', he said, 'that the present state of affairs has been brought about and stems directly from the defiant attitude of U.N.I.P., particularly in the Western Province, and its deliberate flouting of the law regarding public meetings and its resistance to the police in enforcing that law.'

Mr. Kaunda was at that time on a visit to the United States, and the temporary removal of his restraining influence may have contributed to the viciousness of his more disreputable adherents. It is important to realise that the party was lamentably short of men of standing to serve as branch leaders; the better type of educated African usually depended for his livelihood on employment as a teacher or civil servant, and was therefore debarred, understandably if perhaps regrettably, from taking any active part in politics. The local leadership therefore too often

---

[1] Since I cannot bring myself to follow the usual practice of calling it 'Unip', I shall refer to it as the Independence Party.

fell into the hands of third-rate men embittered by their own unfitness for doing anything constructive.

'Those of their people who will not follow them, and they are many, must be terrorised into doing so. Hatred of the whites must be brought to boiling point, particularly of those who in such growing numbers are speeding the necessary reforms which they themselves, though this is not their fault, have failed to achieve. It does not suit them that the reforms should now be made, as a U.N.I.P. leader recently made clear to the Select Committee on Racial Discrimination, which he boycotted and which has secured the abolition of discrimination.' It was the correspondent of the *Guardian*, a paper warmly sympathetic to African interests, who wrote these words.[1]

On his way back from the United States Mr. Kaunda visited London and was received by Mr. Macleod, who gave him an assurance that African opinion would be represented at the conference which was to be held later in the year to review the federal constitution. The Northern Rhodesian delegation, like that from Nyasaland, would not be confined to members of the existing Legislative Councils. With this assurance he had perforce to be content, for he was also told that the territorial constitution would not be altered until after the review of the federal constitution.

By this time it was apparent to everyone outside the Rhodesias, and probably to most of their own electorate as well, that the task of the Federal review conference would not be to prepare for a triumphant transition to complete independent Commonwealth membership, but to try to contrive some compromise which would enable the Federation to survive at all. During the latter part of 1959 a large and cumbrous 'Advisory Commission' had been assembled, with Lord Monckton as

[1] 14th May 1960. A correspondent of the same paper, writing from Nyasaland in December 1961, found a very similar attitude: 'A Malawi leader confessed to me that he was not happy to see the barriers in Southern Rhodesia being broken down, because with them went a focus of nationalist agitation. The same attitude is felt among Africans in Southern Rhodesia itself: they are rapidly losing some valuable grievances.' (*Manchester Guardian Weekly*, 28th December 1961.)

Chairman, and with members representing the British and Federal Governments and the three territorial Governments. Sir Roy Welensky gave his co-operation with reluctance, on the express understanding that the Commission's terms of reference would not include any mention of the possibility that the Federation might be broken up. The Labour Opposition had urged the appointment of the Commission in the hope that its report would help to bring the Federation to an end, and it was so dissatisfied with the terms of reference that it refused to nominate any members, as it was invited and urged to do. The prevailing outlook among the members of the Commission was therefore that of moderate conservatism. All the more startling, therefore, was the report which it presented in October 1960. For it declared that 'the strength of African opposition in the Northern Territories is such that Federation cannot, in our view, be maintained in its present form' (Cmnd. 1148, para. 49). If it were to survive at all, its very name would have to be changed; the Africans would have to be given parity of representation with Europeans in the Federal Assembly, and a majority in the Legislative Council of Northern Rhodesia, where a 'comparable advance' to that recently arranged for Nyasaland would be 'essential . . . in the near future'. The commissioners were less concerned about Southern Rhodesia, where African pressures were so much weaker than in the two Protectorates; but even there they considered that the beginnings of African representation were desirable.

The effect of these proposals would have been to turn the Federation upside down. A constitution devised to strengthen and perpetuate European control over the Federal area would have become an agency for extending African control from the northern Protectorates to Southern Rhodesia. In an unguarded moment Lord Malvern had once said that the partnership of the races was that of a rider and his horse; horse and rider would now change roles.

A reversal of attitudes might therefore have been expected, with the African nationalists demanding that a reformed Federation should in the name of Pan-Africanism be treated as a sacred and indivisible unity, and the Europeans in Southern Rhodesia insisting on their right to secede. On the European side there was, indeed, a slow, sad reappraisal, expressed at last in the rejection of the United Federal Party in the Southern Rhodesian general election of December 1962. But for the Africans the Federation was incarnate in the massive, unshakable person of Sir Roy Welensky, who stood fast, uncompromising and defiant, until he was left with no ground at all to stand on. They remained obsessed with the objective of secession.

From Mr. Kaunda's point of view, as a Northern Rhodesian thinking primarily of the future of his own country, there was indeed no reason for a change of policy. For under federation Northern Rhodesia was subsiding both the other territories, and was gaining little or nothing in return. This was made clear in 1960 by Messrs. A. Hazlewood and P. D. Henderson in a searching analysis of the alleged economic advantages of federation (*Nyasaland: The Economics of Federation* (Blackwell)). But the case of Nyasaland was very different. True, the federal link with *Southern* Rhodesia brought her few if any benefits, and by drawing her inside the Southern Rhodesian customs wall it penalised her consumers in the interests of Southern Rhodesian manufacturers. But such considerations were far less important than the increase in her public expenditure resulting from her link with the wealth of the Copperbelt. When her share of Federal current expenditure is added to the share of the Federal income tax allocated to her own revenue, the annual total was about £4m. more than she could have raised from her own resources. Compare with this the fact that in 1952, the year before federation, her entire revenue was not quite £4m., and even this included grants of £520,000 from the United Kingdom's Colonial Development and Welfare Fund.

If Dr. Banda had been more of a rational statesman, and less of an emotional agitator, he would have recognised the supreme importance to his country of maintaining its link with Northern Rhodesia. By insisting on the establishment of African control over the Federal Government as the price of withdrawing his demand for secession, he could have thrown upon the white

Southern Rhodesians the onus of seceding. The Northern Rhodesian nationalists would then have had no adequate excuse for casting off their embarrassing poor relations to the east. But it was not until the Federation had been finally broken up, and his links with Lusaka as well as with Salisbury irrevocably destroyed, that it occurred to him to express the pathetic hope that a new association with Northern Rhodesia might be formed.

In December 1960, a few weeks after the publication of the Monckton report, the Federal review conference duly assembled in London, amid the splendours of Lancaster House. It met against the background not only of recent events in the Federation itself, but also of the collapse of the Belgian Congo—that apparently solid bulwark against the southward expansion of West African nationalism—immediately after its attainment of formal 'independence'. It might have been confidently predicted that a disaster on such a scale would have cooled the ardour of African nationalists, and that the United Nations, sadly contemplating the near-bankruptcy to which it was being reduced by the demands of its rescue operation, would have learnt to temper its anti-colonialism by some sober thought for the future. But the exact opposite happened. The secession of Katanga with the approval of its Anglo-Belgian mining interests diverted attention from the crimes and follies committed in Leopoldville. Mr. Tshombe, its President, became the scapegoat for all the Congo's ills, and Mr. Patrice Lumumba, the Führer-like demagogue who was more responsible than any other single individual for the ruin of his country, became the symbol of nationalist virtue because he was the champion of the unity of the Congo. With his death he became the martyr of Pan-Africanism. Thus nationalist passions were not cooled but inflamed, and were accompanied by a fervent horror of the bogy of 'neo-colonialism'. And Katanga had a long common frontier with Northern Rhodesia.

In these circumstances, with the Federal Government determined to maintain European control, the Federal review conference decided after some days of fruitless discussion that it could make no progress until the balance of power between the races had been settled in each of the Rhodesias. It therefore adjourned, never to meet again.

The main question concerned Northern Rhodesia, where the nationalists insisted on a clear majority of seats in both the Legislative and Executive Councils, which would enable them to join with Nyasaland in tearing the Federation apart. Both for the Northern Rhodesian section of the United Federal Party and for the Federal Government itself, this was the decisive battle. The conference began in London on 19th December 1960, and ended two months later in acrimonious deadlock. For much of its course the United Federal Party had adopted the tactics more usually followed by the nationalists, boycotting it as a means of coercing the British Government. At the same time Mr. Julian Greenfield, the Federal Minister of Law, went to London to put all possible pressure on Mr. Macleod. By these tactics the Federal Government demonstrated more clearly than ever before that it was the main obstacle to African political advancement. This was, indeed, vehemently denied by Sir Roy Welensky, who told the Federal Parliament on 27th February that he had put forward suggestions which would have given Africans a 'spectacular' increase in representation in the Legislative Council—an increase of up to 150 per cent. But they must be so elected that power would remain in 'responsible' hands. A 'responsible' African, in Sir Roy's view, was one who did not appeal to his own people on the ground of racial solidarity and who was prepared to accept a qualitative franchise. This interpretation eliminated all nationalists. It revealed the fatal limitation in Sir Roy's outlook. For although Mr. Kaunda did indeed rely on the appeal to racial solidarity as the source of his mass support,[1] he was not anti-European by inclination or

[1] 'We do not need to find grounds for unity as does a multi-racial party—our unity is already there in the colour of our skin and our common suffering. This is a great emotional force, and one which can be harnessed for political purposes. . . . Unip does not exclude anyone of any race from its membership, provided he accepts our aims and policies, and would be a suitable member in other ways.' Mr. Kaunda in Morris and Kaunda, *Black Government?*, pp. 93, 95.

policy, and no useful purpose was to be served either by branding him as irresponsible or by so frustrating him that he would be ousted from the leadership by the more impatient and vicious element among his supporters.

During the conference the executive committee of the European miners' trade union called on Sir Roy to proclaim the Federation an independent state and to declare Mr. Macleod a prohibited immigrant. It was subsequently alleged by a prominent left-wing Northern Rhodesian, Mr. Harry Franklin, in his book *Unholy Wedlock*, that the Federal Government planned to use its army to make a *coup d'état*, arresting the Governor and displacing the judiciary. Sir Roy denied the charge. But he had called up the territorials in Northern Rhodesia during the conference, and he called up the Southern Rhodesian force immediately afterwards. It is unlikely that he seriously intended unconstitutional action, but he may well have wished the British Government to believe that he intended it. In concluding his speech of 27th February, he warned the Federal Parliament that they might have to decide whether to 'knuckle down' or to 'fight for what we have created here in the last seventy years'. Undoubtedly he thought that any such fight would be defensive; the Federation would be defending its right to survive. But it was as impossible for the British Government as for the Northern Rhodesian nationalists to accept this view.

Sir Roy afterwards revealed that at the height of the crisis he learnt that British troops and transport aircraft were being concentrated at Nairobi for a possible landing in Northern Rhodesia, but that when he spoke to Mr. Macmillan on the subject, the British Prime Minister assured him that it was unthinkable that British troops would shoot down Rhodesians, their comrades-in-arms in two world wars; the forces in Nairobi were being held in readiness in case there should be an African rebellion in Northern Rhodesia and help might be needed for its suppression; it had been merely an error of omission not to inform the Federal Government. Sir Roy, who already deeply distrusted Mr. Macmillan, was not convinced by the explanation; nor is the present author. The incident seems to show that the British Government thought it might be necessary to call the Federal Government's bluff, and to defend its Protectorate against what, from its point of view, would be armed aggression by the Federal forces.

When it became conclusively evident that the deadlock at the constitutional conference could not be broken, Mr. Macleod produced a hastily devised scheme of his own. It provided only an outline; the details were to be filled in after further discussions conducted by the Governor in Lusaka. There were to be fifteen members elected by upper roll voters, and another fifteen by lower roll voters; in effect, fifteen federalists and an equal members of nationalists. For all these thirty seats the new constitution abandoned the principle embodied in the existing one, that every member of the legislature should be elected by the combined votes of both rolls. It thus tended to divide class from class and—which was the same thing—race from race. On that ground the federalists rightly called it retrograde; but Mr. Macleod might have replied that the division was already so sharp that it had to be recognised. There was, however, to be a third group of fifteen members, known as 'national members', elected by the combined votes of both rolls. For this group of seats the two rolls would carry equal voting strength, since it would be the *proportion* of votes cast for a candidate on the upper roll, added to the proportion of votes cast for him on the lower roll, that would determine the result—not the absolute total of votes. Moreover, a candidate would be disqualified if he did not receive a certain minimum of support from voters on *each* roll, however massive his support from electors on the other. It seemed reasonable to predict that Sir John Moffat's Liberal Party would gain most of these national seats, because it alone would not be disqualified by lack of support on one or other roll. The Liberal Party would thus hold the key position; and if Sir John were called upon to form a Government, he would look to the nationalists, not to the federalists, for partners in a coalition.

The scheme was received with anger and disgust by federalists and nationalists alike. But Mr. Kaunda soon realised that the Government which would result from elections held on such a basis would be a transitional one, which would provide him with a stepping-stone to undisputed power. Very reluctantly he agreed to co-operate. The federalists, however, could see no merit in the scheme, only the ruin of all their hopes. Their ministers resigned from the territorial Government, and Sir John Moffat took office in their place.

The details of the constitution were published in June. During the interval the Federal Government had kept up its pressure for alterations in its favour, and it was supported by a large group of Conservative Members of Parliament who were alarmed by what then seemed to be a gravely deteriorating situation in Kenya, and who were determined that if Kenya was to go the way of the Congo, Mr. Macleod should not send Northern Rhodesia the way of Kenya. And there was another consideration, more important than pressure from either of these sources. In Southern Rhodesia, a referendum was being held on a new constitution which, if adopted by the preponderantly white electorate, would for the first time give Africans a significant place in the constitution. If that electorate believed that Northern Rhodesia was about to be handed over to the nationalists, its attitude might be expected to harden to such an extent that it would repudiate the new constitution, and entrust its future to the Dominion Party.

Accordingly, Northern Rhodesia's June constitution contained modifications sufficient to satisfy Sir Roy Welensky that his party had a reasonable prospect of winning enough of the 'national' seats to control the legislature. The Independence Party reacted vehemently. There was an alarming increase in the number of politically motivated crimes of violence. Within three months enough acts of murder and arson had been committed to persuade Mr. Macleod to reopen the question—thus confirming the truth of the popular African saying that 'violence always pays',[1] although Mr. Macleod himself attempted to maintain the contrary. Repeated assurances had been given

[1] i.e. as a means of putting pressure on the British Government. They would be unwise to suppose that it has any more extended validity.

that the June constitution was final, and the Federal Government rightly regarded the reopening of the question as a breach of faith. By this time the Southern Rhodesian referendum had been won, but many a Southern Rhodesian may well have felt that it had been won on false pretences. Such a feeling doubtless contributed to the result of the general election in December 1962.

It was left to Mr. Macleod's successor, Mr. Maudling, to devise the arrangements under which Northern Rhodesia's elections were eventually held, in October 1962. In those elections the Liberal Party was wiped out, and ten of the fifteen national seats remained unfilled because no candidate had enough support on both rolls to qualify. This was a starting revelation of the chasm which had opened between the races.

The African National Congress, not the Liberal Party, emerged holding the balance between the United Federal Party and the Independence Party. After by-elections to try to fill the vacant seats had been held in December, it had seven seats, while the federalists had sixteen and the Independence Party had fourteen. The last hope of the federalists was that Mr. Nkumbula would so cherish his feud with Mr. Kaunda that he would join them in a coalition. But this would obviously have been political suicide: he had already done himself enough damage by flirting with Mr. Tshombe's secessionist movement in Katanga, and—it was widely believed—drawing a large proportion of his party's campaign fund from Katangan sources. He threw in his lot with Mr. Kaunda, and they took office together in a nationalist and anti-Federal coalition.

By this time Nyasaland was approaching complete internal self-government. A conference was held in London in November 1962, and Dr. Banda told it that he had 'come in the spirit of take, to take what is mine by conquest at the ballot box, and, if I may be forgiven for saying so, Sir, by successful and creditable performance in office'. But he had no need to bluster. The Nyasaland administration was already under his effective control, and the Governor, Sir Glyn Jones, was working with him so harmoniously that he referred to him as 'our beloved Governor'. The British Government had no thought of trying to impede a transition which was progressing so smoothly and amicably. It was therefore unanimously agreed that the Executive Council should be replaced by a cabinet, and on 1st February 1963 Dr. Banda took office as Prime Minister, declaring that Nyasaland was now 'a black man's country in a black man's continent'.

The issue of secession could no longer be evaded or postponed. The British Government's change of policy at the beginning of 1960 implied that the Federation would not be maintained by force, but up to the last possible moment ministers hoped that it might be preserved on a basis of agreement and consent. Perhaps this might have been done if, in 1960, Sir Roy Welensky had approached Dr. Banda with *bonhomie* spiced with a little of the flattery which the doctor loved so much. But if such a thought ever occurred to Sir Roy, he put it aside with scorn. So the Federation drifted to its destruction, and it is not certain whether it was by the deliberate adoption of Fabian tactics or by the total absence of a policy that the British Government stood by and watched it drift. So far as can be judged it was due to a mixture of Micawberism and divided counsels. It was well known that Mr. Macleod at the Colonial Office was a significant distance to the left of Mr. Sandys at the Commonwealth Relations Office; the Colonial Secretary was responsible for the territorial affairs of the two Protectorates while the Commonwealth Relations Secretary handled relations with the Federal Government and with Southern Rhodesia. Even apart from differences of personality, this division of functions was inconvenient and unsatisfactory. But any proposal to make the Colonial Secretary wholly responsible for Britain's dealings with the Federation and its three Governments would have been derogatory to the self-governing status of the Federation and of Southern Rhodesia; while to give the responsibility to the Commonwealth Relations Secretary would have been regarded as a long step towards the withdrawal of British protection from Nyasaland and Northern Rhodesia. At last, in March 1962, when the urgency of the problem became sufficiently pressing, Mr. Macmillan set up a completely separate Central

Africa Office, and placed it under the direction of Mr. R. A. Butler, the most senior member of the Government after the Prime Minister himself.

On 8th May 1962, Mr. Butler told the Commons that it remained the view of the Government that there were 'great advantages for all the peoples in Central Africa in a continued association of the three territories. At the same time,' he added, 'it is clear that there is considerable criticism of the present federation.' He specifically acknowledged that Dr. Banda and the Malawi Party, 'supported by a firm mandate at the last election', were determined to secede. Nevertheless 'we want to take a constructive view of the future and not just pull out bricks and let the structure collapse'. He therefore proposed to appoint a small team of advisers to examine the economic implications of secession and to discuss with the Governments of Nyasaland and the Federation what kind of links between Nyasaland and the Rhodesias would be acceptable for the future. He evidently hoped that, if the full price of secession could be made clear, a recognition of the national interest would constrain the Malawi leaders to modify their intransigence.

When the advisers reached Nyasaland they received all possible co-operation from the Federal Government, which knew that it had a strong case and was determined to make the most of it. It submitted a total of 77 memoranda and other documents, showing how greatly Nyasaland was being subsidised and supported by Rhodesian money. But neither the Nyasaland Government nor the Malawi Party thought it worth while to submit a single written memorandum. For them this was not a matter of reason, of public policy, of the dispassionate weighing of pros and cons; it was a matter of absolutes and categorical imperatives. Rhodesian money was tainted, and they did not want it, whatever the consequences. The Federal Government had been refused permission to invest £3m. in a much-needed hydro-electric scheme at Nkula Falls on the Shiré;[1] it had not

[1] The United Kingdom eventually undertook to finance this undertaking.

298

been allowed to undertake the reclamation of 100,000 acres of good land which formed the Elephant Marsh near Chiromo, although the land was desperately needed to relieve the intense and rapidly growing pressure of population in the Southern Province; the health service had been obstructed and interfered with in quite scandalous ways, merely because it was a Federal service[1]—there had been a Malawi campaign against smallpox vaccination and against anti-malaria measures, and the construction of a leprosarium for 400 patients in the Northern Province had been prevented: all this by a movement headed by an experienced medical practitioner. Students had been forbidden to attend the University College of Rhodesia and Nyasaland because it was a Federally supported institution situated in Salisbury; it was accused of 'brain-washing' them, and this in spite of the fact that one lecturer had already been deported by the Federal Government for being too liberal-minded (another was afterwards deported for being an active member of the Southern Rhodesian nationalist party); when a Nyasaland school-teacher who was a graduate of the College attempted to contradict the Malawi propaganda, she was so persecuted that she had to make a midnight escape from the country.

Malawi ministers were not, indeed, wholly indifferent to their country's economic future. Having exploited for all it was worth the sense of grievance caused among peasants by the enforcement of the Natural Resources Ordinance by district commissioners,[2] they proceeded to implement the ordinance by the use of 'persuasion' instead of 'compulsion', and the methods of their party enthusiasts were more effective than those of the white officials had been: anyone who has read Tocqueville's *Demo-*

---

[1] Yet even Mr. Harry Franklin, in his attack on the Federation (*Unholy Wedlock*), admitted that the health service was 'probably the best of the Federal Government's efforts, and has certainly provided facilities in Nyasaland that would not otherwise have been available'.

[2] See above, p. 233. As Dr. A. I. Richards has remarked, 'It is a striking fact how often modern political parties . . . are said by the villagers to favour a return to the old ways and to a world in which there are no latrines to be dug and no anti-erosion ridges to be made.' (Quoted in Guy Hunter, *The New Societies of Tropical Africa* (O.U.P., 1962), p. 287, n. 15).

cracy in America will understand the reason why. And European civil servants in Zomba are said to have been very favourably impressed by the ability and constructive enthusiasm of their new political masters. In July 1962, at the very time when Mr. Butler's team of advisers was beginning its task, the Nyasaland Government published a £19½m. development plan; obviously much of this money would have to come from Britain or other outside sources. And in that same month a group of economists from Western Europe, the United States, and India met at the invitation of the Nyasaland Government to advise it on how best to develop its economy. But all such thinking and activity were subordinate to the one supreme obsession. Dr. Banda, in a closing address to the gathering of economists, said he knew they thought it madness to secede from the Federation; nevertheless 'we will secede even if we have to go back and eat roots as our ancestors did'.

In face of this attitude, Mr. Butler decided that Nyasaland must be permitted to secede, as the precondition of any constructive achievement. The Federal Government was informed of this decision on 5th November. But, to avoid embarrassing the United Federal Party in the impending general election in Southern Rhodesia, the decision was not made public until 19th December, when the election was over.

From the Rhodesian point of view Nyasaland was an unmitigated liability. It was not the Rhodesians who had pressed for its inclusion in the Federation, but the British Government, which had both overridden their reluctance and disregarded the vigorous objections raised by Sir Geoffrey Colby, who was then Governor of Nyasaland. It had taken this stand partly in order to transfer most of the burden of financial support to Rhodesian shoulders, but also because a balanced federation could not be constructed with only two members. It was this latter consideration which now alarmed the Federal Government. True, there were other anxieties: concerning Nyasaland's share of the Federal debt, its responsibilities towards the Federal civil servants employed in its service, and similar matters on which the Federal Government was entitled to be reassured, and had not been. But the supremely important consideration was the future relationship between the two Rhodesias. It was not merely a general problem in political science— how does one federate two and only two territories in such a way that the one with the larger electorate will not dominate the other?—but also the urgent political reality of the newly formed nationalist coalition Government in Northern Rhodesia, which was certain to insist that the precedent of Nyasaland's secession must be followed in its own case, and followed without delay. If the Federal Government could have received firm assurances on this matter, as well as on the other issues involved, it would have given its consent. But Mr. Butler would have been guilty of disastrous improvidence if he had bought its consent at the cost of involving Britain in a hopeless impasse in Northern Rhodesia.

The British Government decided that Federal consent could be dispensed with; it relied on a statement made in a debate on 27th March by Lord Kilmuir, who was then Lord Chancellor, that 'as a matter of pure law' the United Kingdom Parliament retained unfettered power to legislate how it wished for the Federation; 'legislation for the dissolution of the Federation or the secession of any one of its constituent territories is a matter solely within the legislative competence of the United Kingdom'. The absolute legislative sovereignty of the British Parliament is, of course, a legal truism, which neither Sir Roy Welensky nor anyone else attempted to dispute. But it exists within a controlling framework of constitutional convention, which alone prevents it from becoming an intolerable, arbitrary tyranny, and makes it a flexible and creative instrument of constitutional government. Mr. Butler and his colleagues chose to ignore this fact. The Federal Government, however, strenuously contended that Britain was obliged to respect the autonomy guaranteed to it by the constitutional convention of April 1957.

'It is sometimes suggested', wrote Mr. Greenfield, 'that this communiqué must be so construed as to limit the operation of the Convention to the prevention of interference in matters within the legislative competence of the Federal Parliament, while leaving the British Parliament free to legislate the Federation and its Parliament out of existence. Such a construction is tantamount to saying that a law prohibiting grievous bodily harm permits of murder.' (Letter to *The Times*, published on 26th May 1962.)

Moreover, the British Government itself had defined the constitutional position, in a statement given to the British Council of Churches; this had been quoted by Sir Godfrey Huggins in the Southern Rhodesian Assembly on 30th September 1953:

'The United Kingdom Parliament would not be precluded by law from amending the Federal Constitution without the consent of the Federal or Territorial Governments; but as the Constitution will be based on a scheme which has been agreed between the four Governments concerned and will itself be so agreed, it seems to Her Majesty's Government that it would in any forseeable circumstance be morally and politically indefensible for Parliament to enact amendments which had not been similarly agreed. If amendments to the Constitution were enacted by the United Kingdom Parliament with the agreement of the other Government concerned, the Government of the Federation in agreeing thereto would act in responsibility to the Federal Legislature; but amendments so agreed would not require also to be submitted for the approval of the Federal Legislature.'

In addition to the issue of constitutional propriety, there was the separate though kindred issue of the moral obligation to honour pledges. When reporting the British decision to the Federal Parliament, Sir Roy Welensky quoted from the verbatim record of the discussions during the 1953 conference, when Lord Swinton, who was then Commonwealth Relations Secretary, pointed out that no federal constitution contained, or could contain, a secession clause, because if a federation was to function properly, and in particular if it was to have credit for borrowing money, it must be permanent.[1] He admitted that it

[1] The Monckton Report declared (para. 290) that 'there is nothing in the constitutional theory of this matter which makes a right of secession incom-

was useless to write into the constitution any safeguard for its permanence, because 'you cannot legislate against the United Kingdom Parliament going off its head'; but the whole purport of his remarks was to assure the Rhodesian negotiators that they need have no fear of any such British action.

In the House of Lords, Lord Malvern declared that he would never have signed the conference report which formed the basis of the Federal constitution 'if I had known that all that had been decided in committee was to be repudiated by the British Government'. And Lord Salisbury remarked that while from 'the strictly legalistic point of view' the argument that Parliament could do as it pleased was no doubt correct, 'it does not, I suggest, provide ground on which any self-respecting country could stand in practice. For if it were generally applied, it would deal a death blow to the whole principle of the sanctity of treaties and other international engagements, which is, as we all know, the main base on which peace, and indeed civilisation itself, rests. Especially, I think, is that true of this country of ours, where our whole moral position in the world has always rested on the fact that our word was our bond.'

The British Government was, indeed, in a difficult situation. It had to choose between dishonouring its obligations and persevering in a policy which it knew to be bankrupt and injurious to all concerned, including, in the last resort, the white Rhodesians themselves. In this predicament, the least discreditable course open to it was to explain, with complete candour and considerable humility, why it felt obliged to prefer legality to constitutionality, and reason of state to pledges which ought never to have been given but which were pledges none the less. But the Macmillan Government, talented and tolerably well-intentioned though it was, suffered from a chronic inability to be either candid or contrite. Under pressure from both Houses of Parliament, it published a White Paper in which it proved to its own satisfaction, and to no one else's, that the pledges had no

patible with the federal concept'. But the commission was not so much expressing a considered opinion as trying desperately to reconcile irreconcilables.

relevance to any situation except that with reference to which they happened to have been given: the occasion of the proposed conference to review the Federal constitution.

Mr. Butler still hoped, or said he hoped, to preserve a close association between the two Rhodesias. But by this time the United Federal Party no longer controlled a single one of the three territorial Governments. In both the Protectorates it had been defeated by the nationalists, and in Southern Rhodesia, the inner citadel of the Federation and the possessor of its capital, the fateful general election of 14th December 1962 had been won by the right-wing Rhodesia Front, a new grouping of which the former Dominion Party was the core. Southern Rhodesia thus passed under the control of men who had formerly opposed the establishment of the Federation, as well as the concept of partnership on which it purported to be based. Now that the Federal Government was fighting its last desperate rearguard action against African nationalism, they had no wish to embarrass it. But they had no illusions about its prospects of survival, and Mr. Field, the new Prime Minister, said on 13th February 1963 that 'we shall have been seceded from', that to prolong the process would merely destroy the prospect of establishing a friendly new relationship with Northern Rhodesia and Nyasaland, and that it would be better 'to make a clean break and open up the way to negotiation on an equal footing—as fully independent states'.

On 29th March 1963, Mr. Butler conceded the demand of the Northern Rhodesian ministers that he should recognise their right to secede.

But the ending of the Federation involved a major administrative reorganisation, an allocation and distribution of its assets and liabilities, and provision for the future of its common services. Had the Federal Government chosen to avenge itself by being obstructive, it could have made the operation well-nigh impossible. But Sir Roy Welensky was too patriotic and magnanimous a man to take his revenge in a way which could only injure his own country. And Mr. Butler achieved a notable diplomatic success by persuading all the Governments concerned to participate in a conference at Victoria Falls in the latter part of June, and to agree to the setting up of inter-Governmental committees to arrange the details of the transition. Before the end of the year several major agreements had been negotiated to provide for continued economic co-operation between the three territories, and more especially between the two Rhodesias, which arranged to retain the Kariba hydro-electric undertaking and Rhodesia Railways under joint ownership and control. Even Nyasaland consented to make a trade agreement with Southern Rhodesia as well as with Northern Rhodesia, and to co-operate with both of them in an Agricultural Research Council and in continuing, though decentralising, Central African Airways. The Federal debt was apportioned to the satisfaction of all three Governments, though in the process the bond-holders saw their stocks slump in value and complained that they had been the victims of a confidence trick by the British Government, which had encouraged them to rely on the permanence of the Federation and had then washed its hands of responsibility.

These agreements were in the interests of all concerned, but Southern Rhodesia had particular reason to be relieved that the ending of the Federation had not dealt as heavy a blow to her economy as there had been good reason to fear. Mr. Field had taken great trouble to cultivate friendly personal relations with the nationalist leaders of Northern Rhodesia and Nyasaland, and the results showed the wisdom of his conciliatory approach.

The railway agreement contained a safeguard which was particularly valuable to Southern Rhodesia; the railways were to be indemnified by Northern Rhodesia if they lost revenue as the result of the possible construction of a new line from the Copperbelt to the southern coast of Tanganyika, a project which was almost certainly uneconomic, but which Mr. Kaunda had very much at heart. In return for this concession, Southern Rhodesia undertook not to impose duties on goods in transit to Northern Rhodesia.

On 31st December 1963 the existence of the Federation formally came to an end.

Malawi, Zambia, Zimbabwe

Its ending brought almost to a conclusion the British era in south-central Africa, which has provided the subject of this book. The two Protectorates would become independent, under African rule, within a few months, and although in Southern Rhodesia the people of British origin were still predominant, it was becoming apparent that even they could not retain their position for many more years. In Nyasaland, the Malawi Party had taken the law into its own hands: the functions of the police were largely usurped by party zealots, the lower courts were under party control and were punishing people with imprisonment and hard labour for such offences as not possessing party membership cards, and Dr. Banda was threatening those judges in the higher courts who were still trying to uphold British standards of justice by quashing such convictions on appeal, and who thereby 'make my courts look cheap'. He was also boasting that when the next election was held, in 1964, the 'stupid fools' who formed the opposition parties would not get 'a single cat, chicken or dog' to follow them.

In Northern Rhodesia, Mr. Kaunda was already assured of virtually unfettered and undivided power as soon as the next election was held, a mere three weeks after the ending of federation. A new constitution provided that the Legislative Council and Executive Council should respectively be transformed into a Legislative Assembly and a Cabinet; the former was to be elected in accordance with the nationalist principle of 'one man one vote', except that as a temporary concession to the Europeans there would be ten seats reserved for them out of a total of seventy-five. The African National Congress was almost bankrupt; the suppression of Katangan independence deprived it of any further financial assistance from outside, and it scarcely attempted to conceal the fact that it had no hope of winning the election. Its conflict with the Independence Party had become nothing more than the expression of ancient tribal animosities: the Bemba provided Mr. Kaunda with the core of his support, while Mr. Nkumbula relied on the Ila-Tonga group in the south. In spite of appeals by the leaders, who were still colleagues in the

Government, there were numerous cases of stoning, assault and arson. In a Christmas message, Mr. Kaunda appealed for 'love for mankind'; a few days later he was shocked to learn that his supporters had murdered two children in a raid on a pro-Congress village. A European visiting Kitwe at that time could not fail to observe the bitter hatred in the eyes of almost every African he met; the reason for this hatred, according to an educated African of great goodwill who supported the Independence Party for lack of any better alternative, was that the local leaders of the party had for years been telling the people that when the white man's power was broken they would at once come into possession of the white man's houses, cars, and other possessions.[1] Mr. Kaunda himself was proclaiming that the country's future depended on hard work, and was pleading with European miners, who had been emigrating in large numbers, to remain in the country lest its economy should be seriously weakened. He also showed statesmanlike patience and restraint in dealing with the remote province of Baroteseland, where the upsurge of the masses under the direction of the Independence Party was looked upon by the traditional ruling class with anxiety as well as with aristocratic distaste. It was rightly regarded as a far greater threat to the picturesquely archaic social and political order than British rule had ever been. Mr. Kaunda's strength within the province was steadily increasing, and for the present he could well afford to be patient, in the interests of Northern Rhodesia's precarious national unity, and to concede that the Paramount Chief should retain his veto over the application of Northern Rhodesian legislation to Barotseland.

However incomplete the British achievement in both Protectorates, and however blemished the British record, there was no doubt that an indelible mark had been made on their society during the brief period when they were in tutelage. In

[1] The same informant remarked, by way of illustrating the progress made by Africans in recent years: 'In the 1940s my elder brother worked in the mine for 17s. 6d. a month; now my younger brother is employed there, doing skilled work, for over £100 a month.'

the pre-British era, prestige consisted in numbers of victims slain and of wives possessed; in the post-British era, it consisted in national universities—there was to be one in each territory—national airlines, and national development projects.

On the whole, the men who had opposed federation had gained more from it than those who had supported it. It had given an immense stimulus to the rise of African nationalism, first in Nyasaland, then in Northern Rhodesia, and finally in Southern Rhodesia itself. It had contributed some £41m. to Nyasaland, whose people passionately loathed its name. Yet, by entering into it, the white electorate of Southern Rhodesia had renounced the immediate prospect of full independent membership of the Commonwealth in favour of a vain dream of future greatness.

As soon as the fate of the Federation had been settled, Southern Rhodesia became the focus of controversy, and Mr. Field's Government replaced Sir Roy Welensky's as the target of Pan-African hostility. To understand the position which had then been reached it is necessary to survey developments in that territory during the Federal decade.

When the Federation was formed, Sir Godfrey Huggins took with him into Federal politics all the main figures in Southern Rhodesian public life. Southern Rhodesia's new Prime Minister was a newcomer to politics, a former missionary, Mr. Garfield Todd, who gained the leadership by eloquence and force of personality. A man of passionately liberal convictions, he nevertheless achieved very limited results during more than four years in office. He initiated a major reform of the Industrial Conciliation Act, to enable Africans to obtain the benefits of trade unionism in equal measure with Europeans; but the reform did not become law until more than a year after he had ceased to hold office. He also initiated a notable expansion of African education. But, partly through his own faults of temperament, he antagonised his colleagues and his electorate instead of leading them along the path of progress which he wished to follow. The formation of the Southern Rhodesian African National Congress in 1957 caused a swing of European opinion in favour of discouraging this new phenomenon of African self-assertion; the Dominion Party was showing ominous signs of gaining electoral support. Political anxiety as well as personal resentment therefore prompted a revolt of Mr. Todd's party against his leadership. Early in 1958 he was overthrown. He then rallied his supporters to form a splinter-party as a left-wing opposition, and by so doing he conveyed the impression both to Africans at home and to observers abroad that his successor was a reactionary.

His successor thus took office in a situation of extreme difficulty, with a divided and discredited party, an exhilarated right-wing Opposition, and an increased sense of alienation among the minority of politically conscious Africans. The new Prime Minister was Sir Edgar Whitehead, who had been Finance Minister under Sir Godfrey Huggins and subsequently the Federation's diplomatic representative in Washington. A quiet, shy man, with the temperament of the scholar or administrator rather than of the platform orator or politician, he was preoccupied by his awareness of the alarming rapidity with which the population of Southern Rhodesia was increasing, and of the resulting drift to the towns. Because of this, the country had already ceased to be hungry for all available labour, with the result that it no longer sought workers from other territories but had actually begun to put restrictions on them. Moreover, as the number of work-seekers outpaced the increase in industrial activity, Southern Rhodesia was faced with a serious problem of urban unemployment. If the population was going to go on doubling itself every quarter of a century, and was at the same time to climb from indigence to prosperity, there must be rapid and intensive economic growth, and nothing must be allowed to jeopardise it.

There must also, Sir Edgar believed, be speedy action to remove the social and economic colour bar, which was both objectionable in itself and an impediment to the country's progress; the Government's efforts to this end were assisted by a 'courtesy campaign' by which enlightened citizens endeavoured with considerable success to shame white society into improving its manners towards Africans, and by the end of 1962 racial discrimination in Southern Rhodesia had ceased to be the general rule and had become almost exceptional, though in the rural areas and smaller towns it was still firmly maintained. Even the Land Apportionment Act had been amended, to permit the urban African to own his own house and to make 5,320,000 acres of land in the European area into an unreserved area where there were no restrictions on ownership or occupation on the basis of colour. And these amendments were intended to be a mere preliminary to the total repeal of the Land Appointment Act, promised by the Government if it won the election of December 1962. Repeal would create a free market in land, except for the Tribal Trust Land (formerly the Native Reserves), which would be unaffected. It would also put an end to residential segregation in the towns, and this aspect of the proposal was the one which aroused the sharpest controversy. White Rhodesians had now learnt to accept Africans in hotels and cinemas, and even in public swimming pools, but the idea of having Africans as next-door neighbours was more than they were yet prepared to accept. For this reason, as well as because they had lost faith in the Federation and because they resented the total lack of appreciation shown by African nationalists after the series of concessions which they had made towards the ideal of non-racialism, they rejected the Whitehead Government and gave power to the Rhodesia Front, with its slogan of 'no forced integration'. The era of reform was, for a time, to be followed by a pause for consolidation, though not, as was feared, by a segregationist reaction.

It was a tragic paradox that this great reforming ministry—in which the work of Mr. A. E. Abrahamson, the Minister of Labour, deserves particular mention—should have received, and in a sense deserved, a reputation for being illiberal. It had the misfortune to be suspect from the beginning, owing to the circumstances in which Sir Edgar Whitehead took office; and the suspicion hardened into bitter certainty when, on three successive occasions, Sir Edgar banned the African nationalist organisation. Yet his reason for doing so, however unsound, was not unworthy. His own objective was contained in the slogan 'Build a nation', meaning that Europeans and Africans alike should forget their colour and take pride in being fellow citizens, fellow Rhodesians. It was not as the hard-faced, myopic reactionary that he was often thought to be, but as a constructive planner and an energetic, purposeful reformer, that he opposed a nationalism deliberately based on colour, a movement which divided the people instead of uniting it, setting the emergent masses against the minority which, despite unjust privileges and pretensions, was the modernising leaven which was still needed to complete the work of bringing the country out of Lobengula's era into the twentieth century. African nationalism seemed to him narrow, negative, and destructive; after all, he was an elderly man, and it was a new phenomenon in his experience. Moreover, its agitation was inseparable from violence and intimidation. He was determined that it should not jeopardise his country's progress, and he repressed it with such rigour that most of the better-educated Europeans protested, with good reason, that his legislation for the maintenance of law and order was a serious danger to the liberty of the subject. Even the Chief Justice of the Federation, Sir Robert Tredgold, resigned his office in November 1960 in order to campaign against this legislation. Yet African nationalism flourished under repression, which, while severe enough to discredit the Government, was not nearly consistent enough to achieve its object: for although the leaders were repeatedly prosecuted and convicted, and thereby given publicity and enhanced popularity, they spent most of their time at liberty. The nationalist movement re-emerged with greater strength each time its organisation was banned by the Government.[1] In

[1] Owing to the conservatism of the cattle-owing Matabele, nationalism developed among them somewhat later than among the Mashona. The following figures showing the strength of the successive organisations were given in December 1963 by the Organising Secretary of the Zimbabwe African National Union; the figures are for Matabeleland alone:

African National Congress: 1 branch, with about 500 members.

National Democratic Party: 5 branches, with about 15,000 members.

Zimbabwe African People's Union: 7 branches, with between 30,000 and 40,000 members.

Britain and elsewhere it was looked upon with increasing attention and respect. Mr. Joshua Nkomo, its leader, preoccupied himself with enlisting the support of the anti-colonial states which constituted the majority of the United Nations, where the group of newly independent African members was ready and eager to support his agitation.

In 1961, immediately after the failure of the Federal review conference, the constitution of Southern Rhodesia was substantially altered for the first time since the introduction of self-government in 1923. Four years previously the franchise had been altered by the creation of a second electoral roll with lower qualifications than the ordinary, while the qualifications for the ordinary roll had been appreciably raised. It was in fact Southern Rhodesia which had contrived this expedient of the second electoral roll, afterwards utilised in different ways in both the Protectorates and in the Federation itself. But the lower roll had at first been of negligible political importance. The continued existence of an all-white legislature had become an intolerable reproach; at the same time the Southern Rhodesian Government wished to make its autonomy complete in law as well as in fact by removing the last United Kingdom checks upon the legislative competence of its Assembly. If Britain was to relinquish its powers of disallowance, rusty and useless though they had become, it could only be in return for the extension to the Africans of power to uphold their own interests through their own elected representatives.

Accordingly a constitutional conference was held in Salisbury early in 1961, and resulted in an agreement between Britain and the Southern Rhodesian political parties, including the African nationalists, to relinquish British control over legislation which was alleged to be discriminatory in return for a number of constitutional safeguards, one of which provided that certain 'specially entrenched' clauses of the constitution could not be

Zimbabwe African National Union: 15 branches, with between 15,000 and 20,000 members.

While being grateful to the National Union for its courtesy and helpfulness in providing these figures, I do not accept responsibility for their accuracy. Nor have I any figures for the rival People's Caretaker Council.

amended without the approval of each of the four principal racial groups (European, African, Asian, and Coloured), given in a referendum in which all electors on either roll would be qualified to vote. The Assembly was to be enlarged to consist of fifty members elected mainly (but not entirely) by the upper roll voters, and a further fifteen members elected mainly (but not entirely) by the lower roll voters. And the qualifications for the lower roll were widened in the hope that many thousands of Africans would register for the right to vote. The nationalists could have secured fifteen seats out of sixty-five if they had chosen to claim and exercise their constitutional rights. They would also have had a substantial measure of influence in many of the other fifty. In comparison with Nyasaland's new constitution of 1960, or even with Northern Rhodesia's 'three fifteens' constitution as proposed in February 1961, the Africans' gains were modest, but they were a significant first step; indeed it was reckoned that even if the constitution was not altered again to their advantage, the increasing number of them who would attain the educational and income qualifications for the upper as well as for the lower roll would assure them of a majority of all the seats in about fifteen years. Fifteen years is but a brief moment in the life of a nation, and on any normal reckoning would seem a short enough time in which to effect so great a transition. Besides, Sir Edgar Whitehead felt obliged to submit the new proposals to a referendum of the existing electorate, which was, of course, overwhelmingly European, and they were as large a dose as he could reasonably hope that it would be prepared to swallow at a single gulp. But, with most of Africa already under, or on the point of passing under, some kind of African control, it seemed to Southern Rhodesian nationalists an intolerably long time to have to wait. It was with great reluctance that Mr. Nkomo gave his agreement to the new constitution.

When, however, he received a cable from his representative in London, Mr. Leopold Takawira, rejecting the agreement as 'treacherous to the future of three million Africans', and calling upon him to do likewise, he and his 'national executive' reacted strongly; Mr. Takawira was suspended from the executive, and Mr. Nkomo at once flew to London with the declared intention to take 'disciplinary action' against him.

Four days later, in London, Mr. Nkomo announced that his party repudiated the new constitution. For reasons which would be interesting if made public, he had found that it was he, and not Mr. Takawira, who was exposed to 'disciplinary action', and, rather than lose his position as party leader, he made his *volte-face*. A few months afterwards, a congress of his party denounced the proposals as an 'evil attempt' by the Southern Rhodesian and British Governments 'to entrench settler minority rule'. Ever afterwards, he categorically denied that he had put his signature to the agreement—thus asserting by implication that his signature was required to give validity to his assent, whereas in fact, and in accordance with the usual practice on such occasions, Mr. Sandys as Chairman had signed on behalf of the conference as a whole.

When, in December 1962, the general election was held, the nationalist boycott resulted in a very low poll of lower roll voters, besides provoking European voters on the upper roll to turn away from the existing Government in the disillusioned conviction that the more they conceded to the Africans, the more demanding and uncompromising the Africans became. So the Rhodesia Front won 35 of the main group of 50 seats, leaving the United Federal Party with only 15. As a partial compensation, the United Federal Party won 14 of the 15 seats which the nationalists might have won but had disdained to contest; it thus found itself constituting the Opposition with a total of 29 seats, of which only 14 were occupied by Europeans, while 14 were held by Africans and the remaining seat by a Coloured man. The new Assembly also included one left-wing European, elected by mainly lower-roll votes as an Independent.

The year which followed the Rhodesia Front's victory was the year of the dissolution of the Federation, when both of Southern Rhodesia's unwilling associates in the federal structure were moving unhindered towards the attainment of complete independence. With its forty-year history of internal self-government, and with the removal of the last external controls as a result of the implementation of the new constitution, Southern Rhodesia assumed that it would as a matter of course attain its long-deferred sovereignty at least as soon as either Nyasaland or Northern Rhodesia. Yet, after a year of negotiations with the British Government, no decision had yet been reached. Whatever the British Government's own preferences may have been, it had to take account of the attitude of the Commonwealth, which, since the Second World War, had developed almost as passionate an anti-colonial and anti-settler outlook as the United Nations itself. Led by Ghana,[1] it made clear the fact that it was not prepared to tolerate as a fellow member of the Commonwealth a state in which a white minority was attempting the indefinite prolongation of its own political supremacy. Britain was not prepared to incur the odium of defying this strongly expressed sentiment. And Southern Rhodesian ministers, who had at first thought that it would be easy to seize independence if Britain refused to concede it, had to recognise that by such action they would be isolating their country diplomatically and to a large extent commercially from almost the entire world, so that it would be likely to become a helpless satellite of the Republic of South Africa.

While these inconclusive discussions continued, there was a convulsion within the nationalist movement. Dissatisfaction with Mr. Nkomo's leadership had been growing for a considerable time, and in July 1963 a group of his colleagues declared him deposed because of his 'fumbling, spineless and blunderous leadership' (*The Times*, 10th July 1963). It seemed to them that he spent too much time haranguing the United Nations, whose resolutions would remain idle words as long as the Southern Rhodesian and British Governments chose to ignore them, instead of organising, inspiring and guiding his own people to

[1] Which was about this time demonstrating its own devotion to its professed democratic principles by destroying the independence of its judiciary, deporting a large group of university staff, and legislating for the formal establishment of a one-party dictatorship.

win power by their own endeavours. But in this crisis Mr. Nkomo showed that, whatever his other qualities, he could remain afloat in any storm. Some of his colleagues supported him, declaring that the accusations against him were 'nothing but a chain of most profane lies' (*The Times*, 11th July 1963). Within a few weeks Southern Rhodesia had two nationalist organisations, the People's Caretaker Council led by Mr. Nkomo, and the Zimbabwe African National Union, led by the Rev. Ndabaningi Sithole, who was already widely known as the author of a book entitled *African Nationalism*. Since the National Union alleged that Mr. Nkomo was insufficiently militant, he had to show that he was in fact more militant than they. This was not difficult, since militancy of attitude is easily confused with violence of action. The National Union appealed to most of the better-educated Africans, people who had developed minds of their own; but Mr. Nkomo had the greater financial resources, and, according to Mr. Ian Smith, who was then Deputy Prime Minister, could hire the swarms of urban unemployed to swell his meetings at the rate of a shilling a head, with larger sums for such services as throwing stones (reported in *East Africa and Rhodesia*, 14th November 1963). By the end of 1963 it was fairly clear that if the principle of 'one man one vote', for which both the rival parties contended, could be achieved, it would be Mr. Nkomo who would come to power. It was not an inspiring prospect.

Critics of the existing régime were in the habit of warning that the longer the transition to African control was deferred the more dangerous would the situation become. This assertion was over-simplified. It was, indeed, important that Southern Rhodesia should not become 'another Algeria' through the intransigence of its white population; it was, however, equally important that it should not become another Congo. The tragedy of the Congo could be attributed to the fact that the white men maintained a monopoly of power for far too long; it could equally be attributed to the fact that they relinquished that monopoly far too hastily. Neither statement is adequate; the truth consists in combining the two. It was the suddenness of the transition from complete subjection to complete independence which brought disaster. In Southern Rhodesia, where for over half a century the Africans had quietly accepted the status of a conquered and subject people, despised by their Nyasa neighbours as well as by their white rulers, the danger of a sudden acquisition of power was far greater than whatever danger there might be in insisting that the transition must take place over a reasonable period of time. As Mr. Guy Hunter pointed out, in his penetrating study of *The New Societies of Tropical Africa* (O.U.P., 1962, p. 44):

'The fact that the Africans of Southern Rhodesia are, perhaps, more deeply dependent [than those of Northern Rhodesia or elsewhere] and the Europeans more numerous is not an advantage, but a greatly added danger. It will need skill and determination almost beyond human power to achieve a transition from dependence not to hysterical revolt but to maturity, and to prevent the suicidal resistance of the French *colons* of Algeria from repeating itself south of the Zambesi.'

The policy of the British Government was not to insist on the immediate adoption of 'majority rule' as the price of independence, but to require that a reasonable transition towards the objective should be arranged. The existing constitution had been meant to provide such a transition, but if the majority of Africans who were qualified for the franchise continued to allow themselves to be persuaded and intimidated into boycotting elections, they would never gain the majority which had already been placed within their eventual reach, and they would blame the white man and not themselves for their frustration. Sir Edgar Whitehead, as Leader of the Opposition, now recognised that it was necessary to try to break the deadlock by negotiating concessions to the Africans beyond those made in 1961. But the Government and the electorate were reluctant to agree.

By the end of 1963 there were sporadic acts of petrol bombing, in spite of legislation imposing the death penalty for such crimes; these were sinister portents of the full-scale insurrection which would come in a few years if it were not averted. But as yet it was a gross exaggeration to speak of an 'explosive situation', and the so-called 'grave threat to peace' existed only in the propaganda of those who required a pretext for debating Southern Rhodesia under the terms of the United Nations Charter. No doubt the mass of the people quietly sympathised with the nationalist cause, but they were not yet in any mood to die for it, and the general atmosphere was calm and even friendly—incomparably more so than in the Copperbelt to the north. Southern Rhodesia still had the minimum of time that she required: not time to spare for the prolongation of privilege, but time sufficient for deliberate and constructive statesmanship.

Bibliography

(Books are arranged according to subject matter, as far as possible in chronological order, with some grouping on a territorial basis.)

W. V. Brelsford (ed.): *Handbook to the Federation of Rhodesia and Nyasaland* (Cassell, 1960). Amidst a wealth of other information, includes authoritative articles on the African tribes and on pre-history and early Bantu movements.

E. Colson and M. Gluckman (ed.): *Seven Tribes of British Central Africa* (O.U.P., 1951). A convenient collection of anthropological essays.

C. Northcott: *Robert Moffat, Pioneer in Africa* (Lutterworth, 1961). A good modern biography.

G. Seaver: *David Livingstone, His Life and Letters* (Lutterworth, 1957). A substantial work; the most recent biography of Livingstone, and in some respects the best.

H. M. Hole: *The Making of Rhodesia* (Macmillan, 1926). A full account of the early work of the B.S.A. Company, mainly in Southern Rhodesia, by a former official of the company, unashamedly partisan on its behalf but honest, humane, well-educated and possessing an admirable style. Another of his books, *The Passing of the Black Kings* (Philip Allan, 1932), gives a sympathetic and masterly account of Lobengula, Lewanika, and Khama of the Bamangwato.

P. Mason: *The Birth of a Dilemma* (O.U.P., 1958). An exceedingly well-written survey of the background to British rule and of its beginnings, to about 1920, in Southern Rhodesia, with some attention to Barotseland; the emphasis is on the origins of racial segregation.

J. G. Lockhart and C. M. Woodhouse: *Rhodes* (Hodder and Stoughton, 1963). Whether or not this is the definitive biography, it contains information not to be found in the earlier biographies, of which the most notable is that by Basil Williams.

'VINDEX': *Cecil Rhodes, Political Life and Speeches* (Chapman and Hall, 1900). Important because it gives the text of the speeches, which are well worth reading both for their content and for the impression they convey of the personality of the man who made them.

SIR HARRY JOHNSTON: *British Central Africa* (Methuen, 1897). Surveys in detail, and with an astonishingly wide range of competence, not only the administrative organisation and early history of Nyasaland but everything connected with it, from zoology and anthropology to the equipment needed by settlers. It is illustrated by many dozens of photographs and by a number of the author's excellent sketches and paintings.

A. J. HANNA: *The Beginning of Nyasaland and North-Eastern Rhodesia, 1859–95* (O.U.P., 1956). Supplements Johnston's account with information which had to remain confidential at the time.

G. SHEPPERSON and T. PRICE: *Independent African* (Edinburgh U.P., 1958). A detailed biography of Chilembwe; a massive book, rich in information about the background to the revolt.

S. S. MURRAY: *Handbook of Nyasaland* (Crown Agents for the Colonies, 1932). Much more than a handbook; contains much information of use to the historian.

R. GRAY: *The Two Nations* (O.U.P., 1960). A social history of the three territories during the inter-war and the early post-war years.

C. LEYS: *European Politics in Southern Rhodesia* (O.U.P., 1959). A detailed and authoritative work of reference, dealing with the Federal as well as the territorial constitution.

L. H. GANN: *The Birth of a Plural Society* (Manchester U.P., 1958). A history of Northern Rhodesia to 1914, written mainly for anthropologists; useful as a guide to sources, which the author has skimmed comprehensively if rather perfunctorily. The same author has just published *A History of Northern Rhodesia* (Chatto and Windus, 1964).

Bibliography

K. Bradley: *Copper Venture* (published by Mufulira and Roan Antelope Mining Companies, 1952). An exceptionally readable 'official history' of the companies which published it, and of the Copperbelt in general. *The Diary of a District Officer* (Harrap, 1943). As entertaining as it is informative. *Native Courts and Authorities in Northern Rhodesia* (Longmans, Cape Town, 1941). A short but thorough study of the working of indirect rule, written with wonderful clarity and simplicity for African school-children.

J. W. Davidson: *The Northern Rhodesian Legislative Council* (Faber, 1948). A study of politics and political institutions in Northern Rhodesia to the end of the war.

A. I. Richards: *Land, Labour and Diet in Northern Rhodesia* (O.U.P., 1939). A detailed study of the Bemba, important to the historian for its account of the social consequences of migrant labour.

G. Wilson: *The Economics of Detribalization in Northern Rhodesia* (Rhodes-Livingstone Papers, Nos. 5 and 6, 1941–2). A valuable study of the Africans in Broken Hill, set in the context of foolish generalities about the world economy.

J. A. Barnes: *Politics in a Changing Society: The Political History of the Fort Jameson Ngoni* (O.U.P., 1954). The work of an anthropologist who is also a capable historian.

A. L. Epstein: *Politics in an Urban African Economy* (Manchester U.P., 1958). A valuable study of political and trade-union activity in the Copperbelt, containing a useful short account of the development of Congress.

A. St. J. Wood: *Northern Rhodesia: The Human Background* (Pall Mall, 1961). Contains much information about Northern Rhodesian society, as seen by a former district officer; rather pretentious.

E. Clegg: *Race and Politics* (O.U.P., 1960). A substantial work on the contemporary history of Northern Rhodesia.

Lord Hailey: *An African Survey* (Revised, 1956) (O.U.P., 1957). An enormous storehouse of information, assembled with scholarly thoroughness and presented by a master of exposition. *Native Administration in the British African Terri-*

tories, Part II (H.M.S.O., 1950). Gives the historical background as well as a detailed account of the situation reached by 1947; does not include Southern Rhodesia.

P. SMITH (ed.): *Africa in Transition* (Max Reinhardt, 1958). A collection of broadcast talks, some of them first rate, on social change among the Bantu in southern Africa, mainly in the Federation.

GUY HUNTER: *The New Societies of Tropical Africa* (O.U.P., 1962). A comprehensive work, but it contains some penetrating insights into the situation in both the Rhodesias at the time when it was being written.

P. MASON: *Year of Decision* (O.U.P., 1960). A lucid and reliable account of the Federation in the 1950s, written with scrupulous fair-mindedness and with charity towards all at a time when spiteful partisanship was usually considered a mark of enlightenment.

H. W. WOODRUFF and C. H. THOMPSON: *Economic Development in Rhodesia and Nyasaland* (Dobson, 1954). A good short economic history, mainly concerned with the years 1945–53.

A. HAZLEWOOD and P. D. HENDERSON: *Nyasaland, The Economics of Federation* (Blackwell, 1960). Subjects 'the economic benefits of federation' to a most rigorous and scrupulous analysis; admirable for conciseness and lucidity of exposition.

Two recent elections have each been studied in sufficient detail to form the subject of a book: L. MAIR, *The Nyasaland Elections of 1961* (Athlone Press, 1962), and D. C. Mulford, *The Northern Rhodesian General Election, 1962* (O.U.P., 1964).

A number of books mentioned in the text have been omitted from this bibliography, which is intended as a guide to further reading and not as a list of authorities.

Most of the books listed above contain bibliographies, including information about source material, published and unpublished. There are also full bibliographies in the annual reports on Nyasaland and Northern Rhodesia published by H.M.S.O.; these reports have gradually expanded from mere leaflets in the 1920s to substantial and well-illustrated booklets in recent years. Those on Nyasaland are particularly useful.

This is scarcely a suitable place to discuss source material, but mention must be made of the collection of nineteenth-century correspondence and diaries in the beautifully produced Oppenheimer Series, and in the more humble but still valuable Robbins Series; the publisher in each case is Chatto and Windus.

Index

Index

Index

Hailey, Lord, quoted, 38
Hansard (Nyasaland), 273
Harris, Dr. R., 120
Hartley, H., 70
Hawes, A. G. S., 103–5, 106–7, 121 n. 1
Hazlewood, A., 290
Hellmore, H., 54
Helm, C. D., 81
Henderson, P. D., 290
Henderson Research Station, 233
Hetherwick, A., 60, 122, 217, 242
Hole, H. M., quoted, 85, 90, 135
Hone, Sir Evelyn, 287
Huggins, Sir Godfrey (afterwards Lord
    Malvern), 186–7, 193, 248–53, 259–
    61, 289, 303
Hunter, G., quoted, 317
Hunters' Road, 70

Ibiam, Sir Francis, 267
Ila-Tonga tribal group, 306
Indians, in British Central Africa
    Police, 123; as settlers in Nyasaland,
    216, 217–18, 281; in Southern
    Rhodesia, 176 n. 1, 179, 313
Indians in Kenya (Devonshire White
    Paper), 194–5
Indirect rule, 25
Industrial Conciliation Acts, 188–91,
    308
Inyanga, 23
Inyati, 56
Iron Age, 22, 27

Jameson, Dr. L. S. (afterwards Sir
    Starr), 89–93, 136, 140–1
Jesuits, 61, 70, 236
Johnson, Archdeacon W. P., 107–8
Johnston, H. H. (afterwards Sir Harry),
    39, 109–15, 118–28, 208–10
Jones, A. Creech, 249–52
Jones, Sir Glyn, 296

Kagubi, 142–3
Kariba Dam, 268–9, 305
Karonga, 68, 105–6, 108–9, 124, 203–4,
    214
Kasama, 129, 205
Katanga, 62, 114, 148, 169–70, 221,
    291, 296
Kaunda, K., 267–8, 284–8, 290, 292,
    296, 306–7
Kebrabasa Rapids, 50, 51, 82, 115
Kenya, 99, 174, 180, 203, 232, 243–4,
    279–80, 295
Khama, 63, 130–1
Khami, 23
Kilmuir, Lord, 301
King's African Rifles, 34, 204

Kitwe, 267, 307
Knight-Bruce, Bishop G. W. H.,
    quoted, 74, 79, 178
Kota-Kota, 105, 125, 214
Kruger, P., 75–6
Kuruman (mission-station), 41, 75
Kuruman (son of Mziligazi), 72

Labour, in Southern Rhodesia, 140,
    178–81, 185–6, 188–93, 308–10; in
    Northern Rhodesia, 188–200, 221–5,
    267, 307 n. 1; in Nyasaland, 204–5,
    213–14, 216. See also Migrant labour
Lake people. See Nyanja
Land, in Southern Rhodesia, 136–7,
    152–7, 181–8, 231–3; Land Appor-
    tionment Acts, 184–8, 193, 230, 310;
    in Northern Rhodesia, 167–8, 200–2,
    233; in Nyasaland, 202, 208–13, 233
Landeens, 35
Law and Order (Maintenance) Act
    (Southern Rhodesia), 311, 317
Laws, Dr. R., 58–9, 217, 237; comment
    on slave trade, 32; comment on un-
    healthy mission stations, 64; attitude
    to education, 66, 240
Lealui, 63, 129, 133
Leask, T., 70, 73, 83 n. 1
Lendy, Captain, 91–2
Lennox-Boyd, A. (afterwards Lord
    Boyd of Merton), 275
Letia, 63, 64
Lewanika, 62–4, 129–35
Liberal Party (Northern Rhodesia),
    268, 294, 296
Likoma Island, 61
Limpopo River, 19, 20, 254
Lippert, E. A., 88; Lippert Concession,
    88, 153, 156–7
Livingstone, Dr. D., 32–3, 45–54, 98,
    128
Livingstonia Mission, 58, 66–8, 123,
    240; fear of Portuguese misrule, 97–
    8; Livingstonia Institute, 237–8
Lobengula, 56, 70, 72–95, 138, 156–7
Lobola, 37–8, 228
Loch, Sir Henry (afterwards Lord), 88,
    93, 137
Lochner, F. E., 130–1; Lochner Con-
    cession, 131–4
London Agreement, 1957, 261–2, 274,
    301–2
London Missionary Society, 45; its
    aloofness from politics, 81; mission to
    Makololo, 53, 54; mission to Mata-
    bele, 53, 54–7, 69–70, 83 n. 1, 236;
    mission to Lake Tanganyika region
    (Northern Rhodesia), 60–1, 64, 68,
    237; dissatisfaction with African
    Lakes Company, 68

Index

Index

North Charterland Company, 124, 201–2

North-Eastern Rhodesia, 162–5, 167 n. 1, 245

Northern Rhodesia, tribes of, 29–31; ancient iron-workings, 22; boundary with Nyasland, 118; railway development in, 148, 170, 173, 305; economic development and European population, 161, 163–4, 169–72; unification of (1911), 165; Protectorate status of, 168, 283; constitutional development in, 165–6, 168, 193–8, 282–5, 292–6, 306–7; Labour Department, 233. *See also* Land, Nationalism, Race relations, Zambia

North-Western Rhodesia, 162–5, 167 n. 1

Nyanja, 26, 30, 33

Nyasa, Lake, 18–19, 67–8, 203, 214–15; gunboats on, 121, 203; Nyasa consulate, 103–5, 107–8, 112

Nyasaland, Protectorate declared, 112, 117–18; Treasure control established, 121; railway, 163, 215–16; in two World Wars, 203–6; economic development and race relations, 207–18, 279–80, 282, 290, 298–300, 308, constitutional development, 216–18, 274–5, 280–2, 296–7, 306; emergency (1959–60), 276, 279–80; nationalism, 206, 242, 269–73; antipathy to Southern Rhodesia and Federation, 247–8, 254–6, 258–9, 298–300

Oldham, Dr. H. J. H., 245

O'Neill, Lieut. H. E., 97, 101, 103, 106–7, 109

Orde-Browne, Major (afterward Sir) Granville, quoted, 38 n. 1, 221, 222–3

Oswell, W. C., 46–7, 51

Pan-Africanism, 270, 289, 291, 308

Parliament (U.K.), sovereignty of, 301–2

'Partnership', 193, 196–7, 254, 255, 257, 266–9, 304

Passfield Memorandum, 194–6, 245

People's Caretaker Council, 311 n. 1, 316

Pennefather, Colonel, 87

Pioneers, 85–7, 89, 116

Poison ordeal, 37, 234

Police, 163; British South Africa Company's, 85, 92, 116; Bechuanaland Border, 93; British Central African, 119, 123–7; native (in Southern Rhodesia), 139–40

Polygamy, 38

Ponde, 129

Population, 216, 219, 309. *See also* Northern Rhodesia, Southern Rhodesia

Portugal, 97, 98–103, 108–12, 115–16

Portuguese East Africa, 34–5, 79, 96–103, 115–16; immigration to Nyasaland from, 211

Price, R., 54

Privy Council, Judicial Committee of, 156–7, 167

Protectorate, implications of, 117, 217, 283; Protectorate Council (Nyasaland), 271–2

Providential Pass, 87, 91

Provincial Councils, 271–3

Quilimane, 34, 103, 111

Race relations, 174–202, 207–18, 229–30, 233–42, 245–318. Race Relations Ordinance (Northern Rhodesia), 267

Railways, construction of, 146–9, 215–16. *See also* Rhodesia Railways

Rand. *See* Witwatersrand

Rennie, Sir Gilbert, 252

Reserves, in Southern Rhodesia, 137–8, 182–4, 187–8, 231–3, 310; in Northern Rhodesia, 200–2, 233

Resident Commissioner, 144–5, 165, 180

Rhodes, C. J., acquires Southern Rhodesia for Chartered Company, 76–95; relations with Johnston, Foreign Office and Portuguese, 111, 115–16, 118–21; and Katanga, 114; and naming of Abercorn and Fife, 126; and Barotseland, 130–3; on land rights in Southern Rhodesia, 136–7, 152–3; and Matabele War, 92, 93, 95; and Matabele Rebellion, 140, 143; attitude to constitutional changes of 1896–8, 144–6; views on franchise, 77, 176

Rhodesia, adoption of name, 137

Rhodesia (Administration post on Lake Mweru), 126–7

Rhodesia Front, 304, 310, 314

Rhodesia Herald, quoted, 260

Rhodesia-Nyasaland Royal Commission, 246–9, 271

Rhodesia Railways, 173, 188, 190, 267, 305. *See also* Railways, construction of

Rhodesian Anglo-American Corporation, 199–200

Rhodesian Selection Trust, 199–200

Richards, Dr. A. J., quoted, 299, n. 2

Rift Valley, 18–19, 215

329

Index

Ripon, first Marquis of, 92–3, 95, 140
Roberts, J., 284
Robinson, Sir Hercules, 76
Rowland, Dr. J. W., 233
Royal Geographical Society, 50
Rudd, C. D., 80–1; Rudd Concession, 81–8, 152, 154
Ruo River, 101–3, 112

Sabi River, 115
Salisbury, Southern Rhodesia, 20, 87, 161, 272; communications with, 91, 148; in Matabele War, 93; in Mashona Rebellion, 142; agreement on migrant labour, 230–1, 249; constitutional conference (1961), 312
Salisbury, third Marquis of, 79, 99, 100, 109–12, 116–18
Salisbury, fifth Marquis of, 303
Sandys, D., 297, 314
Scott, D. C., 60
Sebituane, 46–7
Second World War, 197, 205–6, 248, 271
Sekeletu, 48, 54
Select Committee on Racial Discrimination (Northern Rhodesia), 288
Selous, F. C., 70, 85–7
Sena, 34–5
Senga, 129
Sepopo, 61
Serpa Pinto, Major, 111
Shaka, 27–8, 127
Shangaans, 35
Shangani River, 94
Sharpe, A. (afterwards Sir Alfred), 35, 106, 114–15, 122, 217, 238
Sheane, H., quoted, 36, 37, 127–8, 240
Shippard, Sir Sidney, 81
Shiré River, 19, 21, 98–102, 115, 116, 215; Shiré Highlands, 33, 59, 110–15, 208–11, 221
Sikhs, 123
Sithole, Rev. N., 316
Slavery, in Barotseland, 134
Slave trade, 31–6, 49, 51, 105–6; in Angola and Barotseland, 47, 132; Shiré Highlands depopulated by, 208; British efforts to end it by negotiation, 96–7, 100–1, 103–4; suppression of, 122–3, 126, 127, 129
Smith, Dr. (afterwards Sir) Andrew, 44–5
Smith, Colonel Euan, 105
Smith, Sir George, quoted, 205–6
Smith, I., 316
Smuts, General J. C., 159, 244
Sofala, 23
South Africa, 158–61, 193, 244, 246, 254

Southern Rhodesia, Order in Council (1898), 145; relations between British South Africa Company and the settlers, 145–6, 152–9; in First World War, 155, 157–8; railway development in, 146–9, 173; Women's Franchise Ordinance, 158; economic development and European population, 150–4, 157–8, 172–3, 290, 305, 308; annexation of, 161; constitution of, 161, 163, 173–6; reform in, 193, 269, 308–11. See also Land, Race relations
Souza, M. A. de, 116
Stanley, H. M., 52
Stanley, Colonel Oliver, 248–50
Stevenson Road, 61, 112, 128
Stevenson-Hamilton, Colonel J., quoted, 64, 95
Stewart, Dr. J., 57–8, 97–8
Stone Age, 27
Stonehouse, J., 267
Sudan, the, 261; western Sudan, 22
Swinburne, Sir John, 84
Swinton, Viscount, 302–3
Sykes, W., 56

Takawira, L., 313–14
Tanganyika, Lake, L.M.S. mission to, 60–1, 64, 68
Tanganyika Territory, 221, 244, 245
Tatira Akafuna, 63
Taxation, of Africans, 180–1, 227–8, 238; of Europeans, 155, 169
'Technical independence', 259–61
Tete, 34
Thomas, Sir Miles, 250–1
Thomson, J. B., quoted, 57
Thomson, Joseph, 114–15; quoted, 68
'Tickets of Residence', 102
Times, The, quoted, 198–9
Todd, G., 268, 308–9
Tonga (of northern Nyasaland), 30, 58–9; Moir's treaties with, 104; in British Central Africa Police, 123; as migrant labourers, 213–14, 221, 226
Tonga (of North-Western Rhodesia), 61, 129, 306
Tozer, Bishop W. G., 53–4
Trade unions. See Race Relations
Transvaal, 29, 75–6, 79, 81, 85; Jameson's Raid into, 140
Treasury (British), 102, 117–21, 158–9
Treaties with African chiefs, 104, 111–15, 167 n. 1
Tredgold, Sir Robert, 311
Tribal Elders, 224–5
Tribal Trust Land, 310
Tsetse fly, 21, 29
Tshombe, M., 291

Index

Uganda, 32, 99, 217, 243–5
Ujiji, 32, 52, 60, 69
Ummiati-Shasha line, 90–1
Umnombate, 41, 45, 72
Umtali, 147–8
United Federal Party, 260, 263, 268–9, 282–5, 292–6, 300, 309, 314
United Kingdom. *See* British Government, Parliament
United National Independence Party, 268, 287–8, 292 n. 1, 294–6, 306–7
United Nations, 291, 312, 315, 318
United Presbyterians, 58
Universities' Mission to Central Africa, 53–4, 61, 64, 68, 107, 235
University College of Rhodesia and Nyasaland, 239, 297

Victoria. *See* Fort Victoria
Victoria Falls, 49, 148, 164; conferences at, 246, 250–1, 255, 305
Viljoen, J., 70
Vipya tung estates, 214
Vipya, lake steamer, 215
Vryburg, 75, 146, 148

Walker, Prof. E. A., quoted, 75
Wankie, 148
Wankonde, 105–6
War Office, 121
Ware, H., 130; Ware Concession, 130, 133
Watch Tower, 241
Watson, Dr. W., quoted, 222 n. 1, 228
Welensky, Sir Roy, and European immigration, 192; and Northern Rhodesia, 250, 260, 284, 292–5; and the Federation, 250, 260–4, 274, 289–

90, 297, 301–2, 304; and race relations, 263–4, 268–9, 292
Welfare Societies (Northern Rhodesia), 272
Westbeech, G., 62
White Fathers, 65, 128–9
Whitehead, Sir Edgar, 268, 282, 309–13, 317
Wiese, K., 124
Williams, Prof. B., quoted, 77
Wilson, Captain A., 94
Wina, S., 267
Witchcraft, 36–7, 234–5
Witwatersrand, 75, 77, 84–5, 158, 214, 221, 270

Yao, 32–4, 60, 97, 103–5, 123. *See also* Makanjira
Yeta. *See* Letia
Young, Sir Hilton, 224–5

Zambesi River, 28, 102–3, 110; Livingstone's expedition to, 50–1; disputed right to free navigation of, 98–103, 115–16; Lower Zambesi Bridge, 215. *See also* Chinde, Kariba, Kebrabasa Rapids, Victoria Falls
Zambia, 285; Zambia African National Congress, 285–7
Zanzibar, 32, 35, 54, 60, 99–100, 102, 105
Zimbabwe, 22–4, 84
Zimbabwe African National Union, 311 n. 1, 316
Zimbabwe African People's Union, 311 n. 1
Zomba, 107, 121, 164, 211, 216
Zulu tribe, 27–9
Zumbo, 35, 115, 116